"*Rethinking Environmental Justice in Sustainable Cities* is an important book, not only for its examination of the causes and contexts of environmental injustice in US cities, but also as an exemplar of how agent-based modelling can be used to illuminate questions of major policy significance. The book will be of great value to the rapidly expanding community of researchers developing computational models to provide advice in a range of policy fields."

Nigel Gilbert, University of Surrey, UK

"For a qualitative researcher who investigates environmental justice primarily through archival material and interview data, this book is certainly thought provoking. The authors advocate the use of Agent Based Modeling, a method of computational simulation, to understand causes of environmental injustice at the systems level. They argue that injustice might be an "emergent" outcome, unintended by any particular actor or the result of malicious intent. Furthermore, emergence could be used to think more critically about environmental policy and planning for purposes of urban sustainability. Whether or not one is a fan of computational simulation, this book is sure to inspire heated debates in the classroom and engage the important issue of EJ from yet another perspective."

Brinda Sarathy, Pitzer College

# Rethinking Environmental Justice in Sustainable Cities

As the study of environmental policy and justice becomes increasingly significant in today's global climate, standard statistical approaches to gathering data have become less helpful in generating new insights and possibilities. None of the conventional frameworks easily allows for the empirical modeling of the interactions of all the actors involved, or for the emergence of outcomes unintended by the actors. The existing frameworks account for the "what," but not for the "why."

Heather E. Campbell, Yushim Kim, and Adam Eckerd bring an innovative perspective to environmental justice research. Their approach adjusts the narrower questions often asked in the study of environmental justice, expanding to broader investigations of how and why environmental inequities occur. Using agent-based modeling, they study the interactions and interdependencies among different agents such as firms, residents, and government institutions. Through simulation, the authors test underlying assumptions in environmental justice and discover ways to modify existing theories to better explain why environmental injustice occurs. Furthermore, they use agent-based modeling to generate empirically testable hypotheses, which they employ to check if their simulated findings are supported in the real world using real data.

The pioneering research on environmental justice in this text will have effects on the field of environmental policy as a whole. For social science and policy researchers, this book explores how to employ new and experimental methods of inquiry on challenging social problems, and for the field of environmental justice the authors demonstrate how agent-based modeling helps illuminate the complex social and policy interactions that lead to both environmental justice and injustice.

**Heather E. Campbell** is Chair of the Department of Politics and Policy and Field Chair for Policy at the Claremont Graduate University, School of Social Science, Policy, and Evaluation.

**Yushim Kim** is an associate professor at the School of Public Affairs at Arizona State University (ASU) in Phoenix.

**Adam Eckerd** is an assistant professor, at the Department of Political Science, University of Tennessee.

# Routledge Studies in Public Administration and Environmental Sustainability

Edited by Daniel J. Fiorino and Robert F. Durant, American University

Climate change, loss of habitat and bio-diversity, water security, and the effects of new technologies are placing pressure at all levels of government for effective policy responses. Old policy solutions and the administrative processes associated with them not only seem inadequate for managing environmental and energy sustainability issues, but even counterproductive. The challenge for societies worldwide often is how best to harness in the public interest the dynamism of markets, the passion and commitment of nonprofit and nongovernmental organizations, and the public interest oriented expertise of career civil servants at all levels of government. *Routledge Studies on Public Administration and Environmental Sustainability* focuses on core public administration questions as they relate to the topics of environmental, energy, and natural resources policies, and which together comprise the field of environmental sustainability.

# Rethinking Environmental Justice in Sustainable Cities

Insights from agent-based modeling

Heather E. Campbell, Yushim Kim and Adam Eckerd

LONDON AND NEW YORK

First published 2015 by Routledge

2 Park Square, Milton Park, Abingdon, Oxon OX14 4RN
711 Third Avenue, New York, NY 10017, USA

*Routledge is an imprint of the Taylor & Francis Group, an informa business*

First issued in paperback 2017

*Library of Congress Cataloging in Publication Data*
Campbell, Heather E.
    Rethinking environmental justice in sustainable cities : insights from
agent-based modeling / Heather E. Campbell, Yushim Kim, and Adam
Eckerd.
        pages cm. – (Routledge studies in public administration and
environmental sustainability ; 3)
    Includes bibliographical references and index.
    1. Environmental justice–Mathematical models 2. Urban ecology
(Sociology)–Mathematical models. 3. Sustainable development–
Mathematical models. I. Kim, Yushim. II. Eckerd, Adam. III. Title.
    GE220.C36 2015
    363.7'0561–dc23
                2014043515

ISBN: 978-0-415-65744-0 (hbk)
ISBN: 978-1-138-06669-4 (pbk)

Typeset in Sabon
by Taylor & Francis Books

*Heather E. Campbell* dedicates this book to Dr. Gregory Daneke, for early faith, mentorship, and insisting that she pay attention to agent-based modeling and complexity; and to Michael K. Tschudi for love and GIS.

*Yushim Kim* and *Adam Eckerd* dedicate this book to Professor Anand Desai for his mentorship, humor, and willingness to entertain their methodological explorations; and to Professors Andy Keeler and Robert Greenbaum for teaching and support at Ohio State University.

# Contents

# List of illustrations

## Boxes

# Contributors

**Heather E. Campbell**, PhD, is Chair and Professor in the Department of Politics and Policy at the Claremont Graduate University, School of Social Science, Policy, and Evaluation. She is co-author (with E.A. Corley) of *Urban Environmental Policy Analysis* (ME Sharpe, 2012). She has published several refereed articles on environmental policy, particularly on environmental justice. She has served as the editor of the *Journal of Public Affairs Education*.

**Yushim Kim**, PhD, is an Associate Professor at the School of Public Affairs and a Senior Sustainability Scholar at the Julie Ann Wrigley Global Institute of Sustainability at Arizona State University. She is also a faculty associate at the Department of Political Science at the University of Bamberg in Germany. Dr. Kim has published refereed articles on environmental justice, public health emergencies, and social welfare fraud, as well as on spatial and agent-based modeling.

**Adam Eckerd**, PhD, is an Assistant Professor at the Department of Political Science, University of Tennessee. He conducts research on the complex relationship between government decisions and social outcomes, particularly with respect to environmental justice, public participation, and nonprofit organizations. He has contributed two chapters, one on an agent-based model of gentrification and one on an agent-based model of life-cycle costs management for nuclear facilities, to *Simulations for Policy Inquiry* (Springer, 2012), and has published research on environmental justice and neighborhood participation in several refereed journals such as *Policy Sciences* and *Public Administration Review*.

### Contributors to Chapter 10

**Hal T. Nelson**, PhD, is an Associate Research Professor at Claremont Graduate University. He researches environmental, social, and economic sustainability issues, primarily in the energy sector. Dr. Nelson's economic sustainability research centers on low-carbon development strategies, while his social sustainability research focuses on governance, stakeholder participation, and facilitation, as well as decision-support modeling.

**Nicholas L. Cain** is a doctoral candidate and research assistant at Claremont Graduate University. His research uses analytical and empirical approaches to examine the politics and policies of energy and the environment.

**Zining Yang** is a doctoral candidate and lecturer at Claremont Graduate University. Her research applies computational models and statistical models to environmental issues and the policymaking process.

# Series foreword

For visions of truly sustainable cities to become reality, they must become sustainable for all their citizens and not just the most economically secure or politically efficacious among them. To date, a rich, informative, and thought-provoking literature exists on environmental justice, one that has established that minorities and low-income citizens face disproportionate exposure to environmental risks. Less clear is why they find themselves at greater risk than their fellow citizens, a question that has subsequently been explored by researchers from a variety of disciplines. They have tried to discern, among other things, whether the clear patterns of risk exposure established are the result of intentional or institutional racism, income rather than race, or merely disadvantaged citizens moving into riskier areas because of lower housing costs.

In *Rethinking Environmental Justice in Sustainable Cities*, Heather Campbell, Yushim Kim, and Adam Eckerd enter the debate less to resolve these issues than to reconceptualize the way they are studied and hence better inform practice going forward. They argue that scholars and practitioners need a methodological approach to the study of issues like environmental justice in sustainable cities that are less linear, more complex, and incorporate the interconnectedness of decisions in urban settings. They offer agent-based modeling as a means for explaining and anticipating patterns of environmental injustice, and they revisit many of the conventional arguments in environmental justice through a series of agent-based model (ABM)-based computer simulations. In the process, they shed new—and sometimes controversial—light on traditional environmental justice issues as they impact the pursuit of sustainable cities in the United States. Ambitious in conception, rigorous in analysis, yet accessible to newcomers to computer simulations, *Rethinking Environmental Justice in Sustainable Cities* is a breath of fresh air to those who see cities as complex adaptive systems rather than linear static entities.

This book illustrates well the aim of the *Routledge Studies in Public Administration and Environmental Sustainability* series to afford accessible and innovative books for scholars, practitioners, and the general public seeking to understand the relationship between administration, democratic values, politics, and environmental sustainability policies in the United States and abroad. In this case, Campbell and her co-authors are bringing novel ways of analyzing environmental issues as they relate to sustainability by applying a technique used in other fields but seldom used in the study of sustainable cities. Collectively, we envision the books in this series as helping to advance both theory and practice on one of the most significant environmental challenges of our time.

Robert F. Durant
Daniel J. Fiorino
American University

# Acknowledgments

This book is the product of our collaboration over several years. In the process of preparing for and writing this book, we were fortunate to interact with many helpful friends and colleagues at various venues.

Materials for this book were presented at conferences, in particular the Association of Public Policy Analysis and Management (APPAM). We have presented our environmental justice agent-based model (EJ ABM) work at APPAM every year since 2010. We thank the audiences who came to our sessions and commented on the presentations. We would like especially to acknowledge Professor Evan Ringquist of the School of Public and Environmental Affairs of Indiana University, who unfortunately passed away just prior to completion of this book. For many years, Evan Ringquist was an active participant in APPAM, and especially in the area of environmental justice research. We benefited from his meta-analysis of the EJ literature (referenced in later chapters), and also from many interactions at APPAM conference panels. We will miss him.

Each of us also presented parts of this work at various times at our own institutions. We thank the colleagues and the students who participated in these presentations and helped us crystallize our thoughts on environmental justice and agent-based modeling. Thanks also to Dr. Patricia D. Campbell, for reading and editing early chapters.

Special thanks also go to Michael K. Tschudi. And special thanks to Kristoffer Wikstrom, Claremont Graduate University, for exemplary research assistance, including checking and crosschecking references and citations, conforming to Routledge's preferred style, and helping in development of the index. Thanks also to Aye Aye Khaine, Roger Chin, and Nikhil Mathur, also of the Claremont Graduate University, for additional research assistance.

We appreciate the anonymous reviewers of our published papers and this book proposal. Their reviews helped us sharpen the contribution of our work to the fields of environmental justice and urban policy. We also owe our thanks to the editors of the Routledge Studies in Public Administration and Environmental Sustainability, to Natalja Mortensen for her suggestion to write this book, and Darcy Bullock and Lillian Rand for their help on our editorial questions.

Our home institutions during the writing period—Claremont Graduate University, Arizona State University, and Virginia Tech—helped us complete this book by providing us with the necessary time, resources, infrastructure, and mentally stimulating colleagues. Yushim Kim is grateful for financial support received from the National Research Foundation of Korea (NRF-2013S1A3A2053959). Adam Eckerd acknowledges the support of Whitestone Research and the National Nuclear Security Administration, and specifically Cliff Shang, Peter Lufkin, and Jon Miller, for providing support as he learned how to develop agent-based models. We really appreciate this community of support and assistance.

# Preface

Questions of environmental policy are arising worldwide. Among environmental policy questions, consideration of environmental justice (EJ), which began to be examined in the United States during the 1980s, is viewed as increasingly important, not only within the United States and other industrialized countries, but when considering trade between richer and poorer nations. In the literature, environmental injustice usually indicates findings of disproportionate environmental effects based on race or ethnicity, and controlling for other factors such as cost, income, and the movement of minorities into the ambit of environmental "disamenities" (facilities or sites that cause environmental harm). In some cases, the term is used to indicate that the poor receive disproportionate harmful environmental effects. As with any social injustice, environmental injustice can undermine the health and sustainability of societies and communities. Unfortunately, our current understanding of it is limited. We are fairly sure that environmental injustice exists, but there is heated debate as to why.

It is indeed very difficult to tease out EJ issues using our current theoretical and methodological wherewithal. Studies informed by conventional economic theories have largely focused on the location choices of firms or residents; related studies based in other disciplines explore EJ from the perspective of psychology and risk. There are some studies that have framed EJ as a social phenomenon that needs to be understood via aggregate-level dynamics, such as neighborhood change, rather than individual or firm choices. However, none of these frameworks readily allows empirical modeling of the interactions of the many different actors involved, or the emergence of outcomes not necessarily intended. In some sense, EJ research has reached an epistemological deadlock.

*Rethinking Environmental Justice in Sustainable Cities* aims to bring a new perspective to the field of environmental policy and urban sustainability broadly, and EJ research in particular. The specific goal of this book is to reorient EJ research from its common focus on "whether disproportionate minority collocation could actually be due to lower socioeconomic status"— as many analysts argue—to the broader question of "how or why observed environmental inequities come about." Because data-based multivariate statistical analysis can tell us *what* is observed, but not *why*, to move around the epistemological deadlock we rely on a computational simulation approach: agent-based modeling. The computational approach can be used for other environmental and sustainability policy issues, too.

Agent-based modeling is still fairly novel in social science inquiry, but its potential has been well articulated by several scholars such as Epstein; Miller and Page; and Gilbert and Troitzsch.[1] Yet, it is still rare to see published research that utilizes the method for in-depth analysis of policy subjects and problems. *Rethinking Environmental Justice in Sustainable Cities* is at the frontier of this new direction. Such research is only now beginning to arise, and there is new interest in it within the policy community. For instance, the theme of the 2011 Association for Public Policy Analysis and Management (APPAM) research conference was "Seeking Solutions to Complex Policy and Management Problems." This conference fostered the emergence of a new community of inquiry and practice within APPAM. Policy research based on agent-based modeling and other computational methods was presented as part of environment and energy, health, public management, and methods panels.

The key feature of *Rethinking Environmental Justice in Sustainable Cities* is that it is grounded in a unique framework that can illuminate complex social and policy interactions that lead to environmental phenomena including—but not limited to—environmental injustice. The framework includes heterogeneous social entities (e.g., firms, residents, and government institutions) that can simultaneously interact and make coordinated or uncoordinated decisions within a neighborhood or a particular social system. With an agent-based model (ABM), one can explore and analyze both how the interactions and interdependencies among these actors lead to environmental injustice and also, within complex social interactions, what factors can ameliorate environmental injustice. Assumptions underlying existing theories on EJ can be tested within the simulated world and modified for better explanation. New theories can be developed because a virtue of the ABM approach is to shed new light on causal chains that have been overlooked or underemphasized in other research. Additionally, to move analysis from the artificial simulation platform, an ABM can provide new empirically testable hypotheses which can be used to check, using real data, if the findings of the simulated world are supported in the real world.

We hope that *Rethinking Environmental Justice in Sustainable Cities: Insights from agent-based modeling* is an exemplary book for future social science and policy researchers who seek a new method of inquiry on challenging social problems that may not be well understood using other, more standard, modes of inquiry.

# Note

1  Joshua M. Epstein, *Generative Social Science: Studies in Agent-based Computational Modeling* (Princeton, NJ: Princeton University Press, 2007); John H. Miller and Scott E. Page, *Complex Adaptive Systems: An Introduction to Computational Models of Social Life* (Princeton, NJ: Princeton University Press, 2007); Nigel Gilbert and Klaus Troitzsch, *Simulation for the Social Scientist* (Maidenhead: Open University Press, 2005).

# Abbreviations

| | |
|---|---|
| ABM | agent-based model |
| CA | cellular automata |
| CAA | Clean Air Act |
| CBD | central business district |
| CBG | Census block group |
| CBO | community-based organization |
| C-zone | commercial zone |
| DSS | decision support system |
| EJ | environmental justice |
| EJ ABM | Environmental Justice Agent-based Model |
| EP | economic pressure |
| EPA | Environmental Protection Agency |
| ER | eliminating risk |
| GIS | geographic information systems |
| GUI | graphical user interface |
| HVTL | high-voltage transmission lines |
| IAD | institutional analysis and development framework |
| LULU | locally unwanted land use |
| MA | majority |
| MAUP | modifiable areal unit problem |
| MI | minority |
| M-zone | manufacturing or industrial zone |
| NGO | nongovernmental organization |
| NIMBY | not in my back yard |
| OLS | ordinary least square |
| OOP | object-oriented programming |
| R-zone | residential zone |
| SD | system dynamics |
| SEMPro | Sustainable Energy Modeling Program |
| TRIF | toxics release inventory facility |
| TRTP | Tehachapi Renewable Transmission Project |
| TSDF | transport, storage and disposal facility |
| UCC | United Church of Christ |

# 1 Introduction

The possibility of sustainable cities has become of great interest to scholars, governments, and citizens.[1] As the world becomes rapidly urbanized—with more than half the world's population living in cities as of 2014[2]—many are concerned about the ability to maintain quality of life.

Over the last couple of decades since the term came into common use, the concept of sustainability has expanded beyond environmental and economic health to include social and political justice for residents. In other words, sustainability has become a three-pillars concept[3] that includes the "three interacting, interconnected, and overlapping 'prime systems': *the biosphere* or ecological system; *the economy*, the market or the economic system; and *human society*, the human social system."[4] The political system, families and communities, and cultures are all important parts of the human social system. Sustainable cities strive to balance all three prime systems and achieve fully sustainable development.

There are numerous initiatives around the globe to build sustainable cities.[5] As one example, the city of Baltimore is taking action to become a more sustainable city. The 2014 *Baltimore Sustainability Plan* lays out a broad comprehensive agenda with 29 priority goals grouped under seven themes—cleanliness, pollution prevention, resource conservation, greening, transportation, education and awareness, and the green economy.[6] The plan encourages city officials to integrate policy and programs addressing the economic, environmental, and social health of the community and requires collaboration among important actors in the city, such as city government, neighborhoods, community organizations, funders, and state and federal agencies.[7] Balancing environmental, economic, and social systems is essential to a sustainable city, but it poses significant challenges.[8]

Environmental justice (EJ) is a critical element of sustainable cities because social equity, fairness, and progress are core elements of sustainability,[9] especially under the social pillar of the three-pillars concept. Environmental *in*justice can undermine a city's goal of overall sustainability; it can reduce collaboration and create a rift between citizens and their government, or even cause social unrest. Nevertheless, the reality of race- and ethnicity-based environmental injustice is ongoing in many cities.

Existing EJ research has focused on analyzing whether and to what extent environmental injustice exists, and has been weaker in explaining *why* it exists and in providing useful guidance for addressing the problem. The current concept of sustainability is premised on the interaction and inter-dependence of natural and social systems, and we argue that thinking about EJ problems *systemically*—that is, as one part of the entire interlinked *system* of the city—using tools, particularly agent-based modeling, developed to aid this type of thinking can shed light on the stubbornly difficult, wicked problem of environmental injustice.

## Environmental justice

As part of the broader goal of sustainability overall, concerns about the equity of the distribution of environmental quality are arising worldwide. In the United States, consideration of environmental justice began to be examined in the 1980s and was codified into law in the 1990s, when President Bill Clinton signed Executive Order 12898, which stipulated that "each Federal agency shall make achieving environmental justice part of its mission by identifying and addressing, as appropriate, disproportionately high and adverse human health or environmental effects of its programs, policies, and activities on minority populations and low-income populations in the United States."[10] However, the issue is not limited to the United States. The European Union has been working to ensure improvement of the slum-like conditions in which the ethnic minority Romani population often lives.[11] The South African government has passed much stricter standards regarding external-ities of mining to ensure better environmental conditions for the poor who usually live and work close to mines. Environmental justice is also increasingly considered when designing policy for trade—particularly the trade of waste products—between richer and poorer countries.[12]

In the research literature, a finding of environmental injustice most usually is based on statistical evidence of disproportionate environmental effects based on race or ethnicity while (statistically) controlling for other factors such as cost, income, and the movement of minorities into the ambit of environmental "disamenities" (facilities or sites that cause environmental harm). In some cases, the term is used to indicate that the poor receive disproportionate harmful environmental effects. As with any social injustice, environmental injustice can undermine the health and sustainability of societies and communities. Unfortunately, our current understanding of it is limited. We are fairly sure that environmental injustice exists, but there is heated debate as to why.

The study of race- and ethnicity-based environmental injustice has developed into a research subfield of its own since it was first empirically identified in the United States in the 1980s through the famous United Church of Christ report.[13] Despite much evidence of the disproportionate spatial col-location of ethnic minorities and poor environmental conditions, there is still significant disagreement as to whether the cause is race/ethnicity-based, or whether statistical findings supporting it are artifacts of various analytic errors and decisions. Nevertheless, there is sufficient evidence to conclude that race/ethnicity-disproportionate environmental injustice does exist, even when controlling for time ("which came first," the residents or the pollution),[14] residential location economics ("move in" versus "move out"),[15] and many other causal factors including income, politics, and other costs.[16] However, as stated above and as we explicate below, significant evidence of the presence of disproportionate exposure does not tell us why it occurs, and racism is not the only possible answer to this question.

To us, then, the EJ literature presents a troubling puzzle. It is not generally America's self-concept that race and/or ethnicity should still affect living conditions in an involuntary way—this does not seem to be our idea of "justice for all,"[17] as it says in the Pledge of Allegiance of the United States. Even if, as Ringquist argues,[18] the magnitude of race-based environmental injustice effects is small, they have the potential to erode trust between minority residents and their neighbors and governments, and thereby to make cities less governable. This reduces the wellbeing of all.

Some activists and researchers argue that only racism by firm and/or governmental decision makers can explain the oft-observed outcomes in which minority status is an important predictor of disproportionate collocation of residents with environmental disamenities—polluting or polluted land or facilities such as toxics release inventory facilities (TRIFs);[19] Superfund sites;[20] brownfields (plots of polluted land); hazardous waste management facilities (transport, storage and disposal facilities—TSDFs); and excessive noise.[21] However, while in no way denying the continued existence of racism in contemporary America (consider the huge ruckus surrounding the 2013 Cheerios advertisement that showed a multiracial family),[22] we wonder whether the current levels of racism in America are sufficient to explain the observed environmental inequities.

Some researchers suspect that the answer to this conundrum is that minorities are, on average, poorer than majorities in the United States, and it is poverty rather than minority status that drives minority-disproportionate collocation with pollution. However, the persuasiveness of this explanation is diminished by the fact that most recent studies control independently for income and many still find a disproportionate race effect.[23] Further, some research finds race-based environmental injustice in the case of Asian Americans,[24] but Asians are the Census-measured US minority group that actually has a larger average income than white, non-Hispanic Americans.[25] Others wonder if perhaps minorities simply do not care as much about their residential environment as do majority residents, but we also find evidence opposed to this possibility, both through studies of "dread" (the fear of risk),[26] and through some empirical work that explicitly examines related issues.[27]

It is very difficult to tease out the causes of the EJ problem using standard theoretical and methodological wherewithal. Studies informed by conventional economic theories have largely focused on the location choices of firms or residents; related studies based in other disciplines explore EJ from the perspective of psychology and risk. There are some studies that have framed EJ as a social phenomenon that needs to be understood via aggregate-level dynamics, such as neighborhood change over time, rather than individual or firm choices.[28] However, none of these frameworks readily allows the empirical modeling of the interactions of the many different actor types involved, the interdependence of social and natural systems, or the emergence of outcomes not necessarily intended by any. In short, none comprehensively treats the city as a system, with environmental injustice as one outcome of systemic interactions.

However, there are novel research methods available to generate new insights into environmental and sustainability issues and policy designs. One of these is agent-based modeling, a computational simulation method well structured to model dynamic interaction within complex urban systems. The usual statistical approach to environmental policy and planning is at a point of diminishing returns, and the agent-based modeling approach gives us a new route with new insights and new types of implications that can then be tested empirically.

This book invites environmental policy scholars, simulation modelers, and practicing professionals and administrators on an exciting journey of social inquiry with this approach: using agent-based modeling to simulate dynamic, systemic interactions and provide new insight into EJ findings and solutions. In addition, though EJ is the specific topic on which we focus, this method has promise for many other issues in urban policy and planning, and for urban sustainability broadly.

## EJ as emergence, and agent-based modeling

Specific to agent-based modeling, "emergence"[29] is a term that refers to "macroscopic societal regularities arising from the purely local interaction of the agents."[30] Emergence is a systemic attribute, a property of the system rather than of the individuals. As noted by others before, many phenomena of concern in urban policy and planning are inherently emergent.[31] Desai[32] uses the example of traffic jams, which are an emergent outcome of many individual drivers interacting with each other and elements of the cityscape. The behavior of no one driver can explain regular traffic jams; absent a wreck, we cannot tell which additional driver caused the problem, for it is a nonlinear outcome of the system.[33] In 1999, Batty and colleagues argued that "cities are examples par excellence" of phenomena in which "local action … can give rise to global forms which emerge spontaneously."[34] Here the term "global" does not mean for the whole Earth, but global to the structure that is being analyzed: supra or macro.

The importance of emergence as a key to understanding important attributes of cities is embedded in the earliest work on agent-based modeling: In what is considered the first conceptual agent-based model (ABM), Schelling found the emergence of color-based segregation in a city modeled using individual "agents" (black and red checkers) deciding where to live using very simple rules. Racial segregation emerged even when no agent sought to live in a racially segregated neighborhood.[35] However, this decades-old example of the importance of emergence in cities has not fully penetrated the urban policy and planning literature. Agent-based modeling is still fairly novel in social-science inquiry, but its potential has been well articulated by several scholars such as Epstein; Miller and Page; and Gilbert and Troitzsch.[36] Yet, it is still rare to see published research, either in academic journals or professional reports, that utilizes this method for policy and planning subjects and problems.

### What is agent-based modeling?

As indicated in the name, agent-based modeling is a simulation modeling approach based on agents. "Agents" are self-contained subsets of software and data that make decisions based on their own perceptions of the surrounding environment and a set of behavioral rules.[37] An agent is a component "situated within and a part of an environment that senses that environment and acts on it, over time, in pursuit of its own agenda and so as to affect what it senses in the future."[38]

Agent-based modeling can be characterized as follows. Starting from assumptions about the environment and the behavior of agents, agent-based modeling allows us to see what *macroscopic regularities* emerge from the way in which agents interact. As Gilbert says:

> In comparison with variable-based approaches using structural equations, or system-based approaches using differential equations, agent-based simulation offers the possibility of modeling individual heterogeneity, representing explicitly an agent's decision rules, and situating agents in a geographical or another type of space. It allows modelers to represent in a natural way multiple scales of analysis, the emergence of structures at the macro or societal level from individual action, and various kinds of adaptation and learning, none of which is easy to do with other modeling approaches.[39]

The agent-based modeling approach allows testing of decision rules that are hypothesized in the literature, or developed de novo by the researcher. For example, in our case we can compare hypotheses in the literature (e.g., racist decision makers, economically rational decision makers). Therefore, ABMs are often built to understand the behavior of complex adaptive systems that consist of autonomous and/or purposeful heterogeneous agents and the local interactions among agents or between agents and the environment.[40] Like humans, though agents are autonomous, they are embedded within and constrained by the environment; as with market outcomes, macro-level ABM outcomes emerge from interactions of many autonomous, socially embedded agents.

Agent-based modeling allows for the examination of various decision criteria that *could* lead to observed aggregate outcomes, while also dis-aggregating potentially important causal processes from one another. Agent-based modeling is a form of simulation that allows for the examination of processes over time; individual actors and their interactions can be directly represented.[41] Further:

> … agent-based modeling stands beside mathematical and statistical modeling in terms of its rigor. *Like equation-based modeling, but unlike prose, agent-based models have to be complete, consistent, and unambiguous if they are to be capable of being executed on a computer.* On the other hand, unlike most mathematical models, agent-based models can include agents that are heterogeneous in their features and abilities, can model situations that are far from equilibrium, *and can deal directly with the consequences of interaction between agents.*[42]

Agent-based modeling is also a computational method that, like Monte Carlo simulation, allows for experimentation. Monte Carlo simulation can be used to understand what conditions are necessary for a particular estimator to be unbiased and efficient. Agent-based modeling can examine what conditions are necessary for a particular situation to exhibit minority-based environmental injustice. Thus, although in a more dynamic and interactive setting, an ABM can serve the same purpose as the model of perfect competition, which tells us the conditions under which market outcomes will be socially optimal.

Conceptually, an ABM is simple—actors (agents) interact on a spatial (Cartesian) or a-spatial plane. These actors interact with other actors, within the (geographic) constraints of the plane and with the environmental characteristics of the model world. Interactions are based on a set of pre-defined rules of behavior and environmental characteristics. Thus, the behavior of the agents is defined in advance, but the aggregation of their responses is not known, and both the agents' behavior and the nature of the world can change as the aggregation of agent choices alters the landscape.[43] Agent-based modeling takes advantage of three aspects of the social world that other modeling techniques often do not: 1 that actors are heterogeneous and can change their preferences or attitudes over time; 2 emergence; and 3 spatial (or relational in other instances) dependence to account for Tobler's observation that "Everything is related to everything else, but near things are more related than distant things."[44]

It is worthwhile to note that the purpose of agent-based modeling is not to understand individual behavior. ABMs represent complex adaptive systems of which individuals can be a part. What is known about individuals from empirical data, or assumed about them, is used in building an ABM, with the intent of understanding system-level outcomes.

In order to understand the circumstances under which racially based environmental injustice can occur, we propose to use an ABM because thereby we can understand which assumptions can lead to unequal out-comes in the location of environmentally harmful firms. This can also help us understand which conditions are necessary for disproportionality to occur. For example, some have assumed that strong evidence of racially correlated outcomes can only be consistent with explicitly racist behaviors. Is this correct, or might race awareness be enough? Or, even more, can such outcomes arise without even race awareness when other institutional rules and mechanisms are in place? Understanding what is necessary for observed outcomes also presents the opportunity for understanding appropriate policy interventions.

### *Benefits of agent-based modeling for EJ and urban sustainability*

One of the reasons we decided to use agent-based modeling to examine EJ—as opposed to more standard empirical methods (which we have also used)—is our belief that complex interactivity of the many individual deci-sions in a city system may lead to emergent outcomes unintended by any actor.

It is possible that the evidence of environmental injustice that has been found by the empirical-statistical work is at least partly in keeping with Schelling's segregation outcome, an emergent, unintended effect of interactions between many actors and the nature of the city itself. If this is so, standard policies aimed at fixing environmental injustice may be ineffectual. Target-ing a single actor type, such as apparently discriminatory firms, without understanding the many factors leading to an emergent outcome, is unlikely to be successful because it fails to take into account the complex interactions present within cities that often lead to hard-to-predict outcomes. After all, if effects are truly emergent, no individual actor knows what s/he is doing to cause the outcome.[45] This lesson applies more broadly to sustainability itself. Sustainability is an emergent outcome—and one that is much more complex than environmental injustice, which is only one subset of sustain-ability. Thus, sustainability is an outcome of a complex, dynamic system and should be studied using tools that can model such systems.

Second, to fully understand the effects of income, race, mobility, etc., it is helpful to use a method that lets us independently vary these concepts in ways that may not be available in real-world data where, for example, race and income are often highly correlated. Though policy and planning ana-lyses should return to the real world and empirical analysis, in some cases the combinations of different factors necessary to understand independent impacts fully may not be readily observable. For example, to understand the independent effect of minority status and income status, we need to be able to study not only situations in which minorities are poorer, but in which minorities are richer. Such empirical data can be hard to come by, but can be simulated in an ABM.

Third, because the studied behavior may be invidious (if, e.g., racism is a factor), survey and similar methodologies are unlikely to be successful in revealing honest responses on the motives of siting decisions. Fourth, agent-based modeling, with its ability graphically to represent complex phenomena, can be a useful way to communicate with policymakers.

Gaining insights on environmental injustice problems using agent-based modeling is relevant and appropriate for achieving the goal of sustainable cities because it represents values central to all three pillars of sustainability: social, economic, and environmental systems. In addition, the presence of the interlocking pillars, each of which is itself a system, poses serious challenges to sustainability analyses. The ability of agent-based modeling to tackle emergence, interactivity, and hidden processes, and to communicate graphically the nature of interlocking systems to policymakers and practitioners, can provide new and different approaches to analyzing and thus achieving sustainable cities.

### Critiques of agent-based modeling

Like for any modeling effort, there are limitations to agent-based modeling. We address these limitations in detail in Chapter 11, but there are two closely linked critiques that are worth addressing immediately. One has to do with the use of assumptions, and the other with the match between the ABM and the real world, and therefore with the value of the model for real policy and planning.

All models require assumptions. Certainly the commonly used suite of regression techniques makes many assumptions about the nature of the data, the causal process that produces them, and, perhaps most difficult, the structure of the (unobservable) error term (see any econometrics text for discussion).[46] However, as Henri Theil wrote, "Models are to be used, but not to be believed."[47] Models are sets of simplifying assumptions[48] put together in a manner that allows useful analysis, for we cannot directly deal with the "blooming, buzzing confusion"[49] of the real world.

An ABM is constructed to allow the dynamic modeling of a complex system and emergent outcomes—which regression methods are not well suited to do. Cities are certainly dynamic and complex. Our EJ ABM, described in Chapter 3, represents our understanding of environmental injustice as a social outcome that emerges from the city system—that is, we focus on a single emergent outcome, which makes our modeling task plausible, for modeling all emergent outcomes of a city would be extraordinarily difficult, if it is even possible. In order to develop a tractable model, we make distinctions between base assumptions and key assumptions.

Base assumptions are developed simply to make the simulated city look and act like a city in ways that are basically important to our analysis: We need firms to locate, people to locate, pollution and quality to spread, etc. In some cases, we can use assumptions that already exist in the computer-simulation literature—assumptions that have been shown to let ABMs approximate the real world. In other cases, we link the artificial world to the real world through the use of empirical data.

Key assumptions are those we use to test different hypotheses and theories about how the world works. For example, in Chapter 4 we can model both racist firms and economically rational firms, and test the differences in the emergence of environmental injustice under these different assumptions. These are key to developing insights into our understanding of EJ in particular, and would also be key in developing a model of more completely sustainable cities.

The purpose of the EJ ABM presented in this book is twofold: to analyze general insights into how environmental injustice may emerge in cities, and to illustrate the value of agent-based modeling as a technique for urban policy and planning. In order to make a general ABM useful for a specific city or region, it is necessary explicitly to tie a base, generalized model, such as we present here, to explicit real-world data relevant to the problem under study and the specific region under study. We illustrate an example of this linking of a general model and the real world in Chapter 10. Creating a site-specific version of the EJ ABM can help policymakers and administrators understand what is emergent in their jurisdictions, and even allow them to see and anticipate how their decisions in one area interact with decisions made in others to produce consequences perhaps none had expected.[50] However, even a contextualized model will not be a duplication of reality, though it still can help researchers understand and/or explain reality.

Agent-based modeling as a technique can easily use many different assumptions to offer multiple representations of the system under analysis. Though we provide sensitivity assessments of assumptions of the EJ ABM in Table 3.5 in Chapter 3, there are still literally hundreds or maybe even thousands of other experiments we could have done.[51] What experiments are crucial and needed depends upon what questions urban researchers and practitioners are interested in and for what purpose.

As for every model, the quality of assumptions matters in understanding and evaluating the results. In an ABM, good assumptions are driven by appropriate theoretical rationales, empirical observations, thoughtful reasoning, and careful testing. This is no different from any other research method.

## *Uses of computer simulations including ABMs*

We are certainly not the first to incorporate computer simulations in social science and policy analysis; previous uses have been diverse.[52] Their purposes include, but are not limited to, understanding, discovery, decision support, and training.[53]

Many different types of computer simulation models have been used in the social sciences, from system dynamics (SD) models in the early 1960s, to cellular automata (CA), microsimulation, and agent-based modeling.[54] Some simulation approaches are solely based on mathematical equations that specify the relationship between variables, while other approaches can incorporate decision-making actors, events, or objects into the model.[55] SD models use sets of differential equations for macro-level forecasting.[56] Properties and dynamics of a target system are described using a system of equations that drives the future state of the target system from its actual state.[57] A CA model is a primitive form of an agent-based model that consists of neighboring identical cells. Cells can be in states like "alive" or "dead," but are typically less complex in their internal processing and behavior than are an ABM's agents.[58] Microsimulation, developed in the 1970s, used individuals or households as the unit of analysis for macro-level forecasting. Unlike agent-based modeling, individuals or households do not directly interact or adapt in this type of simulation.[59] While the history of computer simulation in the social sciences is relatively short, inventories have been accumulated, including modeling approaches, toolkits, and applications.[60]

In terms of its applications, Heath, Hill, and Ciarallo claim that agent-based modeling has played three different roles in research: as a *generator* of hypotheses; as a *mediator* (or microscope), which enables insight into the system; and as a *predictor*.[61] Which role an ABM plays largely depends on the level of understanding about the real system the model aims to simulate. If the understanding of a system is low, agent-based modeling serves as a hypothesis generator. If a system is very well understood, agent-based modeling plays the role of predictor. When the level of understanding is in between, agent-based modeling can be used as a microscope to peer deep into the system. According to Heath et al., in social science research most ABMs have been used as hypothesis generators, while ABMs have been built as mediators in public policy research. As of 2009, no ABMs in their survey of 279 ABM articles had yet played the role of predictors, even in the areas of biology, ecology, and the military, where ABMs have played an important role for a relatively long time.[62]

The ABM's framework can also be designed to fit with other important frameworks. For example, the institutional analysis and development framework (IAD) developed by Ostrom and others for increasing the sustainability of common pool resources,[63] models the "action situation" as an important part of the framework. Ostrom describes the analytic elements of the Action Arena as a common set of variables used to describe the structure of an action situation, including: 1 the set of participants; 2 the specific positions to be filled by participants; 3 the set of allowable actions and their linkage to outcomes; 4 the potential outcomes that are linked to individual sequences of actions; 5 the level of control each participant has over choice; 6 the information available to participants about the structure of the action situation; and 7 the benefits and costs—which serve as incentives and deterrents—assigned to actions and outcomes.[64] This framework can readily be used as a guide to the elements of a useful ABM for environmental policy and planning.[65]

## The plan of the book

As indicated above, we aim to use agent-based modeling to analyze EJ as a systemic, emergent outcome with the intent of developing policy solutions that may more effectively address the environmental injustice problem than do current policies, and to illustrate the value of agent-based modeling in urban policy and planning for sustainability. In pursuit of these goals, the book is structured according to the following outline.

Chapter 2 provides some background on the empirical EJ research and expands on why we believe that little-used methods, such as agent-based modeling, are needed to move EJ research forward. We believe that in some sense empirical EJ research has reached a methodological dead end, and we explain why. Further, as mentioned above, we fear that policy based in the current research will miss important attributes of emergence and therefore is unlikely to be effective. This chapter also discusses agent-based modeling generally, and steps to follow when building an ABM.

Chapter 3 outlines the ABM we develop to analyze EJ (i.e., the EJ ABM). In order to illustrate how other analysts may develop ABMs for their own urban sustainability purposes, and also to illustrate the use of agent-based modeling as a synthetic experiment, we begin with discussion of a very simple, base EJ ABM, and discuss how we build up to a much more developed one that includes far more attributes of the real world. Of course, mimicking the real world is not the goal of models, so realism is added sparingly and for particular analytic purposes. Chapter 3 also addresses theoretical and empirical justifications for assumptions used in the EJ ABM, and provides a base point to which other chapters refer. Chapters 5 through 9 use variants of the EJ ABM, with key assumptions customized to address particular questions; the structure of these different variants is noted in Table 3.6.

Chapter 4 (and the Appendix) details the simplest EJ ABM specification, our experiments using it, and what we can learn from them. Though this basic ABM is highly simplified, we still begin customization by using US Census information on income and housing prices to link the simulation to key elements of the real world. Using this base model, we are able immediately to begin analysis of certain highly contested issues in the EJ literature. An ongoing tussle within the EJ literature surrounds firm behavior. This first model tests three theoretical assumptions: the economically rational firm, seeking the lowest-priced plot; the politically rational firm, seeking to stay away from the majority; and the discriminatory firm, seeking to locate near the minority. While the firm decision is the focus of this chapter, firms' decisions are made in a dynamic world in which residents also make decisions to locate based on their own decision rules.

Chapters 5, 6, and 7 add additional elements of complexity in residents' decision making to the base EJ ABM used in Chapter 4. Chapter 5 focuses on how constraints on residential choice—differential residential similarity preferences, racial compositions, and population growth rates—affect EJ outcomes. This is a useful question because some urban areas are much more constrained than others, and these tests examine the effects of factors that will differ between specific regions. Chapter 6 addresses a significant debate in the EJ literature: the relative effects of income and race on EJ. We are able to analyze this in the ABM by using US Census information to model income distributions in more detail than in Chapter 4. (Chapter 10 takes this approach further, and provides an example of coupling agent-based modeling with locally explicit geographic information system data.) Chapter 7 explores the role of residential mobility in explaining EJ outcomes. We experiment with key assumptions such that there is: 1 no mobility for residents; 2 perfect mobility, as assumed in the Tiebout hypothesis;[66] and 3 some mobility, based on what has been empirically observed in the United States.

In Chapters 8 and 9, in order to illustrate more clearly policy and planning values of agent-based modeling, we analyze potential solutions to emergent environmental injustice. In Chapter 8, in addition to continuing our focus on the circumstances that bring about EJ problems, we analyze zoning, which is a common local urban policy and planning tool. Here we review some debates on zoning and explicitly address a policy question: Is zoning that is designed to keep pollution separate from residents (that is, to internalize externalities) likely to be an effective solution to emergent EJ issues? Chapter 9 focuses on experimenting with the effectiveness of government cleanup strategies in dynamic neighborhoods. Cleanup assumptions include a government agent that focuses on: 1 the firm that is located on the highest-priced land; 2 the firm that emits the largest amount of pollution; or 3 the firm that is located on the land with the largest concentration of minority residents. Which is best for reducing environmental injustice?

In Chapter 10, Hal T. Nelson, Nicholas L. Cain, and Zining Yang discuss the use of agent-based modeling in the siting of high-power transmission lines. Their ABM is coupled with a geographic information systems (GIS) data structure. This allows contextualization of a general ABM to a very specific locale in the Los Angeles region. Earlier chapters present a limited integration of empirical data into agent-based modeling using income and housing price in the United States, and Chapter 10 illustrates ways to join specific real-world data and an ABM more robustly. This chapter shows versatility of agent-based modeling in extending its capacity to study EJ and other urban sustainability topics with empirical data, thus improving agent-based modeling's empirical validity as well as its ability to support locally specific policy decisions.

Chapter 11 brings together findings from the other chapters, and provides an overview of using the simulation approach presented herein with the goals of making better decisions for addressing environmental injustice in particular, and gaining better insight into environmental policy, planning, and sustainability in general.

The persistence of race- and ethnicity-based environmental injustice in cities in the United States and elsewhere is a troubling puzzle. We take the normative position that policy should be created to reduce environmental injustice, but we also expect that policies are unlikely to be successful without understanding the many complex conditions leading to environmental injustice within cities. The usual statistical approach to environmental policy and planning is at a point of diminishing returns in terms of helping us to understand this persistent problem, and the agent-based modeling approach gives us a new route with new insights and new types of empirical approaches.

## Notes

1 Kent E. Portney, *Taking Sustainable Cities Seriously: Economic Development, the Environment and Quality of Life in American Cities* (Cambridge, MA: The MIT Press, 2003); Annissa Alusi, Robert G. Eccles, Amy C. Edmondson, and Tiona Zuzul, "Sustainable Cities: Oxymoron or the Shape of the Future?" *Harvard Business School Working Paper* 11–062 (2011); Eric S. Zeemering, *Collaborative Strategies for Sustainable Cities: Economy, Environment and Community in Baltimore* (New York: Routledge, 2014).
2 Department of Economic and Social Affairs of the United Nations, *World Urbanization Prospects, 2014 Revision, Highlights* (New York: United Nations, 2014), 1.
3 Daniel J. Fiorino, "Sustainability as a Conceptual Focus for Public Administration." *Public Administration Review* 70, no. s1 (2010): s78–s88.
4 John Robinson and Jon Tinker, "Reconciling Ecological, Economic and Social Imperatives: A New Conceptual Framework," in *Surviving Globalism: The Social and Environmental Challenges*, ed. Ted Schrecker (London: Macmillan, 1997), 77; and see Heather E. Campbell and Elizabeth A. Corley, *Urban Environmental Policy Analysis* (Armonk, NY: ME Sharpe, 2012), Ch. 1.
5 Alusi et al., "Sustainable Cities."
6 City of Baltimore, *The Baltimore Sustainability Plan*, 2009, icma.org/en/icma/knowledge_network/documents/kn/Document/301385/The_Baltimore_Sustainabilty_Plan.
7 Zeemering, *Collaborative Strategies for Sustainable Cities*.
8 See Robert C. Paehlke, "Sustainability," in *Environmental Governance Reconsidered: Challenges, Choices, and Opportunities*, ed. Robert F. Durant, Daniel J. Fiorino, and Rosemary O'Leary (Cambridge, MA: The MIT Press, 2004), 35–68.
9 Fiorino, "Sustainability as a Conceptual Focus for Public Administration."
10 William J. Clinton, "Executive Order No. 12898," *Federal Register* 59, no. 32 (2/11/1994), 1, www.archives.gov/federal-register/executive-orders/pdf/12898.pdf.
11 European Commission, "Justice: EU and Roma" (last update, November 13, 2014), ec.europa.eu/justice/discrimination/roma/index_en.htm.
12 Maja Primorac, *International Political Economy of E-Scrap Trade and the Basel Convention*, unpublished dissertation (Claremont, CA: Claremont Graduate University, 2014).
13 Feng Liu, *Environmental Justice Analysis: Theories, Methods, and Practice* (Boca Raton, FL: CRC Press, 2001); United Church of Christ, Commission for Racial

Justice, *Toxic Wastes and Race: A National Report on the Racial and Socio-economic Characteristics of Communities with Hazardous Wastes Sites* (New York: United Church of Christ, 1987).

14  Heather E. Campbell, Laura R. Peck, and Michael K. Tschudi, "Justice for All? A Cross-time Analysis of Toxics Release Inventory Facility Location," *Review of Policy Research* 27, no. 1 (2010): 1–25.

15  Manuel Pastor, Jim Sadd, and John Hipp, "Which Came First? Toxic Facilities, Minority Move-in, and Environmental Justice," *Journal of Urban Affairs* 23, no. 1 (2001): 1–21.

16  Evan J. Ringquist, "Assessing Evidence of Environmental Inequities: A Meta-Analysis," *Journal of Policy Analysis and Management* 24, no. 2 (2005): 223–47.

17  Campbell et al., "Justice for All?"

18  Ringquist, "Assessing Evidence of Environmental Inequities."

19  Environmental Protection Agency, "Toxics Release Inventory (TRI) Program." Last modified August 27, 2013. www.epa.gov/tri.

20  Environmental Protection Agency, "Superfund." Last modified September 13, 2013. www.epa.gov/superfund.

21  Robin R. Sobotta, Heather E. Campbell, and Beverly J. Owens, "Aviation Noise and Environmental Justice: The Barrio Barrier," *Journal of Regional Science* 47, no. 1 (2007): 125–54.

22  Cheerios, "Heart Healthy." Television advertisement (General Mills, 2013).

23  See e.g., Ringquist, "Assessing Evidence of Environmental Inequities."

24  Campbell et al., "Justice for All?"

25  US Census Bureau, "Income," Table 697 Money Income of Families, 1990–2009, www.census.gov/compendia/statab/2012/tables/1220697.pdf.

26  Liu, *Environmental Justice Analysis.*

27  Pastor et al., "Which Came First?"

28  See Campbell et al., "Justice for All?" for an overview.

29  Emergence is still one of the unsettled concepts in science. Originally, J.S. Mill stated heteropathic laws that "could not be deduced from knowledge of the laws of action of their component parts," in his *A System of Logic* (1872). For the historical development of the concept, see David Blitz, *Emergent Evolution* (Dordrecht, The Netherlands: Kluwer Academic Publishers, 2010), 76–80. Based on Mill's idea, G.H. Lewes termed the "emergent" as something that is incommensurable and cannot be reduced to sums or differences, in contrast to the "resultant," which is a sum or a difference of the cooperant forces. There are different interpretations of the concept depending upon disciplinary areas. See J.H. Holland, *Emergence from Chaos to Order* (Cambridge, MA: Addison-Wesley, 1998); R. Keith Sawyer, *Social Emergence: Societies as Complex Systems* (New York: Cambridge University Press, 2005); Mark A. Bedau and Paul Humphreys, eds, *Emergence: Contemporary Readings in Philosophy and Science* (Cambridge, MA: The MIT Press, 2008). In this book, we take the interpretation that has been used by some agent-based researchers such as Joshua Epstein.

30  Joshua Epstein, "Modeling Civil Violence: An Agent-Based Computational Approach," *Proceedings of the National Academy of Sciences of the United States of America* 99, no. 3 (2002): 7245.

31  Michael Batty, Yichun Xie, and Zhanli Sun, "Modeling Urban Dynamics through GIS-Based Cellular Automata," *Computers, Environment and Urban Systems* 23, no. 3 (1999): 205–33.

32  Anand Desai, ed., *Simulation for Policy Inquiry* (New York: Springer, 2012).

33  It is interesting to note that Downs found that simply building more highway capacity will not generally solve traffic congestion problems. Anthony Downs, *Stuck in Traffic: Coping with Peak-hour Traffic Congestion* (Washington, DC: Brookings Institution Press and the Lincoln Institute of Land Policy, 1992).

34 Batty et al., "Modeling Urban Dynamics through GIS-Based Cellular Automata," 207.

35 Thomas C. Schelling, *Micromotives and Macrobehaviour* (New York: W.W. Norton, 1978).

36 Joshua M. Epstein, *Generative Social Science: Studies in Agent-Based Computational Modeling* (Princeton, NJ: Princeton University Press, 2006); John H. Miller and Scott E. Page, *Complex Adaptive Systems: An Introduction to Computational Models of Social Life* (Princeton, NJ: Princeton University Press, 2007); Nigel Gilbert and Klaus Troitzsch, *Simulation for the Social Scientist* (Maidenhead: Open University Press, 2005).

37 In object-oriented programming (OOP) for agent-based modeling, "objects" are fundamental building blocks that represent elements in the system that the modeler aims to represent (e.g., firms in a city). Each object can be looked at as if it were a little stand-alone computer program: each one stores data and responds to information received from other objects. For instance, objects representing firms in a city can store information about the proportion of majority residents in their neighborhoods and decide to move to another place when the proportion reaches a certain threshold. An agent-based model that represents a certain system is a bundle of such objects.

38 Stan Franklin and Art Graesser, "Is it an Agent or Just a Program? A Taxonomy for Autonomous Agents," in *Intelligent Agents III: Agent Theories, Architecture and Language* (Berlin: Springer, 1996), 21–35.

39 Nigel Gilbert, *Agent-Based Models* (Thousands Oaks, CA: Sage Publication, 2008), 1.

40 "Autonomous agents are computational systems that inhabit some complex dynamic environment, sense and act autonomously in this environment, and by doing so realize a set of goals or tasks for which they are designed." Franklin and Graesser, "Is it an Agent or Just a Program?" 22; Joshua M. Epstein, *Generative Social Science: Studies in Agent-Based Computational Modeling* (Princeton, NJ: Princeton University Press, 2007); John H. Miller and Scott E. Page, *Complex Adaptive Systems: An Introduction to Computational Models of Social Life* (Princeton, NJ: Princeton University Press, 2007).

41 Gilbert, *Agent-Based Models*.

42 Ibid., xi, emphases added.

43 Though agent-based modeling is dynamic, note the similarity between agent-based modeling and "comparative statics" formal modeling in microeconomics, which allow the analyst to derive, based on assumptions, the sign of an unknown partial derivative of interest.

44 Waldo Tobler, "A Computer Movie Simulating Urban Growth in the Detroit Region," *Economic Geography* 46 (1970): 234–40, at 236.

45 This concept is similar to that of market prices in (perfectly) competitive markets. In a competitive market, no one actor—or one set of actor types—determines the market price, nor can the influence of a single actor be understood.

46 For example, Damodar Gujarati and Dawn Porter, *Basic Econometrics*, fifth edn (New York: McGraw-Hill/Irwin, 2008).

47 Henri Theil, *Principles of Econometrics* (New York: Wiley, 1971), vi.

48 Personal communication, Steven Garber, PhD.

49 William James, *The Principles of Psychology* (USA, 1890), Chapter 13.

50 George E.P. Box and Norman Richard Draper, *Empirical Model Building and Response Surfaces* (New York: John Wiley & Sons, 1987).

51 For most parameters, we calculated the local sensitivity as recommended by Steven Railsback and Volker Grimm, *Agent-Based and Individual-Based Modeling* (Princeton, NJ: Princeton University Press, 2011), 293–95.

52  Gönenç Yücel and Els van Daalen, "An Objective-Based Perspective on Assessment of Model-Supported Policy Processes," *Journal of Artificial Societies and Social Simulation* 12, no. 4 (2009), jasss.soc.surrey.ac.uk/12/4/3.html; Harold Guetzkow, ed., *Simulation in Social Science: Readings* (Englewood Cliffs, NJ: Prentice-Hall, 1962); Anand Desai, ed., *Simulation for Policy Inquiry* (New York: Springer, 2012).
53  Nigel Gilbert and Klaus Troitzsch, *Simulation for the Social Scientist* (Maidenhead: Open University Press, 2005); Joshua Epstein, "Why Model?" *Journal of Artificial Societies and Social Simulation* 11, no. 14 (2008).
54  Gilbert and Troitzsch, *Simulation for the Social Scientist.*
55  H. Van Dyke Parunak, Robert Savit, and Rick L. Riolo, "Agent-Based Modeling vs. Equation-Based Modeling: A Case Study and Users' Guide," in *Multi-Agent Systems and Agent-Based Simulation*, ed. Jaime Simao Sichman, Rosario Conte, and Nigel Gilbert (Berlin: Springer, 1998), 10–25.
56  Michael W. Macy and Robert Willer, "From Factors to Actors: Computational Sociology and Agent-Based Modeling," *Annual Review of Sociology* 28 (2002): 143–66.
57  Gilbert and Troitzsch, *Simulation for the Social Scientist.*
58  Ibid.
59  Macy and Willer, "From Factors to Actors."
60  Gilbert and Troitzsch, *Simulation for the Social Scientist.*
61  Brian Heath, Raymond Hill, and Frank Ciarallo, "A Survey of Agent-Based Modeling Practices (January 1998 to July 2008)," *Journal of Artificial Societies and Social Simulation* 12, no. 4 (2009), jasss.soc.surrey.ac.uk/12/4/9.html.
62  Ibid.
63  For an overview, see Elinor Ostrom, "Institutional Rational Choice: An Assessment of the Institutional Analysis and Development Framework," in *Theories of the Policy Process*, ed. Paul Sabatier (Boulder, CO: Westview Press, 2007), 21–64.
64  Ibid., 29.
65  For more thorough discussion of the integration of IAD and ABM, see Amineh Ghorbani, Pieter Bots, Virginia Dignum, and Gerard Dijkema, "MAIA: A Framework for Developing Agent-Based Social Simulations," *Journal of Artificial Societies and Social Simulation* 16, no. 9 (2013), jasss.soc.surrey.ac.uk/16/2/9.html.
66  Charles Tiebout, "A Pure Theory of Local Expenditure," *Journal of Political Economy* 64, no. 5 (1956): 416–24, www.jstor.org/stable/1826343.

## References

Alusi, Annissa, Robert G. Eccles, Amy C. Edmondson and Tiona Zuzul. "Sustainable Cities: Oxymoron or The Shape of the Future?" *Harvard Business School Working Paper* 11–062 (2011).
Batty, Michael, Yichun Xie and Zhanli Sun. "Modeling Urban Dynamics through GIS-Based Cellular Automata." *Computers, Environment and Urban Systems* 23, no. 3 (1999): 205–233.
Bedau, Mark A. and Paul Humphreys, eds. *Emergence: Contemporary Readings in Philosophy and Science.* Cambridge, MA: The MIT Press, 2008.
Blitz, David. *Emergent Evolution.* Dordrecht, The Netherlands: Kluwer Academic Publishers, 2010.
Box, George E.P. and Norman Richard Draper. *Empirical Model Building and Response Surfaces.* New York: John Wiley & Sons, 1987.
Campbell, Heather E. and Elizabeth A. Corley. *Urban Environmental Policy Analysis.* Armonk, NY: ME Sharpe, 2012.

Campbell, Heather E., Laura R. Peck and Michael K. Tschudi. "Justice for All? A Cross-Time Analysis of Toxics Release Inventory Facility Location." *Review of Policy Research* 27, no. 1 (2010): 1–25.

Cheerios. "Heart Healthy." Television Advertisement. General Mills, 2013.

City of Baltimore. *The Baltimore Sustainability Plan.* icma.org/en/icma/knowledge_net work/documents/kn/Document/301385/The_Baltimore_Sustainabilty_Plan, 2009.

Clinton, William J. "Executive Order No. 12898." *Federal Register* 59, no. 32 (February 11, 1994.)

Department of Economic and Social Affairs of the United Nations. *World Urbanization Prospects, 2014 Revision, Highlights.* New York: United Nations. 2014.

Desai, Anand, ed. *Simulation for Policy Inquiry.* New York: Springer, 2012.

Downs, Anthony. *Stuck in Traffic: Coping with Peak-hour Traffic Congestion.* Washington, DC: Brookings Institution Press and the Lincoln Institute of Land Policy, 1992.

Environmental Protection Agency. "Superfund." Last modified September 13, 2013. www.epa.gov/superfund.

Environmental Protection Agency. "Toxics Release Inventory (TRI) Program." Last modified August 27, 2013. www.epa.gov/tri.

Epstein, Joshua M. *Generative Social Science: Studies in Agent-Based Computational Modeling.* Princeton, NJ: Princeton University Press, 2006.

Epstein, Joshua. "Modeling Civil Violence: An Agent-Based Computational Approach." *Proceedings of the National Academy of Sciences of the United States of America* 99, no. 3 (2002): 7243–7250.

Epstein, Joshua. "Why Model?" *Journal of Artificial Societies and Social Simulation* 11, no. 14 (2008). jasss.soc.surrey.ac.uk/11/4/12/12.pdf.

European Commission. "Justice: EU and Roma" Last updated November 13, 2014. ec.europa.eu/justice/discrimination/roma/index_en.htm.

Fiorino, Daniel J. "Sustainability as a Conceptual Focus for Public Administration." *Public Administration Review* 70, no. s1 (2010): s78–s88.

Franklin, Stan and Art Graesser. "Is it an Agent or Just a Program? A Taxonomy for Autonomous Agents." In *Intelligent Agents III: Agent Theories, Architecture and Language.* Berlin: Springer, 1996.

Ghorbani, Amineh, Pieter Bots, Virginia Dignum and Gerard Dijkema. "MAIA: A Framework for Developing Agent-Based Social Simulations." *Journal of Artificial Societies and Social Simulation* 16, no. 9 (2013), jasss.soc.surrey.ac.uk/16/2/9.html.

Gilbert, Nigel. *Agent-Based Models.* Thousand Oaks, CA: Sage Publications, 2008.

Gilbert, Nigel and Klaus Troitzsch. *Simulation for the Social Scientist.* Maidenhead: Open University Press, 2005.

Guetzkow, Harold, ed. *Simulation in Social Science: Readings.* Englewood Cliffs, NJ: Prentice-Hall, 1962.

Gujarati, Damodar and Dawn Porter. *Basic Econometrics.* Fifth edn. New York: McGraw-Hill/Irwin, 2008.

Heath, Brian, Raymond Hill and Frank Ciarallo. "A Survey of Agent-Based Modeling Practices (January 1998 to July 2008)." *Journal of Artificial Societies and Social Simulation* 12, no. 4 (2009), jasss.soc.surrey.ac.uk/12/4/9.html.

James, William. *The Principles of Psychology.* USA, 1890.

Holland, J.H. *Emergence from Chaos to Order.* Cambridge, MA: Addison-Wesley, 1998.

Liu, Feng. *Environmental Justice Analysis: Theories, Methods, and Practice.* Boca Raton, FL: CRC Press, 2001.

Macy, Michael W. and Robert Willer. "From Factors to Actors: Computational Sociology and Agent-Based Modeling." *Annual Review of Sociology* 28 (2002): 143–166.

Mill, John Stuart. *A System of Logic.* 1872.

Miller, John H. and Scott E. Page. *Complex Adaptive Systems: An Introduction to Computational Models of Social Life.* Princeton, NJ: Princeton University Press, 2007.

Ostrom, Elinor. "Institutional Rational Choice: An Assessment of the Institutional Analysis and Development Framework." In *Theories of the Policy Process*, edited by Paul A. Sabatier. Boulder, CO: Westview Press, 2007.

Paehlke, Robert C. "Sustainability." In *Environmental Governance Reconsidered: Challenges, Choices, and Opportunities*, edited by Robert F. Durant, Daniel J. Fiorino and Rosemary O'Leary. Cambridge, MA: The MIT Press, 2004.

Parunak, H. Van Dyke, Robert Savit and Rick L. Riolo. "Agent-Based Modeling vs. Equation-Based Modeling: A Case Study and Users' Guide." In *Multi-Agent Systems and Agent-Based Simulation*, edited by Jaime Simao Sichman, Rosario Conte and Nigel Gilbert. Berlin: Springer, 1998, 10–25.

Pastor, Manuel, Jim Sadd and John Hipp. "Which Came First? Toxic Facilities, Minority Move-in, and Environmental Justice." *Journal of Urban Affairs* 23, no. 1 (2001): 1–21.

Portney, Kent E. *Taking Sustainable Cities Seriously: Economic Development, the Environment and Quality of Life in American Cities.* Cambridge, MA: The MIT Press, 2003.

Primorac, Maja. *International Political Economy of E-Scrap Trade and the Basel Convention.* Unpublished dissertation, Claremont, CA: Claremont Graduate University, 2014.

Railsback, Steven F. and Volker Grimm. *Agent-Based and Individual-Based Modeling.* Princeton, NJ: Princeton University Press, 2011.

Ringquist, Evan J. "Assessing Evidence of Environmental Inequities: A Meta-Analysis." *Journal of Policy Analysis and Management* 24, no. 2 (2005): 223–247.

Robinson, John and Jon Tinker. "Reconciling Ecological, Economic and Social Imperatives: A New Conceptual Framework." In *Surviving Globalism: The Social and Environmental Challenges*, edited by Ted Schrecker. London: Macmillan, 1997.

Sawyer, R. Keith. *Social Emergence: Societies As Complex Systems.* New York: Cambridge University Press, 2005.

Schelling, Thomas C. *Micromotives and Macrobehavior.* New York: W.W. Norton, 1978.

Sobotta, Robin R., Heather E. Campbell and Beverly J. Owens. "Aviation Noise and Environmental Justice: The Barrio Barrier." *Journal of Regional Science* 47, no. 1 (2007): 125–154.

Theil, Henri. *Principles of Econometrics.* New York: Wiley, 1971.

Tiebout, Charles. "A Pure Theory of Local Expenditure." *Journal of Political Economy* 64, no. 5 (1956): 416–424. www.jstor.org/stable/1826343.

Tobler, Waldo. "A Computer Movie Simulating Urban Growth in the Detroit Region." *Economic Geography* 46 (1970): 234–240.

United Church of Christ, Commission for Racial Justice. *Toxic Wastes and Race: A National Report on the Racial and Socioeconomic Characteristics of Communities with Hazardous Wastes Sites.* New York: United Church of Christ, 1987.

US Census Bureau. "Income." Table 697 Money Income of Families, 1990–2009. www.census.gov/compendia/statab/2012/tables/1220697.pdf.

Yücel, Gönenç and Els van Daalen. "An Objective-Based Perspective on Assessment of Model-Supported Policy Processes." *Journal of Artificial Societies and Social Simulation* 120, no. 4 (2009), jasss.soc.surrey.ac.uk/12/4/3.html.

Zeemering, Eric S. *Collaborative Strategies for Sustainable Cities: Economy, Environment and Community in Baltimore.* New York: Routledge, 2014.

# 2 Environmental justice, urban sustainability, and agent-based modeling

Under a market system, we might expect there to be differential environmental outcomes between the wealthy and the poor. The wealthy, having the resources to pay more, can opt to live in areas with high environmental quality, which puts a premium on environmental quality that the poor likely cannot afford. Indeed, the poor do tend to live with worse environmental quality than the wealthy. However, there is also accumulated evidence indicating that the disproportionate collocation of environmentally harmful facilities and locales—referred to as disamenities—with racial and ethnic minorities is not fully explained by socioeconomic status, and that race itself is an important factor.[1] Some studies do not find disproportionate minority-based collocation,[2] but of course failure to find minority-based environmental injustice in one situation does not demonstrate that it does not exist in another. As Noonan points out, choice of the size of the analytic space used for EJ analysis can affect findings.[3] Ringquist's meta-analysis of the EJ literature finds that overall the literature indicates that race/ethnicity-based environmental injustice is present in the United States, though he estimates that the magnitude of the effects is small.[4] His work is in keeping with some earlier meta-analyses, including one by Mohai and Saha.[5] However, there is considerably less clarity with regard to why or how this inequality occurs.

This book analyzes potential pathways that may contribute to observed environmental injustice in society. EJ is important both in and of itself and as a consideration in sustainability analysis. The book uses agent-based modeling, a type of computational simulation that, as we note in Chapter 1, has a particular strength in linking what we observe in society with how it comes about.

Below, we review terminology, issues, challenges, and findings in the empirical EJ literature, and then elaborate on adding agent-based modeling to EJ and other urban research and practice.

## Terminology

It has been noted for at least 25 years that racial and/or ethnic minorities have tended to live in communities with lower levels of environmental quality than white populations, even controlling for many other factors including income. In 1987, the United Church of Christ (UCC) issued a report[6] that drew broad attention to this issue. This report incorporated a normative focus on *outcome* fairness, rooted in the racial and social-justice activist traditions.

Since the UCC report, different terms have been used to describe this social phenomenon, with the dominant term at any given point usually reflecting the causal assumption made in research or political activity related to it. Reflecting the germination of these ideas in the activist community, initially the term *environmental racism* was common. This term not only implies, but outright states, the suspected cause of environmental disparities. However, some argue that the term is inappropriate because it assumes that the observed unjust outcomes are intentional.[7] Others, though, including Bullard, argue that "racism" can indicate any differential outcome, "whether intended or not."[8] Still others, such as Noonan, point out that defining as "racist" differential outcomes that could be based on individual market choices rather than overt discriminatory behavior—such as poorer people choosing to live where housing is less expensive—may be paternalistic.[9] However, with many studies finding that environmental disparities by race are prevalent even when controlling for wealth variability, a market explanation is clearly insufficient.

The term *environmental equity* has also been used, perhaps most prominently by the Environmental Protection Agency's (EPA) Environmental Equity Working Group, formed in 1990, which was the EPA's first formal organizational confrontation of this issue.[10] Although this term gets around the troublesome assumption of cause embedded in the term "environmental racism," some, such as Zimmerman, argue that the term "equity" focuses attention on equal outcomes as opposed to fair procedures.[11] In 1994 the EPA renamed the Office of Environmental Equity as the Office of Environmental Justice.[12]

Implicitly accepting critique of the term "environmental equity," researchers have tended to use the term *environmental justice* (EJ), and although this term has been criticized by some for being too focused on procedural justice, to the detriment of outcome concerns,[13] it has come to be the dominant term in this field. The different terms, and critiques of those terms, both underlie and reflect the lack of a settled explanation for observed race/ethnicity-based environmental disparities.

Regardless of the terminology used, the evidence suggests that environmental disparity, or environmental *in*justice, exists, at least in part, in the disproportionate collocation of minorities with environmental hazards or hazardous facilities (even controlling for other factors). This definition of environmental injustice fits with the EPA's statement that "Fair treatment means that no group of people should bear a disproportionate share of the negative environmental consequences resulting from industrial, governmental and commercial operations or policies."[14]

Throughout this work we use the term environmental justice, or EJ, to indicate this field of study generally, and the term environmental *in*justice to indicate findings of disproportionate environmental effects based on race or ethnicity and controlling for other factors such as cost, income, and the movement of minorities into the ambit of environmental disamenities.

We concur with those who argue that "racism" should be used to denote intentional acts of discrimination, rather than unequal outcomes, though other scholars such as Pulido have articulated forcefully and well that this requirement is too strong.[15] At this point there is little *direct* evidence of environmental racism as here defined, though there is much evidence of environmental injustice (or, in other words, a lack of environmental equity) and some *indirect* evidence of environmental racism.[16] In the EJ ABM we are nonetheless able to model direct racism in some analyses.

In spite of our use of EJ as our preferred term, we do not focus on procedures, but on outcomes; we seek to understand the circumstances under which race- and ethnicity-based environmental injustice occurs so that we can make suggestions about what administrators can do to reduce it. By doing this, we do not intend to undercut the importance of procedures in achieving environmental justice. How environmentally significant decisions are made, in terms of participants, values considered, and remedies allocated, matters in improving EJ,[17] and broadly matters to principles of sustainability, democracy, and citizen perception of government. For example, research finds that governmental actions to remedy environmental injustice—and otherwise to promote sustainability—can be unevenly allocated among communities. Konisky found that the US Federal EJ policy during the mid-1990s increased state enforcement of the Clean Air Act (CAA) in large African-American communities, but decreased enforcement in communities with large poor and Hispanic populations.[18] Studying the implementation of the CAA, Konisky and Reenock further found that firms in minority or poor communities were more likely to be violators of the CAA and less likely to be coded as noncompliant by bureaucrats.[19] These procedural and political dimensions are important to understanding as well as addressing EJ, but are different from the focus of this book. Here we limit our focus, and thus our review of the literature, to ongoing methodological puzzles and to factors that concern economic and social processes that lead to EJ outcomes so that the EJ conversation can be extended to political and broader sustainability dimensions elsewhere.

## Issues in EJ research

### *Measurement of environmental injustice*

One of the key issues in environmental justice literature is the problem of measuring the actual disparities. Ideally, the true measure of environmental injustice would be disproportionate *exposure* to environmental problems, but measurement of actual exposure is sufficiently difficult that only a few authors use exposure measures rather than distance measures. Gen, Shafer, and Nakagawa[20] compare actual wastewater exposures to perceptions, but otherwise when exposure measures are used, they tend to be modeled instead of measured. For example, Jarrett et al.[21] use modeled levels of actual particulate exposure; Sobotta, Campbell, and Owens[22] use modeled levels of actual noise exposure; Eckerd and Keeler[23] create a hazard index based on the presence of pollutants at contaminated sites; and Morello-Frosch, Pastor and Sadd[24] look at modeled cancer risks due to air emission inventories. However, even these uses of modeled exposure measures are exceptions.

The majority of EJ studies use some nearness indicator rather than actual exposure levels, resulting in at least two problems. As advocates point out, these studies fail to take into account the accumulation of risk caused by multiple disamenities, which are often clustered in neighborhoods;[25] and for some pollutants nearness is not so important as are other physical relationships— for example, whether a resident is downwind or upwind of a polluting site, or whether the pollution source and residents share an aquifer.

### The firm decision processes

Another important issue in EJ scholarship is how polluting firms and other facilities—some polluting facilities are government owned—make decisions. From quite early in the EJ research, scholars accepted that no matter what other factors came into play, firms would consider economic factors in deciding where to locate. In reasonably competitive markets, even an overtly racist decision maker would have to consider costs in order to stay in business against non-racist competitors. Hamilton[26] added the important insight that just measuring traditional economic cost factors alone was insufficient since political factors—and in particular factors related to the ability to engage in collective action—matter, too.

In the market-based view of environmental inequity, the goal of firms is assumed to be maximizing profits and minimizing costs. Firms seek to locate where the price of land is cheap and materials are nearby, thus minimizing transportation costs. In this view, environmental inequity is explained because the places where the poor live satisfy such conditions better than areas with a higher proportion of rich residents, and minorities are poorer on average than majorities. Subsequent to the siting of a polluting firm, the poor may opt to live in proximity to it both because of the potential job opportunities offered at such firms,[27] and also because the presence of such a firm is likely to depress property values nearby. This social process can inevitably lead to the disproportionate collocation of firms—these "environmental disamenities"—with minority residents.

One problem with this view is that Ringquist's meta-analysis[28] indicates that, overall, poverty is not as important an explanatory variable as is race/

ethnicity. As other research shows, the market explanation, rooted in the premium some can pay for environmental quality, is sometimes an important factor, but it is not sufficient to explain the problem. If market considerations alone cannot explain disparities, what set of social processes has even the potential to lead to environmentally disproportionate outcomes for minority groups? One possibility that has been proposed is that minorities care less about the environment than majorities, but scholars including Mohai and Bryant have found evidence opposed to this theory.[29] In addition, Manuel Pastor, Jim Sadd, and John Hipp explicitly examined the issue of whether minorities have a tendency to move into polluted areas, and found minorities more likely to live in the studied region prior to disamenities being sited, rather than to move in after the polluting firm was located there.[30]

In some cases, the "discriminatory decision-maker" argument is plausible. For example, Sobotta, Campbell, and Owens[31] examined airport noise—noise caused by airline operations in and out of an airport—and found that being located in a Hispanic community was the best predictor of excess noise exposure. In this case, decisions on exposure were made by a specific, identifiable decision-making body that was provided with detailed information on relevant demographics, including specific identification of the location of traditionally Hispanic communities. In this case, though we cannot know with certainty what the decision criteria were, it is clear how an EJ problem *could* arise from a single, informed, decision-making body if at least some members were racist.

However, in some circumstances the discrimination argument is problematic. For example, in Campbell, Peck and Tschudi,[32] the examined environmental disamenity is newly locating toxics release inventory facilities (TRIFs) during the 1980s, 1990s, and early 2000s. TRIFs are individually owned firms or other facilities, including some that are owned by various levels of government, which release known toxins "'beyond the fence line'—outside of the facility."[33] Therefore, in this case there are many different decision makers, many of whom are unlikely to communicate or collude with one another, making overt coordinated discrimination an unlikely possibility. So, the Campbell, Peck and Tschudi finding of disproportionate collocation of new TRIFs with pre-existing concentrations of Asian populations is confusing. What social process leads to such an outcome? Can it really be the case that many independently acting TRIF decision makers, both public and private, in Arizona's Maricopa County discriminate against Asians holding constant other decision factors such as costs, anticipated political pressures, etc.? Even though Asians are often considered "the model minority"?[34] In Campbell and colleagues' study, the effect of increasing proportions of Asian residents in a community is not only statistically significant, but its coefficient is the greatest in magnitude of any other factor except the previous presence of a TRIF.[35]

There are some social conditions—such as the Jim Crow era in the US South, or the apartheid era in South Africa, for example—in which such consistent discriminatory behavior might be expected, but not in others. This problem of multiple decision makers acting independently affects research using TRIFs and also research using hazardous waste facilities (sometimes called TSDFs for treatment, storage and disposal facilities), and perhaps overall air pollution,[36] or any other disamenity that is produced via a process such that there are many different decision makers in a social context in which preferences for discrimination cannot be expected to be highly similar.

Even if one accepts, as do we, that there is significant evidence of race- and ethnicity-based environmental injustice in at least some situations in the United States, this still does not solve the problem of intent.[37] Even if we know that environmental disamenities are disproportionately placed within minority communities—even controlling for economic and political factors—and that mitigation of these disamenities is slower in minority communities,[38] this does not tell us about the *intent* of the placers or the mitigators. Specifically, we do not know if racist, discriminatory, or other invidious goals are the reason. We expect that simply asking decision makers would not be effective, since racism is socially unacceptable and therefore unlikely to be openly revealed even if it is the reason.

Agent-based modeling is one method particularly suited to beginning to answer the types of questions outlined here. It allows for simulated experimentation with competing explanations, helping us understand what conditions have the potential to lead to observed outcomes. Understanding these conditions can help practitioners ameliorate them.

## Temporal and spatial issues

Beyond the problem of the unobservability of decision-maker intent, other issues in empirical EJ research using traditional analytical techniques have led to disagreements over whether the evidence is strong enough to infer racism or not. Some critiques fundamentally reduce to the well-known axiom that correlation does not imply causation. Though the evidence seems clear that there are often disparities, some scholars (as mentioned above) have argued that these were due to economic efficiency (cost minimization) rather than racism. A key question here is timing: observing that environmental disamenities are disproportionately collocated with minority residents at a particular point in time does not demonstrate that the minority groups were there at the time of the siting of the disamenity (which would be a necessary condition for a racism argument if minorities have residential choice); for a variety of reasons (some discussed earlier), minorities could have moved there afterward, in line with market explanations.

As mentioned previously with respect to timing, both Pastor, Sadd and Hipp (2001, using Los Angeles County),[39] and Campbell, Peck, and Tschudi (2010, using Maricopa County)[40] were able to control for which came first, the minority population or the disamenity, and found evidence that new disamenities tended to be sited in existing minority communities. Both of these studies also controlled for factors that should affect the ability to engage in collective action (as Hamilton notes is important),[41] and Pastor et al. also use a simultaneous equations model and are able to estimate minority move-in and move-out post-siting. Yet, in both studies minority status remained an important predictor of facility siting. Further, Eckerd and Keeler[42] find that cleanup of "brownfields" (plots of polluted land) occurs more slowly in communities with more minority residents than in communities with more majority residents. Thus, in one way or another, all of these directly address timing, and at least to some extent control for the propensity to engage in collective action, and still find evidence of environmental injustice.

In addition to timing considerations, much of the previous research lacks important variables affecting the firm's location decision, such as the presence of other, pre-existing firms in a neighborhood.[43] In 2009, Wolverton's analysis provided evidence that the value of a variable measuring pre-existing disamenities was robust to the inclusion or exclusion of any of the other variables in explaining a firm's location decision.[44] She conjectured that there may be three reasons why a pre-existing disamenity increases the likelihood of a new one: The pre-existing facilities may: 1 signal the lower resistance-level of the community to such facilities; 2 be a proxy for zoning laws; or 3 imply agglomeration economies. "Agglomeration economies" are the assumption that when firms of the same or related types cluster together, that reduces costs for all. Since firms are expected to cost-minimize, this means new firms are likely to locate near existing ones of the same or similar type. Bowen, Atlas and Lee[45] argue that industrial agglomeration should be explicitly incorporated in environmental justice research (and, as discussed later, we include firm agglomeration in our EJ ABM).

Using related ideas, Morello-Frosch et al.[46] emphasized that it is important to consider land-use variables in EJ research (e.g., population density, urbanization, and the percentage of land devoted to residential use); zoning is not neutral and can influence social processes that lead to environmental injustice or subsequent EJ outcomes.

In examining EJ, the issue of spatial scale has also been a major consideration. A substantial body of EJ research has utilized the classic unit-hazard coincident method, which compares demographic characteristics in predefined geographical units that contain hazardous sites or facilities to geographical units without them.[47] This conventional approach is criticized, and alternative approaches (such as a distance-based approach) have been suggested to overcome the limitations of the conventional method.[48] However, it is not easy to answer what an appropriate geographical unit or scale is to examine such a social process as EJ—and this problem also applies to sustainability in general. For instance, there are analyses of the Federal National Priorities List (the Federal Superfund program) that show the sensitivity of empirical evidence to a researcher's choice of spatial scales.[49] Findings were inconsistent based on what geographical units were selected as the units of analysis, including options such as county, ZIP code, Census tract, or Census Block Group. In addition, EJ outcomes can vary depending upon whether analysis is at the national or local levels.[50] Evidence of environmental injustice at the national level does not imply the same result at local levels, and vice versa.

These considerations are directly related to the well-known modifiable areal unit problem (MAUP) in spatial data analysis, which refers to a phenomenon that statistical results depend on scale or partitioning of areal units.[51] However, to study geographic data some spatial demarcation must be used, so the MAUP is not an issue that can be empirically resolved,[52] with the fact that we cannot know the correct areal unit for empirical analysis increasing the likelihood that spatial autocorrelation will be present in data.[53]

In general, scholars using empirical data are forced to use some type of spatial unit, and these structures, usually created for other purposes, are irrelevant to the spatial effects of polluting or polluted facilities. However, distance-based measures are also problematic, in that they assume a concentric quality of impact that may not take other spatial or geographic considerations into account.

Further, some of the statistical critiques that have already been addressed, for example by Pastor et al.,[54] have to do with dynamics of the urban system. In other words, issues of space and timing in the literature—such as which came first, the residents or the disamenities, and do minorities move into or move out from the ambit of the disamenity—are really issues of the dynamism of the urban system, even though analyses have been focused on only two actor types: firms and residents. Yet, there are other actors in this dynamic system, such as local government, and there are other important elements, such as urban form,[55] that potentially affect EJ and other sustainability findings. Dealing with all of these in multivariate regression, using existing data structures (such as ZIP codes and Census tracts), is cumbersome at best. Moreover, unless doing data mining, regression only tests hypotheses that the researcher already considers plausible, but, given the dynamic complexity of the urban form, there are likely to be explanations for the problem that have not yet been considered.

## Why do we believe that empirical-statistical EJ research is at an impasse?

For reasons referenced above, we believe that the traditional, empirical-statistical EJ research has reached a methodological roadblock. Many scholars simply do not accept the results of the large empirical research literature showing race- and ethnicity-based environmental injustice—even when the research controls for many other possible causal factors and even corrects for many identified statistical errors. They do not accept the results because the findings, and the implication of environmental racism, do not accord with assumptions of their disciplines, or with the assumption of competitive housing markets in American cities.

Even more troubling to us, the tools so far used cannot explain why the oft-repeated results are found—whether due to racism or something else—and this has become an important barrier for the EJ literature. In addition, the argument within the literature as to whether "*the* cause" of observed inequity is racism can make members of the majority feel defensive, and distracts research from *solutions* that policymakers and administrators might pursue. If racism is *the* cause, is the only solution to "fix" racism? As we have seen over many decades and societies, this is a tall order. However, if emergent social interactions are causes, we may have some hope of creating a systemic, structural change. We need an analytic method that allows us to consider the dynamism of the urban environment and examine under what conditions we do and do not observe environmentally unjust outcomes. This is one of the key reasons why we have turned to agent-based modeling.

## An agent-based modeling approach

Agent-based modeling can address a number of the issues outlined above. It offers the ability to test the underlying assumptions of existing EJ theories. This is an advantage of the method over other approaches, in large part because of the different nature of the assumptions that underlie other research methods. For example, in empirical statistical analysis, we can include variables measuring economic rationality, and also variables measuring race and ethnicity, with the goal of testing which is correct. However, as is often the case, if support is found for the importance of both economic rationality *and* race and ethnicity—which are often assumed to be mutually exclusive—the reason that race and ethnicity were estimated as important is unclear, leading to many of the methodological arguments in the literature that we have discussed above. In an ABM, we can instead directly manipulate underlying reasons (decision-maker racism, etc.) to see which lead to race and ethnicity being important to outcomes, and which do not.

In addition, in regression analysis with an interval-level dependent variable, it becomes difficult to estimate and interpret many variables interacting with each other, but agent-based modeling directly allows such interactive estimation. In an ABM, we assume that parameters and systems are interdependent—a key assumption for understanding emergent outcomes of systems, rather than independent effects of variables.

Qualitative research can also offer ways around some of these challenges, but such research assumes that causal processes can be gleaned through dialogue and that an anecdotal case can be illustrative of other cases. However, with true interdependence and emergence, the action of a single entity does not clearly affect the emergent outcome, and so understanding it does not actually help us understand the causal process.

Further, an ABM can decontextualize (generalize) a model better to understand underlying causal structures rather than the quirks of the specific empirical data-generating process. Alternatively, general models can be contextualized and applied to a specific context to analyze how underlying causal factors may play out differently within specific circumstances.

Perhaps most importantly, in any ABM we can modify the underlying assumptions of some outcome or theory and explore how changes in those assumptions alter aggregate outcomes. New hypotheses can be generated and tested empirically, potentially leading to new theories and approaches to sustainability practice, because a virtue of the ABM approach is that it can shed new light on causal chains that have been overlooked or underemphasized in other research and practice.

More broadly, we believe that agent-based modeling can be used beyond EJ research and practice better to understand and improve many other facets of urban policy and planning. Many of the factors that make agent-based modeling useful to the EJ conundrum—particularly the dynamism and interactivity—also make it useful for sustainability and other urban questions. Below we briefly describe steps to follow when one wants to develop an ABM for urban sustainability research.

### Steps in the development of an ABM

The development of an ABM is similar to the development of other simulation models, but with some elements specific to the nature of the ABM. Before elaborating on our EJ ABM in Chapter 3, we describe what an ABM is through a discussion of the steps involved in its creation. Though the steps are presented linearly, the process is not linear, but is iterative.

#### Step 1: Systemic patterns

The ultimate goal of an ABM is to understand systemic (aggregate or macroscopic) patterns (i.e., dynamics, behaviors, and complex trajectories of *systems*) emerging from local interactions at a micro level, so the analyst must identify a systemic pattern of interest (i.e., a reference pattern). For instance, EJ researchers have reported statistical and spatial patterns that provide evidence of environmental injustice in various communities. Observed environmental injustice in communities and societies—a disproportionate collocation of hazardous facilities with minorities—is the systemic pattern that we want to understand. Such a conceptual or empirical pattern can serve as the specific pattern of interest that a model attempts to develop and analyze.

#### Step 2: Conceptual model

After a systemic pattern of interest is identified, the analyst must develop a conceptual model. To do this, s/he must define agents, an environment, and a set of rules that guide interactions at the micro level. Agents can be heterogeneous, autonomous, and/or purposeful. In the EJ example, therefore, agents are different types of firms and different types of residents that want to site or live in a community. Environments can be represented as local geographical conditions under which agents make siting or moving decisions. Interaction or decision rules that give rise to the systemic pattern of interest (such as environmental injustice) can be articulated and conceptualized based on existing theories, empirical observations, and so on.

### Step 3: Simulation model

Once the conceptual model is specified, a simulation model that encodes agents and interaction rules can be built using programming languages, toolkits, or platforms. The choices of programming language and toolkit are up to the preferences, skill sets, and experience of the researcher or policy analyst. Researchers and government analysts who are skilled in a specific programming language such as Java can build an agent-based model using that specific language, but there are also many ABM toolkits that were developed to aid beginners and non-programmers. Commonly used ABM toolkits are NetLogo, RePast, MASON, MatLab, and R.[56]

Empirical datasets are sometimes incorporated within the simulation model to enhance the verisimilitude of the model. For example, in the development of our EJ ABM, as described later in the book, we include actual information on household income and housing prices. Models can even incorporate geographic information systems (GIS) data, as illustrated in Chapter 10, and link the simulation to very specific local conditions.

### Step 4: Model verification and validation

A significant amount of time may be spent verifying the model—ensuring that the simulation model was encoded properly and whether each part of the model behaves as designed. For example, an ABM consists of several sub-models since agents perform various functions such as searching areas, calculating the proportion of specific types of agents in the searching area, or sending a message to a chosen group of agents. Modelers can test whether each of these sub-models performs as it is supposed to (e.g., correctly identifies available spaces, updates housing prices, etc.), and whether the model runs without errors. This is not a trivial process. It is always better to have more than one set of eyes to check programming codes and test the behavior of the model.

*Verification* is the process of making sure that a simulation model is built without programming errors (a debugging process). *Validation*, which is the process that involves checking whether the simulation model behaves as key features of the real-world system behave, is a highly controversial concept.[57] Given the difficulty of model verification and validation, *replication* of simulation models by different people in different computing settings has been suggested as an alternative way to evaluate the model.[58]

## Step 5: Model use

Once some confidence in the model and its behavior is achieved, various computational experiments are performed, as presented in Chapters 4–10 of this book.

### Agent-based modeling in action

There are different approaches that one can take when developing ABMs, and because it is a relatively recent mode of analysis, the debate over approaches is not settled. Although we take an approach rooted in simplicity in order to analyze general causal possibilities, we also recognize the potential utility of more detailed and contextualized approaches—especially for local- or regional-level policymakers and administrators.

Our point of view is that no model, whether a statistical, mental, or simulation model, can approach the complexity of the real world. Indeed, as we noted earlier, the nature of models is to make simplifying assumptions; the more detailed a model becomes, the more difficult it is to discern important causes and effects. Our approach is, therefore, to balance simplicity and complexity, starting with a very simple model and then building up as we add complexity that is needed to analyze either issues in the literature or policy solutions. Our aim is to create a model that is complex enough to be a useful representation of the real world, but not so complex that it fits only some specific locale or prevents us from discerning causal relationships.

We conceive of this project as decontextualizing the EJ problem enough to gain insights into the causes and effects of a small, analytically relevant subset of the decisions that are made that could contribute to environmental injustice. Alternatively, we could have approached the problem as a contextual exercise intended to gain specific understanding of a particular locale, and policymakers and administrators may opt to do so for their own jurisdictions. Both approaches are useful, but for different purposes. The first helps with context-independent general insight, while the second is useful for public administrators and policy analysts who need to make decisions that are specific to their locales. Therefore, during the course of this book we provide examples of both. Chapters 4–9 take the decontextualized approach to understand general causes and effects and develop a deeper understanding of the root problem of environmental justice, while Chapter 10 illustrates how an ABM can be used to gain insight into a specific locale and situation in order to guide policy decision making.

The primary model used in this book (as described in Chapter 3 and used in Chapters 4–9) was created with an aim of gleaning an understanding of the EJ problem, primarily focusing on the relationship between firm and residential siting decisions, environmental quality, and policy options, but simple enough to be useful as a tool that can be re-contextualized to specific locations and provide insights into specific EJ problems. In addition, this model should illustrate how agent-based modeling can be used more broadly for sustainability research and practice. Guided by the EJ literature's focus on location choices, we developed the model with this focus.

While any research exercise requires making many assumptions, some assumptions are more relevant to the specifics of the research approach and thus warrant more investigation than others. For example, if one is conducting an empirical-statistical analysis, more time and effort is likely to be expended on the assumptions that underlie the measurement of key variables than on the assumption of independent effects—even though both sets of assumptions are extremely important in understanding the model's results.

Agent-based models are useful in part because they enable us to relax the strict assumption of independent effects, but also because one must be clear and specific about the assumptions made in the ABM. Because the ABM is mathematical and computational, the modeler must fully delineate (and encode in programming language) the nature of all assumptions, rather than leaving those assumptions inexplicit, as can be the case in empirical work. When practical, assumptions should be based on theory and/or empirical evidence, and indeed we use theory and empirical evidence in our assumptions for the EJ ABM. In some cases we specifically focus on disagreement in the literature, altering and contrasting assumptions in order to test different hypotheses. In other cases, we are able to use settled ideas from the literature.

Sometimes neither the literature nor empirics is helpful in knowing what assumptions should be made. In these cases, values of parameters are usually derived through an iterative process of model development and testing until the behavior of the model is consonant with key elements of behavior in the real world. In these cases, the specific nature of the parameters and behavior are less important than the result; if the result of the assumption is a model that behaves appropriately, then it is a sufficient representation. An early example of this perspective is seen in "Boids," in which bird-like flocking behavior—an emergent phenomenon—is simulated through a few simple rules. We do not know what rules birds really follow, but for many purposes we can simulate their action sufficiently with the rules developed by Reynolds.[59] As we describe in Chapter 3, many of our landscape characteristics fall into this latter category, while our location choice behaviors are derived from theory and literature. In some cases behaviorally appropriate assumptions have already been derived in the literature on agent-based modeling, and we are able to use those other modelers' assumptions in our model. In other cases we arrived at the final model through a careful calibration process. In all cases the goal is the same: to develop a model that is a useful representation of the real world.

# Discussion

It is well established at this point that, at least in some contexts, there is a disparity in the environmental quality experienced by different racial/ethnic groups, which is not fully explained by either economic or political factors. There is still significant disagreement in the literature as to what causes this disparity.

In this chapter we explained why disagreement remains, and suggest some reasons agent-based modeling can provide insight into this important policy problem, noting particularly that agent-based modeling provides a useful environment for testing and developing hypotheses while taking into account the dynamism and systemic nature of urban regions. We see agent-based modeling as a way to develop research further on the EJ problem, its relationship to sustainability, and other components of sustainability analysis. In Chapter 3 we develop and explain our attempt to provide this tool: our EJ ABM.

# Notes

1 Evan J. Ringquist, "Assessing Evidence of Environmental Inequities: A Meta-Analysis," *Journal of Policy Analysis and Management* 24, no. 2 (2005): 223–47. In fact, in this work Ringquist concludes that there is significant evidence for the importance of race, but little for the importance of economic class.

2 See e.g., James T. Hamilton, "Testing for Environmental Racism: Prejudice, Profits, Political Power?" *Journal of Policy Analysis and Management* 14, no. 1 (1995): 107–32; Yongwan Chun, Yushim Kim and Heather E. Campbell, "Environmental Inequities in a Sunbelt City: A Bayesian Spatial Analysis," *Journal of Urban Affairs* 34, no. 4 (2012).

3 Douglas S. Noonan, "Evidence of Environmental Justice: A Critical Perspective on the Practice of EJ Research and Lessons for Policy Design," *Social Science Quarterly* 80, no. 5 (2008): 1153–74.

4 Ringquist, "Assessing Evidence of Environmental Inequities," argues that the effect is small enough that there may be more important concerns for policy-makers to focus on.

5 Paul Mohai and Robin Saha, "Reassessing Racial and Socioeconomic Disparities in Environmental Justice Research," *Demography* 43, no. 2 (2006): 383–99.

6 United Church of Christ, Commission for Racial Justice, *Toxic Wastes and Race: A National Report on the Racial and Socioeconomic Characteristics of Communities with Hazardous Wastes Sites* (New York: United Church of Christ, 1987).

7 For a review, see Robin R. Sobotta, *Communities, Contours and Concerns: Environmental Justice and Aviation Noise* (PhD diss., Arizona State University, 2002).

8 Robert D. Bullard, "Environmental Justice: It's More than Waste Facility Siting," *Social Science Quarterly* 77, no. 30 (1996): 497.

9 Douglas S. Noonan, "Defining Environmental Justice: Policy Design Lessons from the Practice of EJ Research," Paper presented at the fall conference of the Association for Public Policy and Management, Washington DC, 2005, cited with permission. However, note that Noonan's argument rests on assumptions of both

full access to information about available choices and no social constraints on choice—but choice constraints are readily observed.

10  Feng Liu, *Environmental Justice Analysis: Theories, Methods, and Practice* (Boca Raton, FL: CRC Press, 2001), 3.

11  Rae Zimmerman, "Issues of Classification in Environmental Equity: How We Manage is How We Measure," *Fordham Urban Law Journal* 21 (1994): 633–69.

12  Liu, *Environmental Justice Analysis*, 4; US EPA, "Environmental Justice, Basic Information," last updated May 24, 2012, www.epa.gov/environmentaljustice/ basics/ejbackground.html.

13  Zimmerman, "Issues of Classification in Environmental Equity."

14  US EPA, August 31, 2010.

15  Laura Pulido, "Rethinking Environmental Racism: White Privilege and Urban Development in Southern California," *Annals of the Association of American Geographers* 90, no. 1 (2000): 12–40.

16  As discussed below, Robin R. Sobotta, Heather E. Campbell and Beverly J. Owens, "Aviation Noise and Environmental Justice: The Barrio Barrier," *Journal of Regional Science* 47, no. 1 (2007): 125–54, can be interpreted as *indirect* evidence of environmental racism—though in no way proven, it is compatible with the findings.

17  Evan J. Ringquist, "Environmental Injustice," in Robert F. Durant, Daniel J. Fiorino, and Rosemary O'Leary, eds, *Environmental Governance Reconsidered: Challenges, Choices, and Opportunities* (Cambridge, MA: The MIT Press, 2004), 255–88; Steven Bonorris, *Environmental Justice for All: A Fifty State Survey of Legislation, Policies and Cases*, fourth edn (San Francisco, CA: American Bar Association and Hastings College of the Law, 2010), www.abanet.org/environ/ resources.html.

18  David Konisky, "The Limited Effects of Federal Environmental Justice Policy on State Enforcement," *The Policy Studies Journal* 37, no. 3 (2009): 475–96.

19  David Konisky and Christopher Reenock, "Compliance Bias and Environmental (In)justice," *The Journal of Politics* 75, no. 2 (2013): 506–19.

20  Sheldon Gen, Holley Shafer and Monique Nakagawa, "Perceptions of Environmental Justice: The Case of a US Urban Wastewater System," *Sustainable Development* 20, no. 4 (2012): 239–50.

21  Michael Jarrett, Richard T. Burnett, Pavlos Kanaroglou, John Eyles, Norm Finkelstein, Chris Giovis and Jeffrey R. Brook, "A GIS–Environmental Justice Analysis of Particulate Air Pollution in Hamilton, Canada," *Environment and Planning A* 33, no. 6 (2001): 955–73.

22  Sobotta et al., "Aviation Noise and Environmental Justice."

23  Adam Eckerd and Andrew G. Keeler, "Going Green Together? Brownfield Remediation and Environmental Justice," *Policy Sciences* 45 (2012): 293–314.

24  Rachel Morello-Frosch, Manuel Pastor and James Sadd, "The Distribution of Air Toxics Exposures and Health Risks among Diverse Communities," *Urban Affairs Review* 36, no. 4 (2001): 551–78.

25  See for example, Bob Bolin, Eric Matranga, Edward J. Hackett, Edward K. Sadalla, K. David Pijawka, Debbie Brewer and Diane Sicotte, "Environmental Equity in a Sunbelt City: The Spatial Distribution of Toxic Hazards in Phoenix, Arizona," *Environmental Hazards* 2, no. 1 (2000): 11–24; and Bob Bolin, Amy Nelson, Edward J. Hackett, K. David Pijawka, C. Scott Smith, Diane Sicotte, Edward K. Sadalla, Eric Matranga and Maureen O'Donnell, "The Ecology of Technological Risk in a Sunbelt City," *Environment and Planning A* 34, no. 2 (2002): 317–39.

26  Hamilton, "Testing for Environmental Racism."

27 Manuel Pastor, Jim Sadd and John Hipp, "Which Came First? Toxic Facilities, Minority Move-in, and Environmental Justice," *Journal of Urban Affairs* 23, no. 1 (2001): 1–21.
28 Ringquist, "Assessing Evidence of Environmental Inequities."
29 Paul Mohai and Bunyan Bryant, "Is there a 'Race' Effect on Concern for Environmental Quality?" *Public Opinion Quarterly* 62, no. 4 (1998): 475–505.
30 Pastor et al., "Which Came First?" 1.
31 Sobotta et al., "Aviation Noise and Environmental Justice."
32 Heather E. Campbell, Laura R. Peck and Michael K. Tschudi, "Justice for All? A Cross-Time Analysis of Toxics Release Inventory Facility Location," *Review of Policy Research* 27, no. 1 (2010): 1–25.
33 US Environmental Protection Agency, October 12, 2010.
34 Tamar Lewin, "Report Takes Aim at 'Model Minority' Stereotype of Asian-American Students," *The New York Times*, June 10, 2008, www.nytimes.com/2008/06/10/education/10asians.html?_r=0 (accessed August 7, 2013).
35 The finding that the presence of a TRIF already in the location is the most important factor associated with the placement of a new TRIF is one reason we include firm agglomeration in the EJ ABM (as described in the next chapters).
36 Rachel Morello-Frosch, Manuel Pastor and James Sadd, "The Distribution of Air Toxics Exposures and Health Risks among Diverse Communities," *Urban Affairs Review* 36, no. 4 (2001): 551–78 (addresses southern California); Manuel Pastor, James Sadd and Rachel Morello-Frosch, "Still Toxic After All these Years: Air Quality and Environmental Justice in the San Francisco Bay Area" (Center for Justice, Tolerance and Community, University of California, Santa Cruz, 2007), cjtc.ucsc.edu/docs/bay_final.pdf (accessed June 2013).
37 Pastor et al., "Which Came First?"
38 Eckerd and Keeler, "Going Green Together?"
39 Pastor et al., "Which Came First?"
40 Campbell et al., "Justice for All?"
41 Hamilton, "Testing for Environmental Racism."
42 Eckerd and Keeler, "Going Green Together?"
43 Ann Wolverton, "Effects of Socio-Economic and Input-Related Factors on Polluting Plants' Location Decisions," *B.E. Journal of Economic Analysis and Policy* 9, no. 1 (2009): 1–32.
44 Ibid.; cf. Campbell et al., "Justice for All?" for related results.
45 William M. Bowen, Mark Atlas and Sugie Lee, "Industrial Agglomeration and the Regional Scientific Explanation of Perceived Environmental Injustice," *The Annals of Regional Science* 43, no. 4 (2009): 1013–31.
46 Rachel Morello-Frosch, Manuel Pastor, James L. Sadd, Carlos Porras and Michele Prichard, "Citizens, Science, and Data Judo: Leveraging Community-based Participatory Research to Build a Regional Collaborative for Environmental Justice in Southern California," in *Methods for Conducting Community-Based Participatory Research in Public Health*, eds Barbara Israel, Eugenia Eng, Amy Shultz and Edith Parker (San Francisco, CA: Jossey-Bass Press, 2005).
47 See e.g., Bolin et al., "The Ecology of Technological Risk in a Sunbelt City"; Pastor et al., "Which Came First?"
48 Greg Kearney and Gebre-Egziabher Kiros, "A Spatial Evaluation of Socio Demographics Surrounding National Priorities List Sites in Florida Using a Distance-Based Approach," *International Journal of Health Geographics* 8 (2009); Paul Mohai and Robin Saha, "Reassessing Racial and Socioeconomic Disparities in Environmental Justice Research," *Demography* 43, no. 2 (2006): 383–99; Campbell et al., "Justice for All?" uses several methods, including a distance method.

49  Brett Baden, Douglas Noonan and Rama Mohana Turaga, "Scales of Justice: Is there a Geographic Bias in Environmental Equity Analysis?" *Journal of Environmental Planning and Management* 50, no. 2 (2007): 163–85; Noonan, "Evidence of Environmental Justice."
50  Morello-Frosch et al., "Citizens, Science, and Data Judo."
51  Stan Openshaw and Peter J. Taylor, "A Million or so Correlation Coefficients: Three Experiments on the Modifiable Areal Unit Problem," in *Statistical Applications in Spatial Sciences*, ed. Neil Wrigley (London: Pion, 1979), 127–44.
52  Ibid.
53  Chun et al., "Environmental Inequities in a Sunbelt City." "Spatial autocorrelation" exists when the error term in regression analysis is correlated across spatial units of analysis.
54  Pastor et al., "Which Came First?"
55  Michael Batty, Yichun Xie and Zhanli Sun, "Modeling Urban Dynamics through GIS-Based Cellular Automata," *Computers, Environment and Urban Systems* 23, no. 3 (1999): 205–33.
56  In Chapter 10 Nelson, Cain and Yang discuss additional ABM programming environments. Some of these, such as NetLogo and R, are freeware.
57  Naomi Oreskes, Kristin Shrader-Frechette and Kenneth Belitz, "Verification, Validation, and Confirmation of Numerical Models in the Earth Sciences," *Science* 263, no. 5147 (1994): 641–46.
58  Uri Wilensky and William Rand, "Making Models Match: Replicating an Agent-Based Model," *Journal of Artificial Societies and Social Simulation* 10, no. 4 (2007), jasss.soc.surrey.ac.uk/10/4/2.html.
59  Reynolds, Craig "Flocks, Herds and Schools: A Distributed Behavioral Model." *SIGGRAPH '87, Proceedings of the 14th Annual Conference on Computer Graphics and Interactive Techniques*, Association for Computing Machinery, 1987: 25–34. As of August 2014, an example of Boids in action can be viewed at www.youtube.com/watch?v=GUkjC-69vaw.

## References

Baden, Brett, Douglas Noonan and Rama Mohana Turaga. "Scales of Justice: Is there a Geographic Bias in Environmental Equity Analysis?" *Journal of Environmental Planning and Management* 50, no. 2 (2007): 163–185.
Batty, Michael, Yichun Xie and Zhanli Sun. "Modeling Urban Dynamics through GIS-Based Cellular Automata." *Computers, Environment and Urban Systems* 23, no. 3 (1999): 205–233.
Bolin, Bob, Eric Matranga, Edward J. Hackett, Edward K. Sadalla, K. David Pijawka, Debbie Brewer and Diane Sicotte. "Environmental Equity in a Sunbelt City: The Spatial Distribution of Toxic Hazards in Phoenix, Arizona." *Environmental Hazards* 2, no. 1 (2000): 11–24.
Bolin, Bob, Amy Nelson, Edward J. Hackett, K. David Pijawka, C. Scott Smith, Diane Sicotte, Edward K. Sadalla, Eric Matranga and Maureen O'Donnell. "The Ecology of Technological Risk in a Sunbelt City." *Environment and Planning A* 34, no. 2 (2002): 317–339.
Bonorris, Steven. *Environmental Justice for All: A Fifty State Survey of Legislation, Policies and Cases.* Fourth edn. San Francisco, CA: American Bar Association and Hastings College of the Law, 2010. www.abanet.org/environ/resources.html.

Bowen, William M., Mark Atlas and Sugie Lee. "Industrial Agglomeration and the Regional Scientific Explanation of Perceived Environmental Injustice." *The Annals of Regional Science* 43, no. 4 (2009): 1013–1031.

Bullard, Robert D. "Environmental Justice: It's More than Waste Facility Siting." *Social Science Quarterly* 77, no. 30 (1996): 493–499.

Campbell, Heather E., Laura R. Peck and Michael K. Tschudi. "Justice for All? A Cross-Time Analysis of Toxics Release Inventory Facility Location." *Review of Policy Research* 27, no. 1 (2010): 1–25.

Chun, Yongwan, Yushim Kim and Heather E. Campbell. "Environmental Inequities in a Sunbelt City: A Bayesian Spatial Analysis." *Journal of Urban Affairs* 34, no. 4 (2012): 419–439.

Eckerd, Adam and Andrew G. Keeler. "Going Green Together? Brownfield Remediation and Environmental Justice." *Policy Sciences* 45 (2012): 293–314.

Gen, Sheldon, Holley Shafer and Monique Nakagawa. "Perceptions of Environmental Justice: The Case of a US Urban Wastewater System." *Sustainable Development* 20, no. 4 (2012): 239–250.

Hamilton, James T. "Testing for Environmental Racism: Prejudice, Profits, Political Power?" *Journal of Policy Analysis and Management* 14, no. 1 (1995): 107–132.

Jarrett, Michael, Richard T. Burnett, Pavlos Kanaroglou, John Eyles, Norm Finkelstein, Chris Giovis and Jeffrey R. Brook. "A GIS-Environmental Justice Analysis of Particulate Air Pollution in Hamilton, Canada." *Environment and Planning A* 33, no. 6 (2001): 955–973.

Kearney, Greg and Gebre-Egziabher Kiros. "A Spatial Evaluation of Socio Demographics Surrounding National Priorities List Sites in Florida Using a Distance-Based Approach." *International Journal of Health Geographics* 8 (2009).

Konisky, David. "The Limited Effects of Federal Environmental Justice Policy on State Enforcement." *The Policy Studies Journal* 37, no. 3 (2009): 475–496.

Konisky, David and Christopher Reenock, "Compliance Bias and Environmental (In)justice." *The Journal of Politics* 75, no. 2 (2013): 506–519.

Lewin, Tamar. "Report Takes Aim at 'Model Minority' Stereotype of Asian-American Students." *The New York Times*, June 10, 2008. www.nytimes.com/2008/06/10/education/10asians.html?_r=0 (accessed August 7, 2014).

Liu, Feng. *Environmental Justice Analysis: Theories, Methods, and Practice*. Boca Raton, FL: CRC Press, 2001.

Mohai, Paul and Bunyan Bryant. "Is there a 'Race' Effect on Concern for Environmental Quality?" *Public Opinion Quarterly* 62, no. 4 (1998): 475–505.

Mohai, Paul and Robin Saha. "Reassessing Racial and Socioeconomic Disparities in Environmental Justice Research." *Demography* 43, no. 2 (2006): 383–399.

Morello-Frosch, Rachel, Manuel Pastor and James Sadd. "The Distribution of Air Toxics Exposures and Health Risks among Diverse Communities." *Urban Affairs Review* 36, no. 4 (2001): 551–578.

Morello-Frosch, Rachel, Manuel Pastor, James L. Sadd, Carlos Porras and Michele Prichard. "Citizens, Science, and Data Judo: Leveraging Community-based Participatory Research to Build a Regional Collaborative for Environmental Justice in Southern California." In *Methods for Conducting Community-Based Participatory Research in Public Health*, edited by Barbara Israel, Eugenia Eng, Amy Shultz and Edith Parker. San Francisco, CA: Jossey-Bass Press, 2005, 371–392.

Noonan, Douglas S. "Defining Environmental Justice: Policy Design Lessons from the Practice of EJ Research." Paper presented at the fall conference of the Association for Public Policy and Management, Washington, DC, 2005.

Noonan, Douglas S. "Evidence of Environmental Justice: A Critical Perspective on the Practice of EJ Research and Lessons for Policy Design." *Social Science Quarterly* 89, no. 5 (2008): 1153–1174.

Openshaw, Stan and Peter J. Taylor. "A Million or so Correlation Coefficients: Three Experiments on the Modifiable Areal Unit Problem." In *Statistical Applications in Spatial Sciences*, edited by Neil Wrigley. London: Pion, 1979, 127–144.

Oreskes, Naomi, Kristin Shrader-Frechette and Kenneth Belitz. "Verification, Validation, and Confirmation of Numerical Models in the Earth Sciences." *Science* 263, no. 5147 (1994): 641–646.

Pastor, Manuel, Jim Sadd and John Hipp. "Which Came First? Toxic Facilities, Minority Move-in, and Environmental Justice." *Journal of Urban Affairs* 23, no. 1 (2001): 1–21.

Pastor, Manuel, James Sadd and Rachel Morello-Frosch. "Still Toxic After All these Years: Air Quality and Environmental Justice in the San Francisco Bay Area." Center for Justice, Tolerance and Community, University of California, Santa Cruz, 2007. cjtc.ucsc.edu/docs/bay_final.pdf (accessed June 2013).

Pulido, Laura. "Rethinking Environmental Racism: White Privilege and Urban Development in Southern California." *Annals of the Association of American Geographers* 90, no. 1 (2000): 12–40.

Reynolds, Craig. "Flocks, Herds and Schools: A Distributed Behavioral Model." *SIGGRAPH '87: Proceedings of the 14th Annual Conference on Computer Graphics and Interactive Techniques*, Association for Computing Machinery, 1987: 25–34. doi:10.1145/37401.37406.

Ringquist, Evan J. "Environmental Injustice." In *Environmental Governance Reconsidered: Challenges, Choices, and Opportunities*, edited by Robert F. Durant, Daniel J. Fiorino and Rosemary O'Leary. Cambridge, MA: The MIT Press, 2004.

Ringquist, Evan J. "Assessing Evidence of Environmental Inequities: A Meta-Analysis." *Journal of Policy Analysis and Management* 24, no. 2 (2005): 223–247.

Sobotta, Robin R. *Communities, Contours and Concerns: Environmental Justice and Aviation Noise*. PhD dissertation, Arizona State University, 2002.

Sobotta, Robin R., Heather E. Campbell and Beverly J. Owens. "Aviation Noise and Environmental Justice: The Barrio Barrier." *Journal of Regional Science* 47, no. 1 (2007): 125–154.

United Church of Christ, Commission for Racial Justice. *Toxic Wastes and Race: A National Report on the Racial and Socioeconomic Characteristics of Communities with Hazardous Wastes Sites*. New York: United Church of Christ, 1987.

US Environmental Protection Agency. "Environmental Justice, Basic Information." Last updated May 24, 2012. www.epa.gov/environmentaljustice/basics/ejbackground.html.

Wilensky, Uri and William Rand. "Making Models Match: Replicating an Agent-Based Model." *Journal of Artificial Societies and Social Simulation* 10, no. 4 (2007), jasss.soc.surrey.ac.uk/10/4/2.html.

Wolverton, Ann. "Effects of Socio-Economic and Input-Related Factors on Polluting Plants' Location Decisions." *B.E. Journal of Economic Analysis and Policy* 9, no. 1 (2009): 1–32.

Zimmerman, Rae. "Issues of Classification in Environmental Equity: How We Manage is How We Measure." *Fordham Urban Law Journal* 21 (1994): 633–669.

# 3 An agent-based model for environmental justice
## The EJ ABM

In this chapter, we explain an agent-based model (ABM) specifically designed to analyze the emergence of the environmental justice (EJ) problem as one component of sustainability analysis (i.e., the EJ ABM). This chapter shows how we conceptualize specific micro-rules (rules at the level of the individual agent) to examine a systemic pattern of emergent environmental injustice in an artificial community. As mentioned before, these are "systemic patterns" because they occur due to interactions within the entire system: Environmental injustice is a macro-level phenomenon (at the level of the city) that emerges from micro-level interactions within the system.

The EJ ABM presented here is grounded in a unique framework that can illuminate complex social and policy interactions that lead to urban phenomena including, but not limited to, environmental injustice. The framework includes heterogeneous social entities (e.g., firms, residents, and government institutions that can have different attributes from each other) that can simultaneously interact and make coordinated or uncoordinated decisions within a city or particular social system. The fundamental behavior of the model is that agents, be they firms or residents, seek a place in which to locate. New firms' and residents' choices are constrained by the choices made by previous firms and residents, with an end result of settlement patterns that emerge as firms and residents seek locations over time. In this process, firms may impose costs if they significantly pollute areas where they site. Thereby, residents experience different levels of environmental quality. Figure 3.1 presents a conceptual framework of our EJ ABM in a graphical format.

With the EJ ABM, one can explore and analyze both:

- Causal processes: How the interactions and interdependencies among these actors lead to environmental injustice; and
- Policy implications: What processes have potential to ameliorate environmental injustice in general.

In essence, the EJ ABM is a fairly straightforward residential sorting model, in the tradition of Tiebout sorting models.[1] We focus most of our

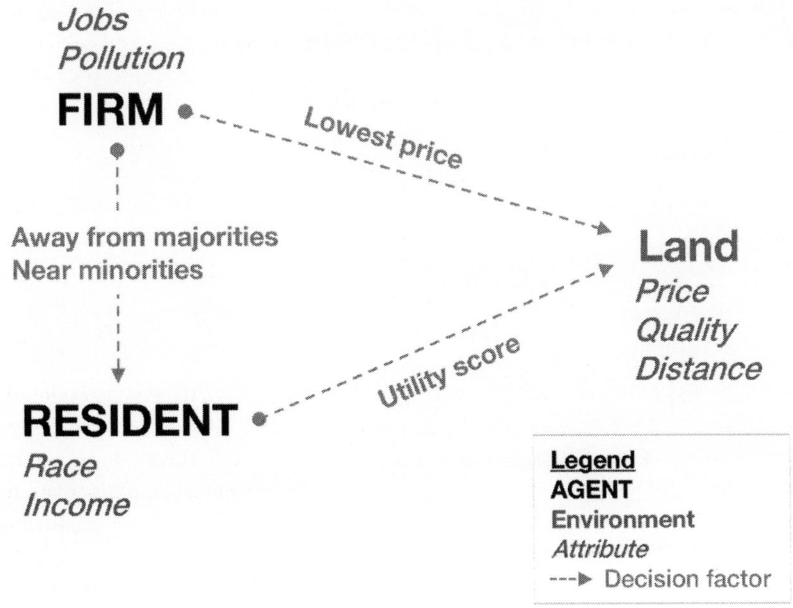

*Jobs*
*Pollution*

**FIRM** •------ L̲o̲w̲e̲s̲t̲ ̲p̲r̲i̲c̲e̲

**Away from majorities**
**Near minorities**

**Land**
*Price*
*Quality*
*Distance*

**RESIDENT** •------ U̲t̲i̲l̲i̲t̲y̲ ̲s̲c̲o̲r̲e̲

*Race*
*Income*

**Legend**
**AGENT**
Environment
*Attribute*
---▶ Decision factor

*Figure 3.1* A conceptual framework of the EJ ABM
(Modified version of Figure 1 in Eckerd, Campbell and Kim 2012: 950)

attention on two key behaviors: how firms make location decisions, and how residents make location decisions. The approach we take is not dissimilar from the approach an economist might take when developing general equilibrium models (although the structure of the model itself is quite different). As detailed in sections below, we create a decontextualized, self-contained world in which there are firms and residents that seek locations based on considering four key aspects of those locations: price, commuting distance, environmental quality, and neighborhood composition. Each of these characteristics has been identified as among the most important factors in location choices.[2] While we could have considered literally hundreds of other factors that affect location choices (like school quality, for instance), we limited the model to these factors in order to ensure a focus on our key variable of interest: environmental inequity.

In the section below, we describe our EJ ABM, and provide some code snippets that detail model behavior. Given the decontextualized nature of the model, the landscape is ancillary to the behavior of the agents. We developed the landscape and necessary natural systems (such as the spread of pollution) through an assessment of the literature and a careful iterative exercise involving repeated testing until the landscape functioned similarly to a city growing over time.

We first describe these landscape and ancillary parameters and the values chosen. We then move to the more important assumptions that deal with the behavior of the residential sorting model (as outlined in Tables 3.1–3.3). After this, we elaborate on the parameter values and our rationales for them (Table 3.4). Next, we describe the sensitivity analyses we conducted to test assumptions, and provide results of these tests (Table 3.5).

In the Appendix, we also provide full code for a base version of this model. The NetLogo code in the Appendix includes all the functionality to replicate simulations such as those described in Chapter 4.

## EJ ABM in NetLogo

Our EJ ABM is built using NetLogo,[3] which is a multi-agent modeling environment developed at the Center for Connected Learning and Computer-Based Modeling at Northwestern University. Other examples of ABMs built in this environment can be found on the OpenABM website (www.openabm. org). NetLogo is not the only ABM toolkit that has been developed to aid researchers and modelers. RePast, Swarm, and MASON are well-known ABM environments developed by different groups. (See Table 10.1 in this book, and Gilbert's detailed comparison of ABM toolkits as of 2008, for additional information.[4]) We used NetLogo primarily because of our familiarity with the programming language, and the overall simplicity of the modeling environment, which meshed well with the modeling approach we describe in Chapter 2.

### The landscape

In the EJ ABM, the landscape is a Cartesian plane consisting of a 101 x 101 grid of cells (10,201 plots of "land"). Each cell has $(x, y)$ coordinates, and the center of the landscape is $(0, 0)$. In the landscape, each 10 x 10 set of plots is defined as a block, and transportation routes run between blocks.[5] Thus, each block contains 100 plots, and 100 blocks exist in the landscape (see the central image in Figure 3.2). The blocks can be viewed as proxies for neighborhoods or for Census block groups (CBGs). Plots, residents, and firms all have specific attributes that affect the others. For example, when residents and firms select plots on which to locate, they use attributes of the plots to make those decisions and, in turn, their choices affect attributes of that plot in the future.

Plots always have three attributes: environmental quality, price, and distance to the nearest firm.[6] Each of the plots within a block is initially homogeneous with respect to environmental quality. At the beginning of the simulation, the environmental quality value of each plot is set to 50.[7] The price of each plot is initially determined through a random assignment of values that mirror median home prices in the United States. Each plot value is drawn from a normal distribution with a mean of US$173,000 and standard deviation of $34,000.[8] In this landscape, resident and firm agents choose which plot they will locate on based on decision criteria described below.

While the term "minority" can have a wide range of different social meanings, throughout all simulations we define the term strictly numerically, so the base simulation is initialized with 140 majority agents (70%) and 60 minority agents (30%). We explored a number of different proportional breakdowns of majority and minority residents (in fact, varying these proportions is a key focus of Chapter 5), and this balance was chosen to ensure a sizable minority, but a clear majority. 70% is also similar to the current percentage in the United States of the "white alone" population.[9]

We set a population growth rate of 5% per time step during the simulation. One of the features of agent-based modeling is that it is iterative, with the entire program running over and over again so that decisions are made multiple times. This allows our model city to grow and develop. Each time that the program is run clear through is referred to as a "time step."

To ensure residential movement, resident agents are "born" and "die" over time; at each time step new residents totaling 7% of the current population are "born." This is accomplished by having 7% of the existing resident agents replicate themselves, and their minority or majority attribute. Then, the oldest 2% of the existing population "dies" once there is a total resident population of at least 500. If there is not a clear set of 2% of the agents who have been in the simulation the longest length of time, agents are selected randomly from those tied as oldest. While of course actual population growth is not so exact, this rate of birth and death was determined reasonably to approximate a rapidly growing urban region such as Phoenix in the mid-2000s.[10] This process keeps the demographic split at roughly 70% and 30% over time steps, with some random variation around those values.

Residents have two behaviors in the model: they have jobs at firms and select residential locations. Each firm agent employs a set number of residential agents, and firm growth is based on a simple assumption of labor supply—that is, when there is a sufficient level of labor supply (i.e., a sufficient number of residents), then a new firm will recognize an opportunity and establish itself. Since employment was not a specific focus of our simulations, for all trials we set the ratio at 50 residential jobs per firm. We settled on this value because this ratio of firms to residents seemed to provide a sufficient amount of variation in environmental quality while retaining as much space as possible for residential location.

Since the simulation is initialized with 200 resident agents, approximately four firms are introduced at random locations at the beginning of a set of simulations.[11] During the simulation, if there is enough job demand (i.e., when the ratio of residents to firms becomes greater than 50), a new firm is introduced. Each plot's distance to the nearest firm is updated whenever a new firm is introduced to the landscape due to population growth.

One of our key behavioral assumptions is the utility score, and we describe it in detail below, but it is worth noting here that each plot has a utility score that is updated based on the three key attributes (environmental quality, price, and distance to the nearest firm) at every time step (see the resident location decision process, below). Unless a specific type of zoning analysis is underway, each plot is considered a residential zone (R-zone).

*Firms*

Because of the focus of the EJ ABM on environmental disparities, we do not specifically vary the nature of jobs provided by the firms. This means that all modeled firms provide the same number of jobs, and we make no distinction between the type or quality of those jobs. A resident is willing to work at any firm, and in fact works at the firm that is closest.

This is a good example of an assumption for which we opted for simplicity over realism. We could have modeled a variety of different firm types and job types, and considered matching residents with appropriate firms given assigned skill sets and education. However, the focus of the model is on environmental disparities, not labor markets. For certain types of analysis, including a complete model of urban sustainability, the type and quality of jobs could be important and could be manipulated in the model. To focus on our research question, we opted to simplify firm characteristics and model only the positive and negative externalities of firms, rather than attributes of firms that are relevant to labor markets. To that end, the only characteristic by which firms vary is the key attribute that affects the environmental quality of plots: pollution levels.

We assume that all firms produce some level of pollution—or, more generally, some negative environmental externality. In addition, all firms produce some social benefit. Whenever labor demand dictates that a new firm be introduced to the landscape, its level of pollution is randomly assigned as an integer between zero and nine (drawn from a uniform distribution). We then make a distinction between firms that produce substantial pollution (greater than five on this scale), which we define as "polluting firms," and those with lower levels of pollution, which we define as "non-polluting firms" (from zero to five on the scale). Polluting firm agents represent land uses such as toxics release inventory facilities (TRIFs) or manufacturing centers, and non-polluting firm agents represent land uses such as commercial centers, museums, and schools. Since we include pollution levels of five with the non-polluting firms, we assume a lesser representation of polluting firms, and thus on average 60% of firms are non-polluting and 40% are polluting throughout the simulations.

We experimented with a number of different proportional breakdowns of polluting and non-polluting firms. We believe that under current regulatory regimes highly polluting firms are currently in the minority in the United States, but we also required enough of them to generate sufficient pollution in our artificial world to allow assessment of environmental differentials; this balance achieved our goals. Were we modeling specific cities, empirically based ratios would be more appropriate. For example, Washington, DC, would have a much higher ratio of non-polluting firms, while Cleveland would have a much higher ratio of polluting firms. Because both cities and residents generally want job-producing firms that do not pollute, we consider non-polluting firms to be *amenities* that enhance plot quality, while polluting firms are *disamenities* that degrade plot quality (but still produce a social good in the form of jobs for residents).

Given the importance of firm location choice in the EJ literature, the computational procedure for firm location choice is a key behavior in the model. A new firm's siting decision is based on two steps. First, considering empirical evidence of agglomeration economies,[12] firms are modeled as preferring to be near firms like themselves. However, to ensure adequate spatial variation, this is limited to no more than four firms within a block at the time of siting. When we allowed more firms per block, then the agglomeration preference overwhelmed firm location choice and all similar firms located on the same block, and the end result was not sufficiently realistic in terms of how firms and pollutants actually are dispersed throughout regions. While similar firms do tend to locate near one another, in most cases all do not locate adjacent to one another.

Although this can change when zoning is introduced in Chapter 8, we found that having firms seek plots where there is at least one other of the same type of firm within 10 concentric rings,[13] on blocks that have fewer than five firms, led to a distribution of firms that looked appropriately realistic. If early in the simulation trial there is no other firm of the same type (polluting or non-polluting), the firm considers plots that have fewer than five firms of any type.[14]

Second, after the agglomeration condition is satisfied, polluting firms make their siting decisions based on one of three plot-selection criteria, hypothesized in the EJ literature and elaborated in Chapter 4: 1 they choose the lowest-priced plot; 2 they prefer to locate away from majorities; or 3 they prefer to locate near minorities.[15] In contrast, non-polluting firms always seek the lowest-priced plot.[16] These decision rules are outlined in Table 3.1. Once firms make location choices, they remain in those locations for the duration of the simulation trial.[17]

### Environmental quality of plots

Once a new firm settles in a plot, polluting firms degrade the quality of a plot, and non-polluting firms improve the quality of a plot. After extensive testing to ensure that our modeled system ended up looking sufficiently like a real (albeit simple) natural system, we modeled these environmental effects in two ways: first, as a reflection of the pollution variable associated with the focal firm, and second, as a function of spatial proximity.

If a new polluting firm is located on a plot during the simulation, the quality value of the plot upon which the polluting firm is located decreases

*Table 3.1* Firm siting rules

| | | |
|---|---|---|
| 1 | | All firms follow the zoning rules, if any. |
| | a | With no zoning scenario, a firm prefers plots where there is at least one other of the same type of firm within 10 concentric rings, and blocks that have fewer than five firms. |
| | b | With zoning rules, a firm considers only appropriate zone types and prefers blocks that have fewer than five firms. |
| 2 | | Non-polluting firms always choose the lowest-priced plot. |
| 3 | | Polluting firms choose a plot based on one of the following decision criteria: |
| | a | The lowest-price plot (modeling an economically rational firm), |
| | b | Plots away from majorities (modeling a politically rational firm), or |
| | c | Plots near minorities (modeling a discriminatory/racist firm) |
| 4 | | Once firms site on a plot, they do not move. |

(Revised version of Campbell, Kim and Eckerd 2014: 11, used by permission)

by between 6% and 9%, depending on the polluting firm's pollution level. For example, if a new polluting firm with a pollution level of six is sited on a plot, the quality of the plot is reduced 6% of the previous quality value. The higher the pollution level, the larger the reduction. The quality of all plots within the block where the polluting firm is located also decreases (between 3% and 4.5%), again depending upon the polluting firm's pollution level.[18] The code block in Box 3.1, displaying NetLogo code, provides more detail on how these are operationalized, and also provides insight into the logic of programming in NetLogo.

> **Box 3.1 NetLogo code I: Decreasing quality of plots due to a polluting firm's siting**
>
> ```
> decrease-rate ( .01 * ( 100 - pollution ) )
> patch-here [ set quality ( quality * decrease-rate ) ]
> neighbor-decrease-rate ( .01 * ( 100 - pollution ) / 2 )
> land with [ block = [ block ] of myself ] [quality ( quality *
> neighbor-decrease-rate ) ]
> ```

Conversely, if a non-polluting firm is introduced to a plot, the quality increases by between 5% and none, again depending upon the non-polluting firm's pollution level.[19] The quality of neighbor plots within the block also increases via the same mechanism as the decrease associated with polluting firms (but here increases are between 0% and 2.5%). These quality operations that are related to the pollution level of the focal firm occur in only one time period, the time step after each new firm is introduced to the simulated world. These operations are also shown, in Box 3.2 on NetLogo code II.

---

**Box 3.2 NetLogo code II: Increasing quality of plots due to a non-polluting firm's siting**

```
increase-rate ( 1 + ( .01 * ( 5 - pollution ) ) )
patch-here [ set quality ( quality * increase-rate ) ]
neighbor-increase-rate ( 1 + ( .01 * ( 5 - pollution ) / 2 ) )
land with [ block = [ block ] of myself ] [quality ( quality *
neighbor-increase-rate ) ]
```

---

Once the simulation starts, two other procedures influence the quality of plots on an ongoing basis. The quality of each plot at time $t$ is updated by negatively adjusting the quality at $t - 1$ by an inverse distance to the nearest disamenity and positively adjusting the quality at $t$ by an inverse distance to the nearest amenity. This procedure is performed to develop a utility score for plots and is sketched in Box 3.3 on NetLogo code III, where *trifdist* is the distance between the plot and the nearest polluting firm, *ntrifdist* is the distance between the plot and the nearest non-polluting firm, and $\delta$ is a quality exponential decay rate that is set at 1.5 in the model.

---

**Box 3.3 NetLogo code III: Quality adjustment procedures**

```
quality ( quality * ( 1 - ( 1 / trifdist ^ δ ) ) )
quality ( quality * ( 1 + ( 1 / ntrifdist ^ δ ) ) )
```

---

After this adjustment occurs, quality changes spread out to adjacent plots (similar to how air pollution might spread in a windless situation), with decreased force based on distance.[20] Finally, each plot diffuses its quality value to the eight neighboring plots based on a diffusion rate. After extensive trial and refinement, we set the diffusion rate to 0.7, so each plot gets one-eighth of 70% of the quality value from each neighboring plot. The quality update and diffusion procedures operate every simulation step, as illustrated in the first line of NetLogo code IV in Box 3.4 (price diffusion, also illustrated here in the second line, is discussed below).

---

**Box 3.4 NetLogo code IV: Quality diffusion procedure**

```
quality diffusion-rate
price diffusion-rate
```

## Residents

As described above, we assume a numerical minority and a numerical majority, and so the simulation begins with more majority than minority residents: 70% to 30%. Within these subgroups, the resident agents are assigned differential incomes. Using overall income levels in the United States as a representation of incomes in what we conceptualize as our decontextualized "average US city," each agent in each racial group is randomly assigned an income from either a normal or gamma distribution roughly approximating the 2010 US Census averages for white non-Hispanics and African Americans.[21] Analysts interested in specific locales should substitute locally appropriate income distributions. In most scenarios, this means that majority residents are assigned an income from a distribution with a mean of $54,000 and standard deviation of $41,000, and minority residents are assigned an income from a distribution with a mean of $32,000 and standard deviation of $40,000[22] (with both constrained to be no less than zero). We hold income constant for both groups in Chapter 4, but the focus of Chapter 6 is on understanding the relationship between income and race, so income distributions are varied in analytic scenarios in Chapter 6.

For analytical purposes, we categorize agents based on these income levels, such that an income level greater than $100,000 is "rich," and this roughly corresponds to the income level at which an individual would be in at least the second-highest federal income-tax bracket. Agents with incomes less than $28,000 are categorized as "poor," corresponding to an income that is, at most, 150% of the defined poverty level for a family of three.[23] All other resident agents are categorized as "middle class." Though this might seem a wide band for the middle class, it accords with the oft-found observation that most Americans consider themselves middle class.

When new residents are introduced to the world, they choose locations based on the utility function described in Equation 3.1, but their location choices are constrained by their incomes and any similarity preferences they have regarding who their neighbors are. For the income constraint, we reason that residents will not always opt to select the lowest-priced home because it may be located in an undesirable neighborhood. Thus, no resident agent will consider a plot that is less than twice its income level and, given the constraints preventing the purchase of a home that is out of one's price range, residents also exclude any plot with a price greater than three times their income level.[24]

Once a resident finds a set of plots that satisfies its income constraints, the similarity preference for living near other residents like itself is considered.[25] If residents have a similarity preference, they first look for any available plots in their income-constrained decision set that meet their similarity preference criterion. For example, if the similarity preference for minorities is assumed to be 80%, minority agents will only consider locating on plots where at least 80% of the agents on neighboring plots are also minorities.[26]

If there is no plot that satisfies their similarity preference, residents choose a plot with the highest utility score within their income constraint.

These income and similarity preference constraints limit residential choice sets; after the constrained set of plots has been identified, residents pick a plot that maximizes their utility within their choice sets given each plot's price, quality, and distance to the nearest job at the moment.[27] In other words, residents locate on the plot with the highest utility score within their constrained choice set, calculated based on the following decision criteria: balance paying the lowest price for the plot, while living with the highest quality, and near their place of work, as described in the following equation:

$$u_{j,t} = p_{j,t}^{-\alpha} \cdot q_{j,t}^{\beta} \cdot d_{jk,t}^{-\gamma}$$   (Equation 3.1)

Where the utility score of a plot $j$ is a function of the price ($p$) and quality ($q$) of the plot $j$ and distance ($d$) between the plot $j$ and the nearest job, $k$, at time $t$. An equal decision weight of 0.5 is set for the three decision variables ($\alpha$, $\beta$, $\gamma$).

Once resident agents choose a plot with the highest utility score, they are assumed to be immobile, except in Chapter 7 and Chapter 9, in which mobility is a focal point of analysis. We chose initially to limit mobility in order to estimate the pure first-order effects of race and income. This also seems reasonable given evidence of increased moving costs and decreased rates of moving in the United States,[28] and the fact that in many other industrialized nations moving rates are much lower than in the United States. When we add residential mobility, a certain proportion of residents who already located on a plot are randomly chosen and assigned to reenter the residential choice process described above (see Chapter 7 for details). These decision rules are outlined in Table 3.2.

### Price of plots

The price of a plot at time $t$ is determined after evaluating several factors, derived again through extensive testing, intended to model relevant attributes of a real-estate market. First, the price at $t - 1$ is weighted by a distance to the nearest polluting firm (*trifdist*), and then the adjusted price at $t$ is weighted by a distance to the nearest non-polluting firm (*ntrifdist*). After that, the price at $t$ is finalized by considering the gap between residential income levels on neighboring plots and the current price of the plot. Specifically, prices are altered based on the income level of the resident agents who settle nearby. If the income level of nearby residents is high, the plot price increases (or decreases if incomes of nearby residents are low) by a multiplier that is calculated by comparing the difference between twice the average income of nearby residents and the current plot price. This procedure is stepwise and completed to be used for the utility score calculation. NetLogo code V in Box 3.5 illustrates this process, where the first line makes the price adjustment for proximity to disamenities, the second line adjusts for proximity to amenities, and the rest of the lines adjust for the wealth of nearby residents.

---

**Box 3.5 NetLogo code V: Price adjustment procedures**

```
price ( price * ( 1 - ( 1 / trifdist ^ δ ) ) )
price ( price * ( 1 + ( 1 / ntrifdist ^ δ ) ) )
ifelse any? residents-on neighbors
[ set area-wealth ( 2 * ( mean [ wealth ] of residents-on
neighbors ) ) ]
[ set area-wealth price ]
price ( price + ( area-wealth - price ) )
```

---

After this adjustment occurs, each plot diffuses its price value to the eight neighboring plots based on a diffusion rate, similar to the procedure described above regarding plot environmental quality. As with quality, the diffusion rate is set to 0.7, so each plot gets one-eighth of 70% of the price value from each neighboring plot at every simulation step. This procedure was previously presented in Box 3.4, NetLogo code IV (line two).

### Government actions

Though a governmental authority is not modeled as a spatially explicit agent with its own location (as are residents and firms), the EJ ABM includes a "government" agent that can set various institutional rules regarding where siting is and is not allowed, or where to clean up in order

*Table 3.2* Residential choice rules

| | |
|---|---|
| 1 | No resident agent considers a plot with a price that is less than twice its income level or greater than three times its income level. |
| 2 | Resident agents may prefer to live near other residents who are like themselves with respect to "race." |
| 3 | From the set constrained by price and racial similarity preference, residents pick a plot that maximizes their utility given price, quality, and distance to the nearest job. |
| 4 | If a reactive zoning rule is in effect, residents living in a block that is zoned must move to other plots. In this case, they follow rules 1–3. |
| 5 | For experiments with mobility, if a resident located at a plot is randomly selected to move, the resident reenters the residential choice process again, following rules 1–3. |

(Revised version of Campbell, Kim and Eckerd 2014: 11, used by permission)

to improve environmental justice. We analyze two government actions: zoning and cleanup strategies.

### Local zoning

The EJ ABM assumes there is a local authority that plans for and manages local land use. In particular, the authority is responsible for zoning. In the United States, local zoning is a common tool of land-use policy[29] that has been used for purposes such as promoting economic development and sheltering residential populations from industrial disamenities. Our zoning procedure is fully explained in Chapter 8, but, briefly, in some scenarios of the EJ ABM, we use three types of government zoning strategies: no zoning, proactive zoning, and reactive zoning (see Table 3.3). Both proactive and reactive zoning scenarios introduce residential zones (R-zones), commercial zones (C-zones), and manufacturing or industrial zones (M-zones) to the artificial community. For these scenarios, our question is how zoning can affect EJ.

### Remediation policies

The government agent can also plan strategies to remedy environmental harm caused by existing hazardous sites. Like the US federal government's Superfund program and various state and local brownfield remediation programs, government can clean up polluting sites according to three different strategies. It can focus on the most potentially risky sites, clean up the sites that have the highest potential economic value, or focus cleanup efforts on sites that have the largest concentration of minority residents nearby. The varying results of the three strategies are discussed in Chapter 9.

Table 3.4 summarizes the initial parameters for the model and our rationale for setting these parameters. In addition to these values, we tested a host of other values for each of our key parameters. We include details of this sensitivity analysis in Table 3.5.

## Model outcome

Our primary interest is in understanding the conditions under which minorities on average end up in lower environmental quality areas than majorities on average—one issue of relevance to sustainable cities. Thus, the model outcome of our interest is the aggregate level of average environmental quality for those plots on which majority residents and minority residents are located.

As mentioned above, each simulation is begun with a random selection of agents and firms. Then, for each time step[30] the entire program is run through once, with new resident and firm agents added according to the outlined rules. In our analyses, the number of time steps is usually 70, which is enough to understand the pattern of environmental quality between

*Table 3.3* Zoning rules

| 1 | | No zoning |
|---|---|---|
| 2 | | Proactive zoning scenario |
| | a | Before the simulation starts, approximately 10 random blocks are designated as M-zones, another 10 random blocks are designated as C-zones, and the remaining plots are assumed to be R-zones. |
| | b | New polluting firms must be located in M-zones and new non-polluting firms must be located in C-zones. |
| | c | Residents cannot locate in M-zones or C-zones. |
| 3 | | Reactive zoning scenario |
| | a | If >2 polluting firms within a block are established, an M-zone is created. |
| | b | If >2 low-polluting firms are established within a block, a C-zone is created. |
| | c | If residents are living in areas that have now been zoned C or M, they move. |
| | d | Zones can be rezoned between C- and M-zones if new firms locate there, but those areas never return to R-zones. |

(Revised version of Campbell, Kim and Eckerd 2014: 11, used by permission)

groups.[31] The entire set of time steps (e.g., 70) for a particular randomized start is a "trial." Throughout each trial we track the average level of quality for plots that have majority and minority residents located on them. We compare these averages dynamically during the simulation, and also the resulting levels at the end of each simulation.

In addition to these average levels for both residential groups, we also calculate a quality gap measure by subtracting the average quality level for minority agents from the average level for majority agents. A positive number indicates that the majority is relatively better off and by how much, while a negative number indicates that the minority is relatively better off and by how much. Zero indicates that there is no difference in the quality level experienced by the two groups.

In most chapters using this model, we ran 200 independent trials for each distinct scenario under examination, where "scenarios" are the specific set of rules under consideration, such as the specific levels of residential mobility, specific firm decision rules, etc. For example, Chapter 4 focuses on the combination of three firm-siting scenarios and three resident similarity-preference scenarios. This yields 127,800 simulated observations (3 firm scenarios x 3 resident scenarios x 200 simulation trials x 71 time steps[32]). The number of simulated observations in each chapter varies depending upon the number of scenarios each chapter experiments with, but all datasets in Chapters 4-9 are created based on the same procedure.

*Table 3.4* Base model parameterizations

| Variables/parameters | Rationales and references |
|---|---|
| **City level** | |
| Number of plots = 101 x 101 (10,201 plots) | Chosen to ensure that the simulation world is big enough to examine the dynamics of society but also reasonable for running the simulation given computing power |
| Growth rate (net) = 5% | Chosen to represent a growing urban area |
| Residents per firm ratio = 50:1 | Chosen given the world size and the initial number of residents |
| Initial plot environmental quality value = 50 | Parameter value chosen as a hypothetical index of environmental quality; given the complexity of environmental quality, many different individual indicators could have been chosen, but we opted for a relative index as the most representative |
| Initial plot price value = $N(\$173,000, \$34,000)$ | Chosen to mirror median housing price in the United States[1] |
| Pollution diffusion rate = 0.7 | The value was chosen based on existing studies[2] |
| Price and quality effects: exponential decay rate = 1.5 | The value was chosen based on existing studies[3] |
| **Agent level** | |
| Initial number of resident agents = 200 | Represents a balance among ensuring enough agents to start interacting, the size of the simulation world, and computing power |
| Initial racial composition = MA 140 (70%): MI 60 (30%) | The concept of a majority requires more residents than in the minority, so the current composition was chosen as a starting point |
| Majority income = $N(\$54,000, \$41,000)$ | Chosen to mirror the US income distribution for white non-Hispanics[4] |
| Minority income = $N(\$32,000, \$40,000)$ | Chosen to mirror the US income distribution for African Americans[5] |
| Initial number of firms = ~4 | A function of initial number of residents and jobs per firm |
| Firm's pollution level = $U(0,9)$ | A hypothetical starting point to represent the variation of pollution levels of firms |
| Residential similarity preference = 0%, 20%, 50%, or 80% | Chosen for simplicity or based on empirical studies that report similarity preferences[6] |
| Utility balancing parameters = 0.5 | Chosen based on existing studies[7] |

Notes: 1) US Census 2010.
2) A. Tom Veldkamp and Peter H. Verburg, "Editorial: Modeling Land Use Change and Environmental Impact," *Journal of Environmental Management* 72, no. 1–2 (2004): 1–3; Daniel G. Brown, Scott E. Page, Rick Riolo, Moira Zellner and William Rand, "Path Dependence and the Validation of Agent-Based Spatial Models of Land," *International Journal of Geographical Information Science* 19 (2005): 153–74.
3) Veldkamp and Verburg, "Editorial: Modeling Land Use Change and Environmental Impact," 1–3.
4) US Census 2010.
5) Ibid.
6) William A. V. Clark, "Residential Preferences and Residential Choices in a Multiethnic Context," *Demography* 29, no. 3 (1992) 451–66.; Michael O. Emerson, George Yancey and Karen J. Chai, "Does Race Matter in Residential Segregation? Exploring the Preferences of White Americans," *American Sociological Review* 66, no. 6 (2001): 922–35.
7) Daniel G. Brown and Derek T. Robinson, "Effects of Heterogeneity in Residential Preferences on an Agent-Based Model of Urban Sprawl," *Ecology and Society* 11, no. 1 (2006): 46; Paul M. Torrens and Atsushi Nara, "Modeling Gentrification Dynamics: A Hybrid Approach," *Computers, Environment and Urban Systems* 31 (2007): 337–61.

*Table 3.5* Sensitivity assessments

| Parameters | Model value | Range of values tested | Sensitivity (S) | Result |
|---|---|---|---|---|
| **Firms** | | | | |
| Jobs per firm | 50:1 | 10, 30, 70, 90 | 1.6 | At higher numbers, fewer firms were established, resulting in less environmental quality variability. Results at high levels showed few discernible trends, but as the number of employees per firm was lowered, similar patterns to those presented emerged. At low values, more firms were established resulting in more overall environmental variation. |
| Pollution | 0–9, uniform distribution | 0–9, from normal distribution ~ N(5, 2) | NA | The normal distribution resulted in many firms near 5, and little variation in pollution and its effects. Overall environmental quality was much less variable, so the environmental quality gaps between groups was much lower. |
| **Residents** | | | | |
| Number of residents | 200 | 100, 500 | 8.1 | With more initial residents, space became constrained more quickly in the model, and more clustering of minorities was noted near both amenities and disamenities. With constrained space, more residents of both races saw more extremes of environmental quality. |
| Racial composition | 70%/30% | 55%/45%, 90%/10% | -15.6 | With more parity, the environmental quality gap between the groups was much smaller. With the higher proportion of the majority, the results were very similar to the 70/30 scenario but with larger gaps (see Chapter 4). |
| Similarity preference | 80% | 20%, 50% | -12.5 | In line with previous studies, at lower similarity preferences, the results were conceptually the same, but with much smaller environmental quality gaps between the two groups. |

| Parameters | Model value | Range of values tested | Sensitivity (S) | Result |
|---|---|---|---|---|
| Quality, price, and distance preference weights | 0.5, 0.5, 0.5 | Combinations of 0, 0.5, and 2 for each parameter | 2.1 (quality); 4.2 (price); 1.8 (distance) | If residents preferred quality more relative to price and distance, trends were the same but more pronounced, and if they preferred quality less, trends were the same but muted. Altering price preferences relative to quality and distance was very similar to altering quality preferences. Altering distance relative to price and quality resulted either in more pronounced trends if distance preference was increased, or virtually no trends if the distance preference was decreased. Altering all three together produced results nearly identical to those presented. |
| *Patches* | | | | |
| Diffusion rate | 0.70 | 0.10, 0.50, 0.90 | 2.4 | Lower diffusion rates tended to concentrate pollution only on patches where polluting firms were located, while higher rates watered down pollution of these focal patches, while providing a bit more variability with respect to the overall environmental quality gaps between groups. Overall results were similar regardless of the rate used. |
| Pollution decay rate | 1/d | 1/d², 1/d³ | NA | More rapid decay rates tended to concentrate high pollution in relatively few places, not creating a realistic spread of pollution across a geographic area. Since high pollution was constrained, residents tended to settle away from polluted patches until the population size so constrained choice that there were no alternatives. Therefore, results were muted (but similar) with more rapid decay rates. |

| Parameters | Model value | Range of values tested | Sensitivity (S) | Result |
|---|---|---|---|---|
| *System* | | | | |
| Agglomeration (firm search) radius | 10 patches | 5, 10, 20, 30, 40, 50 | 1.3 | Agglomeration effects seemed to have little effect on the extent of the environmental quality gap between groups, but the smaller the agglomeration search radius, the more clustering by minorities near both amenities and disamenities was observed. With less agglomeration there was lower variability in minority environmental quality. |
| Population growth rate | 5% | 0%, 1%, 10% | 6.4 | Results were similar regardless of population growth rate, although at higher growth rates space became more constrained, so initially the trends were amplified and the gaps remained relatively larger through the end of the trial. |

Note: We provide both a calculation of sensitivity (where appropriate) as well as a descriptive review of the overall trends observed in the model results given changes in each parameter. As recommended by Railsback and Grimm (2011), sensitivity is calculated as $[(G_1 - G_2) / G_1] / [(P_1 - P_2) / P_1]$ where: $G_1$ is the average environmental quality gap between majorities and minorities at time-step 70 for trials using the parameter value noted in the "model value" column; $G_2$ is the average of the same variable when the parameter value is the most extreme difference noted in the "range of values tested" column; $P_1$ is the value of the parameter in the "model value" column and $P_2$ is the most extreme value noted in the "range of values tested" column. The Sensitivity value shown is the result for the most extreme value assessed. In some cases (indicated by NA), this value could not be computed. For most parameters we examine the sensitivity of the results to multiple outcomes. However, for simplicity we report only one S value per variable: the most extreme value, indicating the greatest sensitivity found for the tested set. For our analysis, sensitivity values greater than 1 are generally of less concern than those smaller than 1; with numbers greater than 1 environmental gaps are bigger than under the base model, indicating that the base model is conservative. This metric is in essence an elasticity: it computes the percentage change in the key variable (here, the environmental quality gap) as a ratio of the percentage change in a parameter. Thus, if the value is greater than one in magnitude, the key variable is elastic to changes in the parameter (a 1% change in the parameter leads to a more than 1% change in the key variable). However, the closer the value is to one in magnitude, the less sensitive the model results are to changes in the sensitivity-analyzed parameter. Further, positive values indicate that a parameter change led to an environmental quality gap *larger* than in the base case, and negative values indicate that the parameter change led to an environmental quality gap *smaller* than in the base case.

As noted, simulations produce data from sets of assumptions and scenarios tested. The data can be analyzed in various ways. Some analyses are performed during the simulation using the agent-based modeling toolkit. For example, in NetLogo the quality gap between social groups during the simulation can be monitored (see the bottom charts in Figure 3.2). In most instances, simulation data are stored in files such as .csv or .txt files. We extract simulation data as .csv files and analyze them using statistical software. This stage of analysis is not different from the analysis of empirically based datasets.

### EJ ABM interface

Figure 3.2 presents a snapshot of the EJ ABM in NetLogo. This snapshot shows output from one trial that has been allowed to run for about 56 time steps. The NetLogo graphical user interface consists of the central "landscape," where firms and residents are displayed, as well as "buttons," "sliders," and "switches" on the left-hand side of the panel,[33] and output monitors at the bottom and right. The landscape in Figure 3.2 shows the segregation of residents by racial group over time, along with the level of quality of the area. The visualization capability of NetLogo and other ABM toolkits helps researchers, policymakers, and administrators examine whether the encoded model runs as intended.

Users can interactively change values of important variables using sliders and switches. Various scenarios beyond those considered in this book can be tested by adjusting these. The development of an environmental quality gap among social groups can be monitored on the output monitors, which appear at the bottom. In Figure 3.2, these output monitors show not only racial gaps, but also quality gaps between income groups.

### Discussion

In this chapter, we began explaining and testing a simple, stylized base model. We have reviewed the basic behavior and functionality of the EJ ABM, and described how the model was designed, programmed, and presented in NetLogo (see the Appendix for greater detail). While the process has been explained in a linear manner, modeling is a highly iterative process and the model described above is not an ultimate product, but a base we use to analyze systemic questions regarding EJ, and a base that could also be used for other analyses, particularly regarding urban sustainability.

With this as background, in subsequent chapters we turn some features on or off and add complexity and different focuses to the model. However, for consistency, the basic processes remain the same, as described in this chapter. For example, our first EJ ABM experiments in Chapter 4 include only a few very basic characteristics: resident agents, who seek land, are either minorities or majorities, and otherwise identical; and firms, which seek land, are

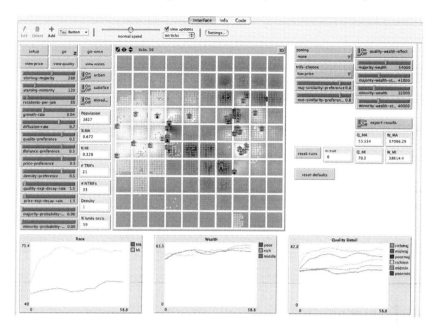

*Figure 3.2* Model interface in NetLogo

either non-polluting firms or polluting firms (depending on the level of randomly drawn pollution), and otherwise identical. Next, based on Schelling's path-breaking work on segregation,[34] and on some empirical work by Clark,[35] we add similarity preferences such that the otherwise identical residents prefer to be near others of their same "race" (majority or minority).

To understand better the other factors that determine environmental justice outcomes, in following chapters we build upon this platform by experimenting with base assumptions and adding income, mobility, and policy interventions. Table 3.6 summarizes features that are turned on or off for the main questions analyzed in each chapter. Readers can refer to Table 3.6 to check which scenarios or conditions are set in each chapter.

## Notes

1 H. Spencer Banzhaf and Randall P. Walsh, "Do People Vote with their Feet? An Empirical Test of Tiebout's Mechanism," *American Economic Review* 98, no. 3 (2008): 843–63.

2 For price, see Jennifer Roback, "Wages, Rents, and the Quality of Life," *Journal of Political Economy* 90, no. 6 (1982): 1257–78; for commuting distance, see Richard Voith, "Transportation, Sorting and House Values," *Real Estate Economics* 19, no. 2 (1991): 117–37; for environmental quality, see Banzhaf and Walsh, "Do People Vote with their Feet?"; and for neighborhood composition, see Su-Yeul Chung and Lawrence A. Brown, "Racial/Ethnic Residential Sorting

Table 3.6 EJ ABM setup for each chapter

| System | Variables | Scenarios | Firms | Residents | | | Government | |
|---|---|---|---|---|---|---|---|---|
| | | | Siting motives | Residential constraints | Race vs. income | Mobility | Local zoning | Cleanup policy |
| | | | Ch.4 | Ch.5 | Ch.6 | Ch.7 | Ch.8 | Ch.9 |
| Firms | *Non-polluting firm siting decision* | | | | | | | |
| | | Lowest-priced plot | ✓ | ✓ | ✓ | ✓ | ✓ | ✓ |
| | *Polluting firm siting decision* | | | | | | | |
| | | Lowest-priced plot | * | ✓ | ✓ | ✓ | * | ✓ |
| | | Away from majorities (MA) | * | ✓ | | | * | ✓ |
| | | Near minorities (MI) | * | ✓ | | | * | ✓ |
| Residents | *Similarity preference* | | | | | | | |
| | | Both: none | * | | * | * | | |
| | | Both: 20% | * | | | | | * |
| | | Both: 80% | * | * | * | * | ✓ | * |
| | | MA: 80% / MI: 50% | | * | * | * | | * |
| | | MA: 80% / MI: 20% | | * | | | | |
| | *Income* | | | | | | | |
| | | Normal distribution | ✓ | ✓ | ✓ | ✓ | ✓ | ✓ |
| | | Right-skewed (γ) distribution | ✓ | ✓ | | | | |
| | | MA=MI | | ✓ | ✓ | ✓ | ✓ | ✓ |
| | | MA>MI | | * | * | ✓ | ✓ | |
| | | MI<MA | | | * | | | ✓ |

| System | Variables | Scenarios | Firms | Residents | | | Government | |
|---|---|---|---|---|---|---|---|---|
| | | | Siting motives | Residential constraints | Race vs. income | Mobility | Local zoning | Cleanup policy |
| | | | Ch.4 | Ch.5 | Ch.6 | Ch.7 | Ch.8 | Ch.9 |
| | *Mobility* | | | | | | | |
| | | No mobility | ✓ | ✓ | ✓ | * | ✓ | |
| | | Limited mobility | | | | * | | ✓ |
| | | Tiebout mobility | | | | * | | |
| Community | *Race composition* | | | | | | | |
| | | MA 70%: MI 30% | ✓ | * | ✓ | ✓ | ✓ | ✓ |
| | | MA 55%: MI 45% | | * | | | | |
| | | MA 90%: MI 10% | | * | | | | |
| | *Population growth rate* | | | | | | | |
| | | 5% | ✓ | * | ✓ | ✓ | ✓ | ✓ |
| | | 1% | | * | | | | |
| Government | *Zoning rule* | | | | | | | |
| | | No zoning | ✓ | ✓ | ✓ | ✓ | * | ✓ |
| | | Proactive | | | | | * | |
| | | Reactive | | | | | * | |
| | *Cleanup policy* | | | | | | | |
| | | No cleanup | ✓ | ✓ | ✓ | ✓ | ✓ | * |
| | | Economic pressure | | | | | | * |
| | | Environmental risk | | | | | | * |
| | | Environmental injustice | | | | | | * |

Note: ✓ basic setup; * analytical focus.

in Spatial Context: Testing the Explanatory Frameworks," *Urban Geography* 28, no. 4 (2007): 312–39.

3  Uri Wilensky, *NetLogo* (Evanston, IL: CCL, Northwestern University, 1999), ccl.northwestern.edu/netlogo/.

4  Nigel Gilbert, *Agent-Based Models* (Thousand Oaks, CA: Sage Publication, 2008), 50.

5  In the analyses presented in this book we do not experiment with transportation, but we recognize the importance of the overall built environment and intend to analyze this in future research.

6  In some scenarios plots also have a zone type, or a percentage of minorities nearby, etc.

7  It is not uncommon to find that there are no good empirical data or evidence upon which to base some parameters in an ABM. Modelers often use reasonable hypothetical values for such parameters in an ABM, providing some rationales. In the literature, two perspectives on this are the following: 1 it may sound arbitrary, but it would have been much more unscientific if some important variables were left out of the model because of unknown empirical values (Donella H. Meadow, *Thinking in Systems* (White River Junction, VT: Chelsea Green Publishing, 2008)); and 2 a pattern-oriented modeling approach is suggested as a way of calibrating unknown parameters in an ABM, especially in the area of ecology (Volker Grimm, Eloy Revilla, Uta Berger, Florian Jeltsch, Wolf M. Mooji, Steven F. Railsback, Hans-Hermann Thulke, Jacob Weiner, Thorsten Wiegand and Donald L. DeAngelis, "Pattern-Oriented Modeling of Agent-Based Complex Systems: Lessons from Ecology," *Science* 310, no. 5750 (2005): 987–91).

8  Both of these numbers are based on results of the 2010 US Census.

9  See US Census Bureau, "Quick Facts," quickfacts.census.gov/qfd/states/00000.html.

10  William H. Frey, *Population Growth in Metro America Since 1980: Putting the Volatile 2000s in Perspective* (Washington, DC: Brookings, 2012), www.brookings.edu/~/media/research/files/papers/2012/3/20%20population%20frey/0320_population_frey.pdf.

11  An analyst who aims to focus on industrial development rather than environmental injustice could change this so that firms are located near rivers or other transportation corridors. For our purposes, initial random location is sufficient.

12  Paul Krugman, "On the Relationship between Trade Theory and Location Theory," *Review of International Economics* 1, no. 2 (1993): 110–22; Ann Wolverton, "Effects of Socio-Economic and Input-Related Factors on Polluting Plants' Location Decisions," *The B.E. Journal of Economic Analysis & Policy* 9, no. 1 (2009): 1–32.

13  We used a primitive, *in-radius*, that was built into the agent-based modeling toolkit we used (NetLogo). The primitive reports plots that include only those agents whose distance from the caller is less than or equal to *number*. This can include the agent itself. The distance to or from a plot is measured from the center of the plot. The 10 concentric rings (*in-radius 10*) return 316 surrounding plots of the plot that is the caller (the focal plot).

14  With zoning scenarios in place (see Chapter 8), a firm considers zone types given its own category as either a polluting firm (industrial) or a non-polluting firm (commercial), and also the number of firms settled within each block (again, firms prefer blocks that have fewer than five firms).

15  As shown in Chapter 4, choices 2 and 3, which can respectively be thought of as politically rational and discriminatory, lead to different outcomes.

16  Adam Eckerd, Heather E. Campbell and Yushim Kim, "Helping those Like Us or Harming those Unlike Us: Agent-Based Modeling to Illuminate Social Processes Leading to Environmental Injustice," *Environment & Planning B* 39, no. 5 (2012): 945–64, DOI:10.1068/b38001.

17 As noted by a reviewer, in real life some firms move, but our interest is not on a specific firm that may stay or go, but on the distribution of polluting and non-polluting firms within the region.

18 As described above with respect to other assumptions, these assumptions were iteratively designed to create an appropriate level of variation in pollution and quality.

19 The "non-polluting firm" case can be considered one in which the benefits provided by the firm (jobs, services, etc.) exceed the costs (e.g., pollution).

20 Dawn C. Parker and Vicky J. Meretsky, "Measuring Pattern Outcomes in an Agent-Based Model of Edge-Effect Externalities Using Spatial Metrics," *Agriculture Ecosystem & Environment* 101 (2004): 233–50.

21 The true US income distribution is not normally distributed, but is skewed to the right. While most chapters in this book are based on the right-skewed gamma distribution, we experiment with a normal distribution in Chapter 4. In unreported analyses, we compared the simulation results based on the normal distribution and the right-skewed distribution and did not find much difference in outcomes.

22 2010 US Census averages for white non-Hispanics and African Americans.

23 As noted by Heather E. Campbell, Laura R. Peck and Michael K. Tschudi (in "Justice for All? A Cross-time Analysis of Toxics Release Inventory Facility Location," *Review of Policy Research* 27, no. 1 (2010): 1–25), this percentage of the official poverty level is consistent with what the populace generally considered poverty.

24 Dawn C. Parker and Tatiana Filatova, "A Conceptual Design for a Bilateral Agent-Based Land Market with Heterogeneous Economic Agents," *Computers, Environment and Urban Systems* 32, no. 6 (2008): 454–63.

25 Thomas C. Schelling, *Micromotives and Macrobehavior* (New York: W.W. Norton & Company, 1978); William A.V. Clark, "Residential Preferences and Residential Choices in a Multiethnic Context." *Demography* 29, no. 3 (1992): 451–66.

26 During the simulation each plot calculates the proportion of majorities and minorities within 10 concentric rings from its location. Resident agents use this information to narrow down their choice set based on similarity preference.

27 These decision behaviors are similar to, but not the same as, Daniel G. Brown, Scott E. Page, Rick Riolo, Moira Zellner and William Rand, "Path Dependence and the Validation of Agent-Based Spatial Models of Land," *International Journal of Geographical Information Science* 19 (2005): 153–74; John W. Pratt, "Risk Aversion in the Small and the Large," *Econometrica* 32, no. 1–2 (1964): 122–36; William Rand, Moira Zellner, Scott E. Page, Rick Riolo, Daniel G. Brown and L.E. Fernandez, "The Complex Interaction of Agents and Environments: An Example in Urban Sprawl," Conference on Social Agents: Ecology, Exchange and Evolution, Chicago, 2002.

28 K.R. Cox, "Housing Tenure and Neighborhood Activism," *Urban Affairs Review* 18 (2007): 107–29.

29 W. Fischel, *The Economics of Zoning Laws: A Property Rights Approach to American Land Use Controls* (Baltimore, MD: Johns Hopkins University Press, 1987).

30 Time steps can generally be considered as any measurement of time, including seconds, hours, months or years. In the context of our urban region, we have generally conceived of these time steps as years, and we thus are considering how environmental quality is distributed over a long period of time.

31 We made an exception for Chapter 8, in which we stop the simulation at time-step 60 due to the limited residential plots as a result of zones introduced. Once

M- or C-zones are introduced, it reduces the number of plots available for residents, and the R-zoned plots are quickly filled.
32  A simulation run starts from time-step 0, so if it stops at time-step 70, it includes simulation data from 71 time steps.
33  Buttons, sliders, and switches are pre-made features in NetLogo. Buttons named "setup," "go," etc. in Figure 3.2 execute instructions once or multiple times (as appropriate). Sliders, used for "starting majority," etc., are accessible by all agents. Users can move the slider to different values and observe what happens in the model. Switches, used for "urban," etc., are a visual representation of a true/false variable. Users can set the variable to either on (true) or off (false) by flipping the switch.
34  Schelling, *Micromotives and Macrobehavior.*
35  Clark, "Residential Preferences and Residential Choices in a Multiethnic Context."

# References

Banzhaf, H. Spencer and Randall P. Walsh. "Do People Vote with their Feet? An Empirical Test of Tiebout's Mechanism." *American Economic Review* 98, no. 3 (2008): 843–863.

Brown, Daniel G., Scott E. Page, Rick Riolo, Moira Zellner and William Rand. "Path Dependence and the Validation of Agent-based Spatial Models of Land." *International Journal of Geographical Information Science* 19 (2005): 153–174.

Brown, Daniel G. and Derek T. Robinson. "Effects of Heterogeneity in Residential Preferences on an Agent-Based Model of Urban Sprawl." *Ecology and Society* 11, no. 1 (2006): 46–66.

Campbell, Heather E., Yushim Kim and Adam Eckerd. "Local Zoning and Environmental Justice: An Agent-based Model Analysis." *Urban Affairs Review* 50, no. 4 (2014): 521–552.

Campbell, Heather E., Laura R. Peck and Michael K. Tschudi. "Justice for All? A Cross-time Analysis of Toxics Release Inventory Facility Location." *Review of Policy Research* 27, no. 1 (2010): 1–25.

Chung, Su-Yeul and Lawrence A. Brown. "Racial/Ethnic Residential Sorting in Spatial Context: Testing the Explanatory Frameworks." *Urban Geography* 28, no. 4 (2007): 312–339.

Clark, William A.V. "Residential Preferences and Residential Choices in a Multiethnic Context." *Demography* 29, no. 3 (1992): 451–466.

Cox, K. R. "Housing Tenure and Neighborhood Activism." *Urban Affairs Review* 18, (2007): 107–129.

Eckerd, Adam, Heather E. Campbell and Yushim Kim. "Helping those Like Us or Harming those Unlike Us: Agent-based Modeling to Illuminate Social Processes Leading to Environmental Injustice." *Environment & Planning B* 39, no. 5 (2012): 945–964.

Emerson, Michael O., George Yancey and Karen J. Chai. "Does Race Matter in Residential Segregation? Exploring the Preferences of White Americans." *American Sociological Review* 66, no. 6 (2001): 922–935.

Fischel, W. *The Economics of Zoning Laws: A Property Rights Approach to American Land Use Controls.* Baltimore, MD: Johns Hopkins University Press, 1987.

Frey, William H. *Population Growth in Metro America Since 1980: Putting the Volatile 2000s in Perspective.* Washington, DC: Brookings, 2012. www.brookings.

edu/~/media/research/files/papers/2012/3/20%20population%20frey/0320_population_frey.pdf.

Gilbert, Nigel. *Agent-based Models*. Thousand Oaks, CA: Sage Publication, 2008.

Grimm, Volker, Eloy Revilla, Uta Berger, Florian Jeltsch, Wolf M. Mooij, Steven F. Railsback, Hans-Hermann Thulke, Jacob Weiner, Thorsten Wiegand and Donald L. DeAngelis. "Pattern-Oriented Modeling of Agent-based Complex Systems: Lessons from Ecology." *Science* 310, no. 5750 (2005): 987–991.

Krugman, Paul. "On the Relationship between Trade Theory and Location Theory." *Review of International Economics* 1, no. 2 (1993): 110–122.

Meadow, Donella H. *Thinking in Systems*. White River Junction, VT: Chelsea Green Publishing, 2008.

Parker, Dawn C. and Vicky J. Meretsky. "Measuring Pattern Outcomes in an Agent-based Model of Edge-effect Externalities Using Spatial Metrics." *Agriculture Ecosystem & Environment* 101 (2004): 233–250.

Parker, Dawn C. and Tatiana Filatova. "A Conceptual Design for a Bilateral Agent-based Land Market with Heterogeneous Economic Agents." *Computers, Environment and Urban Systems* 32, no. 6 (2008): 454–463.

Pratt, John W. "Risk Aversion in the Small and the Large." *Econometrica* 32, no. 1–2 (1964): 122–136.

Railsback, Steven and Volker Grimm. *Agent-Based and Individual-Based Modeling*. Princeton, NJ: Princeton University Press, 2011.

Rand, William, Moira Zellner, Scott E. Page, Rick Riolo, Daniel G. Brown and L.E. Fernandez. "The Complex Interaction of Agents and Environments: An Example in Urban Sprawl." Conference on Social Agents: Ecology, Exchange and Evolution, Chicago, 2002.

Reynolds, Craig. "Flocks, Herds and Schools: A Distributed Behavioral Model." *SIGGRAPH '87: Proceedings of the 14th Annual Conference on Computer Graphics and Interactive Techniques*, Association for Computing Machinery, 1987: 25–34. doi:10.1145/37401.37406.

Roback, Jennifer. "Wages, Rents, and the Quality of Life." *Journal of Political Economy* 90, no. 6 (1982): 1257–1278.

Schelling, Thomas C. *Micromotives and Macrobehavior*. New York: W.W. Norton & Company, 1978.

Torrens, Paul M. and Atsushi Nara. "Modeling Gentrification Dynamics: A Hybrid Approach." *Computers, Environment and Urban Systems* 31 (2007): 337–361.

US Census Bureau. "Quick Facts," quickfacts.census.gov/qfd/states/00000.html.

Veldkamp, A. Tom and Peter H. Verburg. "Editorial: Modeling Land Use Change and Environmental Impact." *Journal of Environmental Management* 72, no. 1–2 (2004): 1–3.

Voith, Richard. "Transportation, Sorting and House Values." *Real Estate Economics* 19, no. 2 (1991): 117–137.

Wilensky, Uri. "NetLogo." Evanston, IL: CCL, Northwestern University, 1999. ccl.northwestern.edu/netlogo/.

Wolverton, Ann. "Effects of Socio-Economic and Input-Related Factors on Polluting Plants' Location Decisions." *The B.E. Journal of Economic Analysis & Policy* 9, no. 1 (2009): Article 14.

# 4 Economic rationality, political rationality, or racial targeting

## Focusing on firm behavior[1]

Much of the EJ research has focused on firms' or other organizations' siting decisions to explain minority-collocated environmental disamenities. Indeed, the "environmental racism" claims made by EJ advocates include arguments that harmful intentionality is key in disamenity placement. As such, with EJ a key component of any sustainable future envisioned, this chapter discusses theoretical rationales regarding firm placement and tests whether assumptions about the firm can explain environmental injustice outcomes.

As previewed in Chapter 2, there is accumulated evidence indicating that the disproportionate collocation of environmental disamenities with racial and ethnic minorities is not fully explained by economic rationales,[2] and that racial characteristics may affect outcomes more than, for example, the economic factor of poverty.[3] However, given complications in disaggregating race from poverty, and targeted damage to the minority from unintended results of majoritarian politics,[4] there is considerably less clarity with regard to the circumstances under which environmentally unjust outcomes occur.[5]

In this chapter, we disentangle racially motivated behavior from economically and politically motivated behavior to understand how different sets of circumstances may result in environmental injustice by race, even if overt racist action is not the social norm. This analysis is important because the lack of understanding about the fundamental social processes leading to racial inequity in the placement of environmental disamenities inhibits the design of useful policies to combat it, and thus hinders our ability to attain a truly sustainable future.

## Theories of firm siting in EJ research

State-level policies to address environmental injustice have primarily centered around two mechanisms: 1 education and participation; and 2 rules and programs focusing on "permitting and facility siting decisions,"[6] including regulations to discourage firms from locating hazardous facilities in areas with a high proportion of minorities, and incentives for firms to locate away from clusters of minority residents.[7] The latter policies implicitly assume that firms have some specific interest in siting facilities in minority areas and that such location decisions are the culprit in observed environmental inequity. The validity of this assumption is debatable—and much debated.[8]

Relying on conventional methods such as surveys in order to differentiate incidents of decision-maker "environmental racism" from other rationales is difficult; for one thing, asking people about socially unacceptable behavior is unlikely to yield honest responses. Though asking disamenity-bearing firm decision makers how their locations were chosen might be interesting and even useful for a variety of purposes, it is unlikely that—even were it true— many decision makers would tell a researcher that they located their pol- luting facility near certain minority groups because they did not like, or wanted to harm, those groups.

Second, disamenity location does not occur in a static world. Firms and resi- dents make location decisions in a dynamic urban system[9] that can also exhibit durability.[10] Especially in the case of old disamenities,[11] it is often difficult to discern whether the hazardous firm or the minority population was there first. Even if indeed discrimination was a motive of firm decision makers, the *current* composition of a neighborhood—the dominant temporal unit of analysis in this area of research[12]—within which a site is located is not necessarily relevant to EJ concerns (though it is relevant to pollution expo- sure); a more relevant consideration is the composition of the community at the time the siting decision was made.[13] Some studies examining community composition at the time the hazardous facility was sited, or the siting deci- sion or expansion plan was made, have found that minority composition was an important predictor,[14] but others find that chosen locations generally were not disproportionately minority or poor,[15] except in some geographic contexts with a history of racial discrimination.[16]

When considering the dynamism of urban interaction, it is also worth noting that in some cases "which came first" may not be especially mean- ingful—transformation of a neighborhood can partake of elements of a tip- ping point, with what seems a simultaneous movement of firms and residents. Nevertheless, in the end, minorities still tend to be clustered near environmental disamenities.[17] If the cause is not overt discrimination on the part of firm decision makers—or at least that is not the only cause—then other social mechanisms, including perhaps the decisions made by residents themselves, must be at work.[18]

What if it is not the case that firm behavior is the primary driving factor of environmental injustice? What if residential choices, and interactions between firm decisions and resident decisions, have a part to play in this result? Although the residential choice mechanism has been studied includ- ing income and wealth,[19] the effect of residential choices on observed envir- onmental injustice has gone largely unexplored as it relates to racial disparities.[20] An exception to this is research by Pastor, Sadd and Hipp, who find "that disproportionate siting matters more than disproportionate min- ority move-in in the [southern California] sample area."[21] One value of their work is the explicit recognition that the observation at any one point of an urban area's commercial and demographic attributes is simultaneously determined by firm decisions as well as resident decisions—and that there is constant change.

One reason for minority move-in to be under-examined may be the fear that to consider this possibility is to "blame the victim." Yet, if we do not understand what social processes lead to undesirable urban outcomes, it may be harder for us to solve them, and policy solutions may be weak at best. Schelling showed that urban neighborhood segregation can arise from the dynamics of very simple location preferences.[22] This of course does not demonstrate that racism does not exist—indeed, we can be sure that it does—but warns us that simple views of complex outcomes are not necessarily correct.

As outlined in Chapter 2, what decision processes have even the potential to lead to environmentally unjust location decisions is confusing in some cases though not in others.[23] When a single decision-making entity makes a pollution-location decision, especially with good information about residential demographics, then racism is at least possible. However, a number of actors separated by industry, space, and time are less likely as a collective to be acting in an explicitly racist or even discriminatory way, even though environmentally unjust outcomes may result.

As discussed in more detail in earlier chapters, for about a decade there was also much concern in the EJ literature as to whether disproportionate minority collocation with environmental disamenities was due to correlation between race and income of residents and was caused simply by the fact that minority groups are disproportionately poorer, and polluting firms were more likely to be sited on the least expensive land. In this vein, the usual causal explanation is the following: 1 disamenities are located on relatively low-priced land, which already has a higher proportion of poorer residents; 2 when a disamenity locates in a community, nearby land values decline as those who can afford to leave do so; 3 this makes properties more affordable to poor people, who tend to be disproportionately minorities; and 4 thus we find a high concentration of poor people near disamenities.

However, as mentioned earlier, Ringquist's meta-analysis—and various other individual studies including Mohai and Saha, and Campbell, Peck, and Tschudi—indicate that although income is an important socioeconomic factor, the environmental injustice story is not simply about income alone.[24] For example, some cross-time studies referenced above have shown cases where minority presence was a more important predictor of the location of *new* facilities than poverty presence. These studies break the hypothesized causal chain described in the previous paragraph.

In this chapter, for the base EJ ABM analysis, we remove the issue of income by modeling all residents' incomes—whether minority or majority—as coming from the same income distribution. This lets us study the issue of minority status in isolation from the debate about income and its correlation with race and/or ethnicity. Then, in subsequent chapters we add back factors stripped out in this first model.

## Modeling firms' and residents' decisions

The basic setup of the EJ ABM for this chapter is presented in Table 3.6 (marked with checks). For example, non-polluting firms choose plots based on the lowest price. Residents are assigned an income drawn from a normal distribution with a mean of US$54,000 and a standard deviation of $41,000 (based on US Census data for "white alone" residents), and there is no difference between majorities and minorities in terms of the distribution of income levels. In the next sections we focus on explaining in detail key aspects of the EJ ABM that are relevant for this chapter—firms' siting decisions and residents' similarity preferences (marked with asterisks in Table 3.6).

### Firms' siting decisions

The goal of both types of agents—firm and resident—in the simulation is to find a plot that they can occupy. Agent decision rules are centered on agents scanning plots and selecting the one that best suits their preferences at any given time and space. For firms, in all scenarios we assume that there are agglomeration benefits[25] such that non-polluting firms prefer to locate near non-polluting firms, and polluting firms prefer to locate near polluting firms. This assumption accords with Wolverton's finding of the importance and robustness of pre-existing disamenities in the location of new disamenity-bearing firms.[26] This also fits with our understanding of path dependence in cities.

We modeled this agglomeration preference as a constraint in firm location decision making.[27] In words, when a *new* firm is introduced to the modeled world (due to labor demand), the firm looks around for plots on which there is at least one other of the same type of firm within a radius of 10,[28] and fewer than five firms within a block.[29] If there is no other firm of the same type, the firm considers blocks that have fewer than five firms of any type as candidate plots.[30] If there are plots that meet these preferences in the firm's decision set, it will limit the consideration to those plots. If there are no plots in the decision set that meet this preference, then the firm will make a siting decision according to the scenario under consideration.

In addition to preferring to be near other similar firms, polluting firms and non-polluting firms behave somewhat differently in deciding where to locate. In all scenarios, non-polluting firms simply seek the plot with the lowest price—that ideally meets their agglomeration preferences. In this chapter, polluting firms are modeled with three different siting criteria that are hypothesized in the EJ literature:

- *PFS1*: In the first set of experiments, polluting firms seek the plot with the lowest price among plots that satisfy the agglomeration preference (i.e., firms are economically rational).

- PFS2: The second set of experiments is informed by political rationality. In it, the polluting firm seeks to locate away from majority residents, who may carry more cost risk than do minority residents.[31] Hamilton outlines the reasons for this, particularly focusing on the idea that majorities are more politically active (vote at a higher rate) than minorities. Related work suggests that majorities have more political access than do minorities.
- PFS3: In the third set of experiments polluting firms act with discriminatory (racist) motives and purposely site in minority communities.

An implicit assumption of the model is that firms are owned by majority residents and are therefore susceptible to pressures from other majority residents, and to discriminating against minority residents.

When the "lowest price" scenario (PFS1) is set for polluting firms, a new polluting firm first finds plots that meet its agglomeration preference, and then settles in the lowest-priced plot among them. When the political rationality scenario is set for polluting firms (PFS2), a new polluting firm settles in a plot with the lowest proportion of majorities among plots that satisfy its agglomeration preference. When the discrimination scenario is set for polluting firms (PFS3), a new polluting firm first satisfies its agglomeration preference, and then settles in a plot with the highest proportion of minorities.

The proportion of majorities and minorities nearby for each plot is calculated by identifying the number of residents who settled in plots within a radius of 10 of each plot, and the resident types (i.e., majority or minority) in those plots. At every time step in the simulations, a plot examines the surrounding 316 plots and identifies how many residents live in those plots and how many belong to the majority or minority group. In all of these scenarios, if there is a tie between the lowest price, the highest proportion of minorities, or the lowest proportion of majorities, one random plot among the tied plots with the highest (or lowest) value is selected.

### Residential choices

Since firms' siting decisions are made in a neighborhood where residents also live and to which they may move, it is important to explain how residents make their residential choices in the model. It has long been recognized that the process of finding a residence is quite complicated.[32] The process can be disentangled into its component parts, but, in the end, the decision to move is complex, followed by an additional complex set of criteria for determining one's preferred location.[33] Once the relocation decision has been made, people are limited in their abilities to see all available properties in a timely manner,[34] afford properties that may best meet their preferences, and have access to informal information that may be available to those in large social networks.[35]

Of the initial 200 residents, 140 (70%) are categorized as members of the majority and 60 (30%) as members of the minority. As discussed in Chapter 3, analysts with a focus on a particular region can adjust these percentages to reflect reality in that region. For the analyses in this chapter, residents are otherwise assumed to be homogeneous in all other attributes, and seek a residential location near a firm at which they will work; in seeking "employment" they do not differentiate between polluting firms and non-polluting firms, though pollution levels affect their residential utility function.

When *new* residents are introduced to the world based on the population growth rate, their location choices are constrained by their incomes and similarity preferences as we described in Chapter 3. In this chapter, the income distribution for both resident types is set at the same level: a mean of $54,000 and a standard deviation of $41,000. While we use residents' income drawn from the right-skewed gamma distribution throughout Chapters 5 through 10, we use a normal distribution in this chapter.[36]

As described in Chapter 3, we reason that wealthy residents will not always opt for the lowest-priced home because it may be located in an undesirable neighborhood, so no resident agent will consider a plot that is less than twice its income level and, given the constraints preventing the purchase of a home that is out of one's price range, residents also exclude any plot with a price greater than three times their income level.[37]

Once residents find plots that satisfy their income constraints, in some experiments the similarity preference for living near other residents like themselves is considered.[38] During the scenarios in which residents have a similarity preference, they first look for any available plots in their income-constrained decision sets that meet their similarity preference criterion. For example, if the similarity preference for minority agents is assumed to be 80%, minority agents will only consider locating on plots where at least 80% of the agents on neighboring plots are also minorities.

In this chapter, for comparison purposes we focus on three conditions for similarity preference:

- *SP1*: Residents do not consider similarity preference at all in making the residential location choice.
- *SP2*: Residents hold similarity preferences at a modest level of 20%.
- *SP3*: Residents hold similarity preferences at a high level of 80%.

In the SP1 scenario, residents exhibit no preference regarding whether their neighbors are majorities or minorities, so they behave in a purely economically rational way. Alternatively, we examine the situation in which residents hold a similarity preference at a modest level, with both groups preferring to locate where 20% of neighbors are of the same "race." This assumption is further changed in SP3, in which we introduce highly race-conscious residents to the model, with an 80% similarity preference for both groups. In all cases there is no difference between majority and minority agents in preferred similarity of neighbors.

These income and similarity preference constraints limit residential choice sets; after the constrained set of plots has been identified, residents pick a plot that maximizes their utility within their choice set given a price, quality, and distance to the nearest job.[39] In other words, within the confines of the income and similarity constraints, residents make a siting decision based on the following decision criteria: pay the lowest price for the plot, live on a high-quality plot, and live near their place of work, as described in Chapter 3 (Equation 3.1).

### Experimental scenarios

Altogether, this first analysis results in a set of nine possible combinations of scenarios, each of which focuses on firms' siting decision choices and residential similarity preference and their interactions (see Table 4.1 for the combinations: C1–C9). In all nine scenarios, non-polluting firms choose based solely on agglomeration and price. Of these cases, only those including the PFS3 scenario are obviously compatible with firm "racism," or invidious practices of firms (or, more broadly, decision makers) in their location decisions. PFS1 fits with a purely neoclassical, perfect-competition world.

In each case, polluting firm decisions are extreme; beyond its agglomeration preference, the specified criterion is the only information considered by a polluting firm when finding a location. While in reality no firm would consider only two pieces of information in determining an ideal location, using these extreme cases should allow us to differentiate fully the effects on EJ of these decision scenarios, which span the space of relevant firm decision criteria discussed in the EJ literature.

It is worth mentioning that we do not see "race consciousness" as the same as racism. In racism, actors believe that one group is superior to the other, and therefore they believe that one group deserves a better outcome than another. In a race-conscious world, people note difference and feel some level of discomfort in being outnumbered by the other group, but need not feel that one group is superior to the other, nor that one group deserves better (or worse) outcomes than the other. It seems clear that many societies are certainly race conscious, and that there is also racism. An important question is whether racism is necessary to observe EJ outcomes.

### Model outcome

We ran each of the nine scenarios for 200 trials (with 70 time steps per trial). For each of the scenarios (and sets of scenarios) we track the average environmental quality level, both overall and for each race group. Thus, we can compare average majority quality with minority quality in these different scenarios. We also calculated a quality gap by subtracting the average minority quality level from the average majority quality level. As previewed, a positive number indicates that the majority is relatively better off and by how much, while a negative number indicates that the minority is relatively better off and by how much. Zero indicates that there is no difference in the average quality level experienced by the two groups.

## Economics, politics, discrimination, and race consciousness

Over all nine decision-making scenarios under consideration, at the end of each simulation trial the average level of quality with which majority residents lived ($Q_{ma}$) was 60.6 compared with an average minority quality level ($Q_{mi}$) of 58.5. Regardless of the decision-making scenario under consideration, during each simulation run approximately 61 firms were created, and about 24 of these were polluting firms (40%).

### Comparison of environmental quality between majorities and minorities

In Table 4.1, we summarize simulation outcomes, including mean quality scores for both types of residents, the difference between the quality scores for both types of residents, and t-statistics at the end of the simulation (time-step 70). C1–C3 present simulation outcomes under the three polluting firms' location decision scenarios with residents having no similarity preference. For example, Case 1 (C1) represents the economically rational choice of the location with the lowest price, C2 assumes the firm seeks to avoid harming or annoying majority residents, and C3 shows the results of the discriminatory decision of firms to choose the location with the most minority residents nearby. C4–C6 present simulation outcomes under the three polluting firms' location decision scenarios with residents preferring to have 20% of residents nearby of the same "race" type (minority or majority). Finally, C7–C9 present simulation outcomes under the three polluting firms' location decision scenarios with residents preferring to have at least 80% of the same "race" type nearby.

Overall, average quality levels between groups in each case somewhat differ, regardless of the cases. Noticeable differences in means are especially found in C5, C6, C8, and C9, in which both types of residents have a modest or high level of similarity preference and polluting firms use different criteria from the economically rational one. We see some quality gaps in other cases, but they are not as large as we see from those four scenarios.[40] In particular, in C1, C2, and C7, the magnitudes are very small and the differences are not statistically significant, meaning that we can attribute the differences in these cases to random noise.

The results depicted in Table 4.1 are limited, however, because they compare only the results recorded at the end of each simulation trial. In order to gain a more dynamic view, we examined environmental quality differences between majorities and minorities as simulation trials were ongoing. For ease of comparison, each row in Figure 4.1 presents environmental quality differences between the groups over time under three different

*Table 4.1* Environmental quality by scenarios at $t=70$, using t-tests

|  |  | Polluting firms' siting decision criteria | | |
|---|---|---|---|---|
|  |  | Lowest price (PFS1) | Away from majorities (PFS2) | Near minorities (PFS3) |
| Resident similarity preference | None (SP1) | C1 $Q_{ma} = 62.27$ $Q_{mi} = 62.30$ diff. = -0.03 $t = -0.75$ $(p = 0.45)$ | C2 $Q_{ma} = 60.71$ $Q_{mi} = 60.66$ diff. = 0.05 $t = 1.45$ $(p = 0.15)$ | C3 $Q_{ma} = 60.83$ $Q_{mi} = 60.72$ diff. = 0.11 $t = 2.66$ $(p < 0.01)$ |
|  | 20% (SP2) | C4 $Q_{ma} = 62.33$ $Q_{mi} = 61.51$ diff. = 0.83 $t = 4.31$ $(p < 0.001)$ | C5 $Q_{ma} = 61.63$ $Q_{mi} = 58.46$ diff. = 3.18 $t = 19.54$ $(p < 0.001)$ | C6 $Q_{ma} = 61.77$ $Q_{mi} = 58.54$ diff. = 3.22 $t = 20.12$ $(p < 0.001)$ |
|  | 80% (SP3) | C7 $Q_{ma} = 58.36$ $Q_{mi} = 58.57$ diff. = -0.21 $t = -0.51$ $(p < 0.61)$ | C8 $Q_{ma} = 58.71$ $Q_{mi} = 53.15$ diff. = 5.56 $t = 11.58$ $(p < 0.001)$ | C9 $Q_{ma} = 58.58$ $Q_{mi} = 52.50$ diff. = 6.08 $t = 12.83$ $(p < 0.001)$ |

Note: $n = 200$ for each cell; 1,800 overall.

polluting firm decision scenarios, holding constant a specific residential preference scenario. When residents do not have any similarity preference (row a),
both agent types have about equal environmental quality over time regardless of the polluting firm's siting decision. When residents hold a modest
level of similarity preference (wanting one of five neighbors to be "like
them"), environmental quality for the majority becomes slightly higher than
when there is no similarity preference (row b). However, minorities are
disadvantaged. Significant quality gaps between the two resident groups
emerge around time-step 20 and a quality gap continues to exist throughout.

In Figure 4.1, there are two cases where the minority is better off than the
majority for a short period (and at a small magnitude): when residents have
an 80% similarity preference, and polluting firms either seek the lowest-
priced plot or the plot with the most minorities. However, when both resident agents hold an 80% similarity preference, the environmental quality
that both groups experience is lower than in other cases (quality level is
measured on the vertical scale) and the gap between the majority and the
minority eventually becomes the largest when firms are also race aware.

### Relative importance of the different decision scenarios

The results above show the differential effects of the different scenarios.
From them, we can see that in this simple modeled world, residential

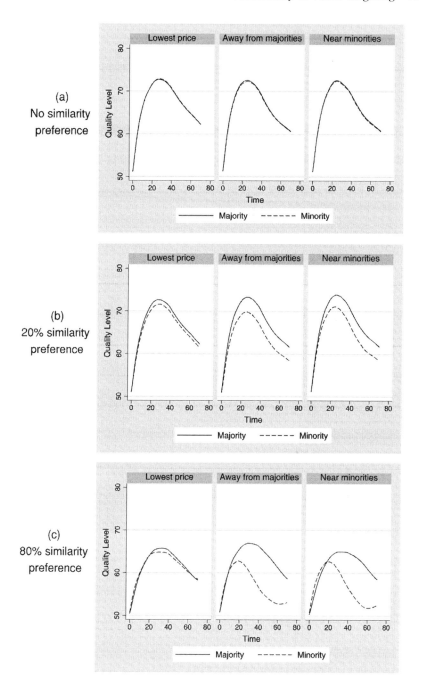

*Figure 4.1* Environmental quality over time

similarity preferences are more important than firm behavior, though the two clearly interact. When residents have no racial component in their decision making, there is essentially no quality gap, no matter how firms behave. Only once residents incorporate race in their decisions does a quality gap begin to open, and then firms' race-based decisions also have an effect.

However, the results shown so far do not give us an easy way to compare the magnitudes of the relative importance of the different residential and firm decision factors. Table 4.2 shows the result of ordinary least square (OLS) regression using the data at time-step 70 across all 1,800 outcomes (200 trials for each of nine scenarios). The quality gap between majorities and minorities was used as the dependent variable, and the explanatory variables are the different decision rules. Positive values for the coefficients indicate that the presence of the characteristic increases the quality gap between majority and minority groups. These results allow direct comparison of the magnitudes of effects, and show that in this model resident behavior is more important to unequal outcomes.

## The effect of "neighborhood" size

As discussed in Chapter 3, in the use of agent-based modeling to give insight into real-world phenomena, an important factor is analysis of the sensitivity of the results to assumptions that are necessary but fairly arbitrary. For example, the above results indicate that residents' similarity preference and firms' agglomeration preference are important factors in this model's outcomes; but could it be that the assumed "neighborhood" size importantly drives results?

*Table* 4.2 Ordinary least squares regression results—dependent variable is quality gap at $t=70$

|  | $\beta$ | Standard error | p-value |
|---|---|---|---|
| Polluting firms locate where fewest majorities are nearby | 2.77 | 0.24 | 0.000 |
| Polluting firms locate where most minorities are nearby | 2.96 | 0.24 | 0.000 |
| Residents have a 20% similarity preference | 2.34 | 0.24 | 0.000 |
| Residents have an 80% similarity preference | 3.75 | 0.24 | 0.000 |
| Percentage of polluting firms sited during the simulation | 0.08 | 0.03 | 0.001 |
| Constant | -3.89 | 0.65 | 0.000 |

Note: N = 1,800; $F_{(5, 1,794)} = 91.86$; Adjusted $R^2 = 0.20$

This model uses a certain radius to define neighborhoods. As mentioned before, during the simulation each plot updates the proportion of majority and minority as well as the proportion of polluting firms and non-polluting firms within a radius of 10. New residents consider this information when exercising a similarity preference, and new firms use the information as they seek to agglomerate. A radius of 10 includes 317 plots, including the center (focal) plot. It covers less than four blocks (each block consists of 10 plots x 10 plots). How sensitive are the simulation results to the chosen radius, which seems reasonable to us, but for which we have no ready empirical evidence? We experimented with radii of 5, 10, 15, 20, and 30 (see Table 3.5). Note that the world size is 101 x 101 and the radius of 30 covers an area of approximately 60 x 60. Therefore, any larger than that seems less like a neighborhood effect and more like a city effect.

Quality gap distributions in cases C1–C3 under all five neighborhood size conditions are quite consistent. When residents hold a 20% similarity preference (C4–C6), distributions of quality gaps become narrower as neighborhood size becomes larger. Regardless of neighborhood size, quality gap distributions are quite large when residents hold an 80% similarity preference (C7–C9). In these scenarios, regardless of neighborhood size, the gap becomes larger, favoring majorities, and at almost the same level regardless of whether polluting firms site in areas with the fewest majorities or target minorities, compared to when they site at the lowest-price plot. Also, the high level of similarity preference brings a larger variance in quality gaps between majorities and minorities.

Taken together, these results suggest that the findings are not overly sensitive to the size of the neighborhood, though it does have some impact. When neighborhood size seems particularly important, analysts with a focus on a particular locale could use data to determine the appropriate neighborhood size.

## Discussion

The goal of the research presented in this chapter is to understand circumstances under which variations in environmental quality might exist between two groups, one of which is in the minority, while holding income constant, in an urbanizing environment. The just distribution of environmental costs of social benefits is one necessary element of an overall sustainable city.

From our virtual experiment, we observe that environmentally unjust outcomes resulted from social interactions between firms and residents rather than being solely based on the independent decisions of firms. In the world modeled here, only two conditions led to environmental injustice in the form of lower levels of aggregate environmental quality for the minority: a goal by polluting firms to locate near minorities, or a preference by residents to live near other residents like themselves. A race-blind world in which neither firms nor residents consider the demographic makeup of possible locations did not lead to environmental injustice.

We expected that when polluting firms specifically chose to locate in minority areas, the quality differential between majority and minority residents would be higher than if polluting firms chose the lowest-price plot or a plot that was located away from large majority populations. In the simulation, there were small but statistically significant quality differences for residents if polluting firms specifically chose to locate in minority areas. Though the magnitude is small, the gap between majority quality and minority quality was consistently larger when polluting firms located near minority residents than when they located away from majority residents, regardless of whether or not residents had a similarity preference. If polluting firms begin to make location choices that are not strictly economically rational, differences in quality begin to emerge. Though these trials test extremes of polluting firm siting choices, if polluting firms make discriminatory location decisions it seems clear that there is potential for real differences in environmental quality for different ethnic populations.

However, this difference is only part, and perhaps only a small part, of the larger story. As soon as we introduce even a relatively modest assumption regarding residents' similarity preferences, differences in environmental quality become substantially more pronounced. For example, moving from C1 to C2 has much less effect on the environmental quality gap than does moving from C1 to C4, or from C2 to C5. Based on empirical findings, an assumption of no race-based residential similarity preference is probably unrealistic,[41] yet our results point to the conclusion that polluting firm siting choices do not appear to have as much impact on quality differentials as residential siting choices. These ABM experiments suggest that even slight preferences by residents to live near others like themselves have a substantially larger effect than even overt, discriminatory behavior by polluting firms.

This provides an unexpected and potentially fascinating insight. Many researchers have pointed out that any current collocation cannot be due only to firm decisions, but must also incorporate resident decisions.[42] However, the implications of many such critiques have been that minority residents disproportionately choose locations near polluting firms and other disamenities, because either they are disproportionately poor or they do not value environmental quality as much as majorities do.[43] This study presents a different reason that has nothing to do with either residential income or preferences for quality—both of which are constant across races in these analyses—or even with firm location choices, but only with preferences for at least some (even one in five) racially similar neighbors.

Within our simplified, experimental world, it is evident that polluting firm decisions have less substantial effect on the variation in quality between majority and minority residents than does residential similarity preference. Within each similarity preference set (rows in the table), the variation in environmental quality between the three polluting firm decision-making criteria is relatively low, with the largest "bump" caused by polluting firms deviating from pure rationality. In the case for which residents had no similarity preference, the only case in which there was a statistically significant difference in quality outcomes between majority and minority residents was when polluting firms chose the plot near the largest concentration of minority residents.

However, an assumption that residents have no similarity preference with regard to their neighbors is problematic according to the extant literature.[44] The relaxation of this assumption reveals the key findings of this experiment: although polluting firm decision making had a substantive effect on environmental quality variation, its effects are dwarfed by even a small residential similarity preference of 20%. Regardless of the polluting firm siting choice, the quality difference between majority and minority residents was considerably larger for all simulation trials with this 20% preference compared with the no similarity preference alternatives, and larger still with an 80% similarity preference.

Why might the residential similarity preference have so much of an impact on a seemingly unrelated outcome: environmental quality? We view this result as an extension of Schelling's segregation model.[45] Whenever people self-select into neighborhoods with residents similar to themselves, they constrain the set of choices that are available to them. When minority residents constrain their choices, they constrain the set of potential locations from which they may choose, and they may have to sacrifice other preferences for this similarity preference. When environmental quality is variable across space, one of those tradeoffs may involve environmental quality.

These findings are at the same time both troubling and somewhat encouraging. It is encouraging in the sense that it is unlikely that all polluting firms will focus exclusively on harming minority residents as we have assumed here in cases C3, C6, and C9. While some firms no doubt have nefarious intent, it is doubtful that other considerations such as land cost are not just as important in the siting choice, and it is also doubtful that all polluting firms would have nefarious intent, as was the case in our trials where polluting firms chose to locate near the most minority residents. Most industrialized nations today, though far from perfect, are neither apartheid South Africa nor the Jim Crow US South.[46] However, even if this extreme situation were the case, the *independent* effect on the equity of environmental quality is moderate at worst.

Using what we hope is the more likely assumption that polluting firms opt to locate via some choice mechanism incorporating both low prices and a lower likelihood of encountering "not in my back yard" (NIMBY) opposition (as Hamilton implies), the effect on environmental quality differences is more marginal, and depends importantly upon the assumed residential similarity preference. Further, in reality some firms are minority owned (as of 2007, more than one-fifth of all US firms were minority owned),[47] so even the widespread use of explicitly minority-targeting decision rules by majority-owned firms should not have the same magnitude of effect.

The findings are troubling but useful in that they imply there is likely little that firm-targeted regulatory policy can do if observed environmental injustice is substantially based on residential proportions and similarity preferences. If residents have similarity preferences, then they will likely automatically exclude certain neighborhoods from their consideration when finding a residence, as was the case in our model. With more options simply because they are the majority, majority residents can quickly gain more of the higher environmental quality plots. With fewer options meeting their similarity preference—if for no other reason than simply because those they want to be near are in the numerical minority—minority residents may have to opt for plots with lower environmental quality. This line of reasoning is very much in line with Clark's[48] work suggesting that minority residents tended to have more relaxed similarity preferences than majority-white residents, potentially because of the paucity of residential options that would be available under their ideal preferences, especially while maintaining high levels of concern for environmental quality.[49] In our model, minority residents did not relax their similarity preferences, so they did make residential choices with fewer alternatives than their majority counterparts.

Therefore, we believe the main insight this set of scenarios provides is that an important facet of environmental injustice may be due to "preferring to be near people like us" rather than the choices of firms to "help those like us" or "harm those unlike us." This has very important policy and planning implications since it suggests the solution to environmental injustice may not be where it has been looked for. If our ABM is, as designed, relevant to the real world, it suggests that EJ policies may be more effective at reducing environmental inequity if they focus more on reducing preferences for racial similarity in residential location than on changing firm location decisions. Of course, the former task is far more difficult than the latter.

Finally, it is also worth noting the difference in quality that comes about during different polluting firm decision-making scenarios. In our limited region, quality differences were small in the different polluting firm cases with no residential preference (C1–C3). However, as the residential similarity preference was larger, the marginal effect of the polluting firm's decision criterion also increases. This indicates a type of interaction effect. In a real community, these marginal differences could be extremely important and merit further consideration, particularly given the likelihood that people do indeed prefer their neighbors to be similar to them.

In general, these results imply that a race-conscious *society*, rather than just race-conscious firms or decision makers, produces the environmental injustice that we observe. These interaction effects also have implications for how we understand urban sustainability more broadly.

# Notes

1 Material presented in this chapter is based on the more up-to-date version of the EJ ABM described in Chapter 3, but the analysis performed and discussed here is similar to that in Adam Eckerd, Heather E. Campbell, and Yushim Kim, "Helping those Like Us or Harming those Unlike Us: Agent-Based Modeling to Illuminate Social Processes Leading to Environmental Injustice," *Environment & Planning B* 39, no. 5 (2012): 945–64. Any overlapping elements are used by permission.

2 Liam Downey, "Environmental Injustice: Is Race or Income a Better Predictor?" *Social Science Quarterly* 79, no. 4 (1998): 766–78; Evan J. Ringquist, "Assessing Evidence of Environmental Inequities: A Meta-Analysis,"*Journal of Policy Analysis and Management* 24, no. 2 (2005): 223–47.

3 Robert Bullard, "Environmental Justice in the 21st Century: Race Still Matters," *Phylon* 49, no. 3/4 (2001): 151–71; Ringquist, "Assessing Evidence of Environmental Inequities"; Heather E. Campbell, Laura R. Peck, and Michael K. Tschudi, "Justice for All? A Cross-Time Analysis of Toxics Release Inventory Facility Location," *Review of Policy Research* 27, no. 1 (2010): 1–25.

4 James T. Hamilton, "Testing for Environmental Racism: Prejudice, Profits, Political Power?" *Journal of Policy Analysis and Management* 14, no. 1 (1995): 107–32.

5 Paul Mohai and Robin Saha, "Reassessing Racial and Socioeconomic Disparities in Environmental Justice Research," *Demography* 43, no. 2 (2006): 383–99.

6 Steven Bonorris, *Environmental Justice for All: A Fifty-State Survey of Legislation, Policies and Initiatives*, fourth edn (San Francisco, CA: American Bar Association and Hastings College of Law, February 15, 2010), iv.

7 Ibid.

8 Warren Kriesel, Terence J. Centner, and Andrew G. Keeler, "Neighborhood Exposure to Toxic Releases: Are there Racial Inequities?" *Growth and Change* 27, no. 4 (1996): 479–99; Vicki Been and Francis Gupta, "Coming to the Nuisance or Going to the Barrios?" *Ecology Law Quarterly* 24, no. 1 (1997): 1–56.

9 H. Spencer Banzhaf and Randall P. Walsh, "Do People Vote with their Feet? An Empirical Test of Tiebout's Mechanism," *American Economic Review* 98, no. 3 (2008): 843–63.

10 That is, though the system is dynamic, specific features may remain for long periods.

11 Been and Gupta, "Coming to the Nuisance or Going to the Barrios?"; Manual Pastor, James Sadd, and John Hipp, "Which Came First? Toxic Facilities, Minority Move-in, and Environmental Justice," *Journal of Urban Affairs* 23, no. 1 (2001): 1–21.

12 Douglas S. Noonan, "Evidence of Environmental Justice: A Critical Perspective on the Practice of EJ Research and Lessons for Policy Design," *Social Science Quarterly* 89, no. 5 (2008): 1153–74.

13 Been and Gupta, "Coming to the Nuisance or Going to the Barrios?"

14 Mohai and Saha, "Reassessing Racial and Socioeconomic Disparities in Environmental Justice Research"; Campbell et al., "Justice for All?"

15 Hamilton, "Testing for Environmental Racism"; Been and Gupta, "Coming to the Nuisance or Going to the Barrios?"

16 Kriesel et al., "Neighborhood Exposure to Toxic Releases."

17 John A. Hird, "Environmental Policy and Equity: The Case of Superfund," *Journal of Policy Analysis and Management* 12, no. 2 (2001): 323–43.

18 Paul Mohai and Bunyan Bryant, "Is there a 'Race' Effect on Concern for Environmental Quality?"*Public Opinion Quarterly* 62 (1998): 475–505.

19  Been and Gupta, "Coming to the Nuisance or Going to the Barrios?"; Banzhaf and Walsh, "Do People Vote with their Feet?"

20  Mohai and Bryant, "Is there a 'Race' Effect on Concern for Environmental Quality?"

21  Pastor et al., "Which Came First?" 1.

22  Thomas C. Schelling, *Micromotives and Macrobehavior* (New York: W.W. Norton & Company, 1978).

23  Paul Mohai and Robin Saha, "Reassessing Racial and Socioeconomic Disparities in Environmental Justice Research," *Demography* 43, no. 2 (2006): 383–99.

24  Ringquist, "Assessing Evidence of Environmental Inequities"; Mohai and Saha, "Reassessing Racial and Socioeconomic Disparities in Environmental Justice Research"; Campbell et al., "Justice for All?"

25  Paul Krugman, "On the Relationship Between Trade Theory and Location Theory," *Review of International Economics* 1, no. 2 (1993): 110–22.

26  Ann Wolverton, "Effects of Socio-Economic and Input-Related Factors on Polluting Plants' Location Decisions," *The B.E. Journal of Economic Analysis & Policy* 9, no. 1 (2009): 14.

27  In addition to applying the constraint in this manner, we modeled this agglomeration preference in two other ways, including directly including it in firms' utility calculations, and also applying the constraint prior to the derivation of the plot set that the firm would consider for its location. Results under each of these variations were interpretively the same, so we modeled the agglomeration as a constraint subsequent to the derivation of the plot set because, under the two alternative approaches, it was programmatically possible that firms could find themselves with no possible locations that met preferences, which could prematurely halt a simulation trial.

28  The number of plots belonging to a radius of 10 is 317, including the center plot that looks around the area. It includes approximately four blocks (400 plots) in the current simulation.

29  As indicated in Chapter 3, we iteratively analyzed these assumptions to make the developing city sufficiently realistic for our purpose.

30  Daniel G. Brown, Scott Page, Rick Riolo, Moira Zellner, and William Rand, "Path Dependence and the Validation of Agent-Based Spatial Models of Land Use," *International Journal of Geographical Information Science* 19, no. 2 (2005): 153–74.

31  Hamilton, "Testing for Environmental Racism."

32  James W. Simmons, "Changing Residence in the City: A Review of Intraurban Mobility," *Geographical Review* 58, no. 4 (1968): 622–51.

33  Grace K.M. Wong, "A Conceptual Model of the Household's Housing Decision-Making Process: The Economic Perspective," *Review of Urban & Regional Development Studies* 14, no. 3 (2003): 217–34.

34  Fulong Wu, "Simulating Temporal Fluctuations of Real Estate Development in a Cellular Automata City," *Transactions in GIS* 7, no. 2 (2003): 193–210.

35  Andrea Röper, Beate Völker, and Henk Flap, "Social Networks and Getting a Home: Do Contacts Matter?" *Social Networks* 31, no. 1 (2009): 40–51.

36  The model here is the simplest model in the book, and use of the normal distribution is an additional simplifying assumption. When we used the gamma distribution there was no noticeable difference in simulation results.

37  Dawn C. Parker and Tatiana Filatova, "A Conceptual Design for a Bilateral Agent-based Land Market with Heterogeneous Economic Agents," *Computers, Environment and Urban Systems* 32, no. 6 (2008): 454–63.

38  Schelling, *Micromotives and Macrobehavior*; William A.V. Clark, "Residential Preferences and Residential Choices in a Multiethnic Context," *Demography* 29, no. 3 (1992): 451–66.

39 Similar to, but not the same as, Daniel G. Brown and Derek T. Robinson, "Effects of Heterogeneity in Residential Preferences on an Agent-Based Model of Urban Sprawl," *Ecology and Society* 11, no. 1 (2005): 46–66; John W. Pratt, "Risk Aversion in the Small and the Large," *Econometrica* 32, no. 1–2 (1964): 122–36; William Rand, Moira Zellner, Scott E. Page, Rick Riolo, Daniel G. Brown and L.E. Fernandez. "The Complex Interaction of Agents and Environments: An Example in Urban Sprawl," Conference on Social Agents: Ecology, Exchange and Evolution, Chicago, 2002.

40 Note that the results here are somewhat different from those reported in Eckerd et al., "Helping those Like Us or Harming those Unlike Us." The differences are occasioned by the introduction of income, housing prices, and other complexities that are present in the model used here and absent in the model used for that paper.

41 Brown and Robinson, "Effects of Heterogeneity in Residential Preferences on an Agent-Based Model of Urban Sprawl"; William A.V. Clark, "Residential Preferences and Neighborhood Racial Segregation: A Test of the Schelling Segregation Model," *Demography* 28, no. 1 (1991): 1–19; William A.V. Clark, "Residential Preferences and Residential Choices in a Multiethnic Context," *Demography* 29, no. 3 (1992): 451–66.

42 See e.g., William M. Bowen, "An Analytical Review of Environmental Justice Research: What Do We Really Know?" *Environmental Management* 29, no. 1 (2002): 3–15; Hamilton, "Testing for Environmental Racism."

43 See Mohai and Bryant, "Is there a 'Race' Effect on Concern for Environmental Quality?" for a discussion of this.

44 Brown and Robinson, "Effects of Heterogeneity in Residential Preferences on an Agent-Based Model of Urban Sprawl"; Clark, "Residential Preferences and Neighborhood Racial Segregation"; Clark, "Residential Preferences and Residential Choices in a Multiethnic Context."

45 Schelling, *Micromotives and Macrobehavior*.

46 During the "Jim Crow" era in the southern states of the United States, racism was ingrained into every aspect of society.

47 US Bureau of the Census, "US Firms—Ownership by Gender, Ethnicity, Race, and Veteran Status: 2007," www.census.gov/compendia/statab/2012/tables/12s0769.pdf.

48 Clark, "Residential Preferences and Neighborhood Racial Segregation"; Clark, "Residential Preferences and Residential Choices in a Multiethnic Context."

49 Mohai and Bryant, "Is there a 'Race' Effect on Concern for Environmental Quality?"

# References

Banzhaf, H. Spencer and Randall P. Walsh. "Do People Vote with their Feet? An Empirical Test of Tiebout's Mechanism." *American Economic Review* 98, no. 3 (2008): 843–863.

Been, Vicki and Francis Gupta. "Coming to the Nuisance or Going to the Barrios?" *Ecology Law Quarterly* 24, no. 1 (1997): 1–56.

Bonorris, Steven. *Environmental Justice for All: A Fifty-state Survey of Legislation, Policies and Initiatives*, fourth edn. San Francisco, CA: American Bar Association and Hastings College of Law, 2010.

Bowen, William M. "An Analytical Review of Environmental Justice Research: What Do We Really Know?" *Environmental Management* 29, no. 1 (2002): 3–15.

Brown, Daniel G., Scott E. Page, Rick Riolo, Moira Zellner and William Rand. "Path Dependence and the Validation of Agent-based Spatial Models of Land Use." *International Journal of Geographical Information Science* 19, no. 2 (2005): 153–174.

Brown, Daniel G. and Derek T. Robinson. "Effects of Heterogeneity in Residential Preferences on an Agent-based Model of Urban Sprawl." *Ecology and Society* 11, no. 1 (2005): 46–66.

Bullard, Robert. "Environmental Justice in the 21st Century: Race Still Matters." *Phylon* 49, no. 3/4 (2001): 151–171.

Campbell, Heather E., Laura R. Peck and Michael K. Tschudi. "Justice for All? A Cross-time Analysis of Toxics Release Inventory Facility Location." *Review of Policy Research* 27, no. 1 (2010): 1–25.

Clark, William A.V. "Residential Preferences and Neighborhood Racial Segregation: A Test of the Schelling Segregation Model." *Demography* 28, no. 1 (1991): 1–19.

Clark, William A.V. "Residential Preferences and Residential Choices in a Multi-ethnic Context." *Demography* 29, no. 3 (1992): 451–466.

Downey, Liam. "Environmental Injustice: Is Race or Income a Better Predictor?" *Social Science Quarterly* 79, no. 4 (1998): 766–778.

Eckerd, Adam, Heather E. Campbell and Yushim Kim. "Helping those Like Us or Harming those Unlike Us: Agent-based Modeling to Illuminate Social Processes Leading to Environmental Injustice." *Environment & Planning B* 39, no. 5 (2012): 945–964.

Hamilton, James T. "Testing for Environmental Racism: Prejudice, Profits, Political Power?" *Journal of Policy Analysis and Management* 14, no. 1 (1995): 107–132.

Hird, John A. "Environmental Policy and Equity: The Case of Superfund." *Journal of Policy Analysis and Management* 12, no. 2 (2001): 323–343.

Kriesel, Warren, Terence J. Centner and Andrew G. Keeler. "Neighborhood Exposure to Toxic Releases: Are there Racial Inequities?" *Growth and Change* 27, no. 4 (1996): 479–499.

Krugman, Paul. "On the Relationship between Trade Theory and Location Theory." *Review of International Economics* 1, no. 2 (1993): 110–122.

Mohai, Paul and Bunyan Bryant. "Is there a 'Race' Effect on Concern for Environmental Quality?" *Public Opinion Quarterly* 62 (1998): 475–505.

Mohai, Paul and Robin Saha. "Reassessing Racial and Socioeconomic Disparities in Environmental Justice Research." *Demography* 43, no. 2 (2006): 383–399.

Noonan, Douglas S. "Evidence of Environmental Justice: A Critical Perspective on the Practice of EJ Research and Lessons for Policy Design." *Social Science Quarterly* 89, no. 5 (2008): 1153–1174.

Parker, Dawn C. and Tatiana Filatova. "A Conceptual Design for a Bilateral Agent-based Land Market with Heterogeneous Economic Agents." *Computers, Environment and Urban Systems* 32, no. 6 (2008): 454–463.

Pastor, Manuel, James Sadd and John Hipp. "Which Came First? Toxic Facilities, Minority Move-in, and Environmental Justice." *Journal of Urban Affairs* 23, no. 1 (2001): 1–21.

Pratt, John W. "Risk Aversion in the Small and the Large." *Econometrica* 32, no. 1–2 (1964): 122–136.

Rand, William, Moira Zellner, Scott E. Page, Rick Riolo, Daniel G. Brown and L.E. Fernandez. "The Complex Interaction of Agents and Environments: An Example in Urban Sprawl." Conference on Social Agents: Ecology, Exchange and Evolution. Chicago, 2002.

Ringquist, Evan J. "Assessing Evidence of Environmental Inequities: A Meta-Analysis." *Journal of Policy Analysis and Management* 24, no. 2 (2005): 223–247.

Röper, Andrea, Beate Völker and Henk Flap. "Social Networks and Getting a Home: Do Contacts Matter?" *Social Networks* 31, no. 1 (2009): 40–51.

Schelling, Thomas C. *Micromotives and Macrobehavior.* New York: W.W. Norton & Company, 1978.

Simmons, James W. "Changing Residence in the City: A Review of Intraurban Mobility." *Geographical Review* 58, no. 4 (1968): 622–651.

US Bureau of the Census. "US Firms—Ownership by Gender, Ethnicity, Race, and Veteran Status: 2007." 2007. www.census.gov/compendia/statab/2012/tables/12s0769.pdf.

Wolverton, Ann. "Effects of Socio-Economic and Input-Related Factors on Polluting Plants' Location Decisions." *The B.E. Journal of Economic Analysis & Policy* 9, no. 1 (2009): 14.

Wong, Grace K.M. "A Conceptual Model of the Household's Housing Decision-making Process: The Economic Perspective." *Review of Urban & Regional Development Studies* 14, no. 3 (2003): 217–234.

Wu, Fulong. "Simulating Temporal Fluctuations of Real Estate Development in a Cellular Automata City." *Transactions in GIS* 7, no. 2 (2003): 193–210.

# 5    Residential choice constraints[1]

This chapter further examines residents' location choices under various constraints, including and going beyond residential similarity preferences. Residential similarity preference, though considered in urban demography, has been overlooked in environmental justice (EJ) research.[2]

In Chapter 4, we noted the importance of the residential similarity preference on EJ outcomes, but our focus in that chapter was on the role of firms' siting-decision motives. In this chapter we focus on several factors that may constrain residential choices. For example, empirical research suggests that minorities may have a relatively lower residential similarity preference. The effect of residential similarity preference may constrain or expand plot options,[3] which may be important in EJ outcomes, and hence affect efforts to create truly sustainable cities.

## What can cause minority-correlated environmental disparities?

As discussed in Chapter 4, the dominant view in the EJ field on the link between race and environmental risk (or quality) disparity is that environmental injustice mainly results from organizations' siting processes.[4] That is, if someone or something is responsible for observed environmental risk disparities, the responsible party may be the managers of hazardous facilities.

As outlined in other chapters, in an alternative view the firm's intention is not necessarily discriminatory nor does it serve as a sufficient explanation of environmental risk disparity. The firm's main intention is to maximize profits and reduce the cost of doing business, seeking a location where the land, labor, or materials are cheap, and where the potential costs of an accident are low—an important consideration for a hazardous use.[5] It may be coincidental, or a facet of broader societal characteristics, but these could be areas where lower-income minority groups also live.

Thus, it is not firms' intention to discriminate against racial and ethnic minority groups, but in making location decisions based on economic rationales, the end result is a spatial proximity of minorities and hazardous firms. Beyond this initial siting effect, the racial and ethnic composition of a community may change after disamenity-producing firms and facilities are located within a neighborhood because these firms produce negative effects. Some residents may want to leave such areas, and those individuals who are able to leave are more likely to be comparatively affluent.[6] The movement of affluent people out of the area may depress property values, making housing more affordable, which further attracts the poor to move in. This dynamic aggravates environmental risk disparities. Since minority residents are disproportionately poorer than white residents, observed racial disparities will appear to be caused by racial factors.

As the market dynamics view illuminates, a minority-correlated environmental risk disparity observed in society could be a result of some combination of various contingent motives and decision criteria within changing environmental conditions—and there may be no intention from any of the actors to bring about this outcome. However, this view is difficult to disentangle using standard analytical tools, which assume away this complexity. A virtue of the simulation modeling process is that it offers a new view of causal chains that have been overlooked or underexplored in research due to the structures of previously used statistical techniques.

In the EJ ABM, firms' and residents' decisions occur interactively within a dynamic system, leading to variation in the environmental quality experienced by residents. Therefore, we can disaggregate how the heterogeneous preferences of different social groups to live in mixed-race communities alter EJ outcomes, especially in combination with other factors that add constraints, such as growth rates and the racial compositions of different regions.

### Residential similarity preference

Our approach to modeling similarity preference is in line with that of Schelling, who suggested that a fraction of the micro-motives (micro-preferences or micro-choices) of individuals could lead to an unexpected macro pattern in neighborhoods: "These several processes of separation, segregation, sharing, mixing, dispersal—sometimes even pursuit—have a feature in common. *The consequences are aggregate but the decisions are exceedingly individual.*"[7] Individual uncoordinated behaviors can lead to highly structured aggregate patterns, such as segregation in a neighborhood.

In his self-forming neighborhood model for dichotomous mixing (of any two social groups such as white versus black, girls versus boys, speaking English versus speaking French), Schelling developed a thesis on residential preference, assuming that people's preference-based decisions are dynamic: people move around until a location satisfies their preferences. In particular, people may have a preference for being near some fraction of others who are "like them" along some dimension (such as those listed above). In his examples, residential location decisions are assumed to be driven by these preferences, but Schelling recognized that it is not always easy to isolate individual preference, or individual color-based discriminatory segregation, from other reasons such as economically induced and collectively enforced factors.

In Chapter 4, we considered how EJ problems could emerge from firms and residents making uncoordinated decisions given decision rules and constraints. Firms' siting decisions and their impacts on environmental quality disparity were examined using three scenarios: siting based on the lowest cost, a political rationale to stay away from the majority, and/or a discriminatory motive to be close to the minority. In this simulation model, when residents seek a location to settle in, they first consider their income level and a similarity preference as constraints and then utilize decision criteria such as price, quality, and proximity to a job to select a residence. While residential choice is not directly determined by the similarity preference, the preference limits the potential locations that are available for residents. In Chapter 4, we assume that both the majority and minority hold the same level of similarity preference (i.e., 0%, 20%, or 80%). This assumption, which is contradicted by some empirical work, could affect environmental justice outcomes.

Clark empirically examined Schelling's thesis regarding residential similarity preferences and found that his conception of residential choice is generally correct, but the magnitude of similarity preferences regarding neighborhoods is in fact much larger than Schelling imagined.[8] Further, residential similarity preferences vary by city and region,[9] as well as by race and ethnicity.[10] In a household survey in Los Angeles, Clark asked: "What mixture of people would you prefer? Would you prefer a neighborhood that is ...? (combinations of 100% white and 0% black, 90% white and 10% black, and so on through 0% white and 100% black for white and black households; similar combinations were read for other groups)."[11] White respondents held strong preferences for neighborhoods that were 70% or more white in terms of composition.[12] No white respondents expressed a preference of less than 50% white for their neighborhood compositions. In contrast, the neighborhood composition preferences of other racial/ethnic groups were to have approximately 45% to 60% of residents coming from their own racial and ethnic groups, and a plurality of Hispanics preferred to have a composition of about 50% Hispanic residents in their neighborhoods. In addition, an individual's preferences may understate his or her actual choice. Clark reported that the revealed choice of the respondents showed higher preference for the same racial group than the stated preference in the survey.[13] These results are corroborated by Farley et al.[14] in a study of Detroit, and by Krysan and Farley's multi-city survey.[15]

In general, these studies conclude that observed segregation is best explained by white residential preferences to live in neighborhoods that are nearly entirely white, while blacks settle in more mixed communities. On the other hand, it is important to recognize that simple agent-based models developed to study segregation—such as computerized versions of Schelling's original model[16]—show that agents who are completely honest in their preference revelations will usually still end up in neighborhoods that are more segregated than their preferences.

The studies reviewed here do indicate that minority groups tend to have more relaxed similarity preferences than whites, possibly because of the scarcity of residential options that would be available for minorities under higher similarity preferences, and possibly because minority residents seeking neighborhoods that mirror society should seek neighborhoods with fewer minorities than majorities. Based on these considerations, assuming that the minority's similarity preference is equal to that of the majority (as we assumed in Chapter 4) may be too rigid. Under this assumption, precisely because they are in the numerical minority, in the simulation the minority groups make residential choices with far fewer alternatives than their majority counterparts.

So, the question arises: When relaxing the minority similarity preference to a level in Clark's 1992 study (or even lower), is the environmental quality gap smaller than when the minority group holds the same level of similarity preference as the majority? Therefore, our first analysis of residential choice constraints involves testing the effect of relaxing the minority's similarity preference while holding the majority's similarity preference at a high level. We wish to know if this reduction in minority choice constraint reduces the environmental quality gap.

### Experiment one: Minorities hold lower similarity preferences

As outlined above, we account for residential similarity preferences by subjecting the residential utility function to a constraint based on the residential makeup of locations nearby. If residents have a similarity preference, they will look first for any of the available plots that meet their preference criterion; for example, if the similarity preference is assumed to be 50% (or 20%) for minority residents, minority agents will only consider locating on plots where at least 50% (or 20%) of the agents on neighboring plots are also minorities, unless there are no such plots available in their decision set, in which case they will maximize their utility within the full decision set. In this case, majority agents will have a higher similarity preference than minority agents, seeking areas where 80% of the agents on neighboring plots are also majorities. The scenarios of differential similarity preference give us a good picture of the possible impact of differential similarity preference on environmental justice outcome in the current EJ ABM.

### Relative racial composition

If we think of similarity preferences as particularly constraining the minority, we might expect that this is due to limiting the residential choices for minorities. A numerical minority with a similarity preference would have fewer location options simply due to its lower percentage of the population. If the EJ problem is partially a matter of limited choices available to the minority, there may be other ways to increase the choice set for minorities beyond changing similarity preferences. For example, in an environment with a racial ratio closer to parity, we expect the minority to have more choice sets even if it holds a relatively high similarity preference.[17] Will this improve EJ outcomes?

In some geographic areas there will be proportionally larger minority populations, which would suggest more choice of places to live that meet a given similarity preference constraint. We are not suggesting that the numerical difference is the only, or even the most important, factor to define minority status, but the hypothesis follows that in areas where there are proportionally more minorities, there will be proportionally more choice of places for minorities to live even if they hold the same level of similarity preference as do majorities. Further, this reduction in location constraint might possibly lead to more equitable environmental outcomes. If the relative balance in the size of minorities to majorities indeed matters, this could be one factor explaining why environmental injustice is more likely to be found in some areas than others. Therefore, we experiment with the proportion of minorities as another constraint.

### Experiment two: Adjusting minorities' relative population proportions

We have used 70% majorities and 30% minorities as a base racial composition in Chapter 4. Here we expand the possibilities of minority status, assuming two other scenarios of population composition: 1 a community of 90% majority and 10% minority (i.e., extreme racial disparity); and 2 a community of 55% majority and 45% minority (i.e., near parity). Thereby, we can examine how extreme racial composition disparity or close-to-parity scenarios influence environmental justice outcomes.

### Population growth rate

If there indeed are interdependencies among residents' similarity preferences, minority/majority composition, and the location choice sets available, would the EJ outcome emerging from these interdependencies remain the same under different residential conditions, such as varying neighborhood characteristics? It is not a new argument that certain neighborhood characteristics matter for EJ outcomes, especially as a pressure factor on firms' decisions and behaviors, such as siting toxics release facilities.[18] From a residential choice point of view, a high population density indicates limited residential choice sets remaining.

Using this line of reasoning, we can consider the effect of altering a city-wide condition—i.e., growth rate—to analyze if such conditions can alleviate or aggravate environmental quality disparities by influencing residential choice sets within a finite neighborhood. In a rapidly growing region, for example, the finite land can be quickly filled by residents and firms, continually decreasing the residential choice sets available for newly introduced members of the numerical minority who are also constrained by a similarity preference. In a slower-growing region, we expect fewer constraints on all agents' choices. Therefore, we propose this hypothesis: With faster population growth in a region (holding constant region size and residential similarity preferences), the overall quality gap between the majority and minority groups is expected to be greater due to decreasing residential choice options.

### Experiment three: Adjusting growth rates

The base model assumes a relatively fast-growing region (5% rate of net growth). By altering the growth rate to 1%, we can examine how this rate, along with other constraints, influences environmental justice outcomes.

Figure 5.1 summarizes factors affecting residential choice sets and how constraints on them may contribute to environmental justice via interaction with firms' siting decisions.

### Model setup

To better account for the effects of similarity preferences, racial parity, and regional growth, we used the same model as in Chapter 4 except regarding the income distribution. We relaxed the assumption of a single, normal income distribution used in Chapter 4, and assigned different income levels for both groups, drawn from a gamma distribution of income as described in Chapter 3.[19] That is, majorities are assigned incomes from a higher income distribution (with a mean of US$54,000 and standard deviation of $41,000)

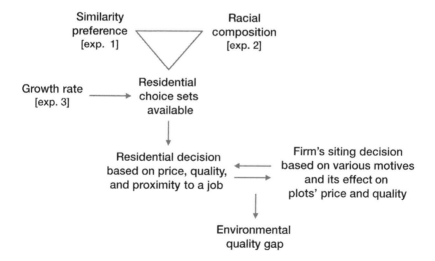

*Figure 5.1* Expanded model framework: Constraints on residential choice
Note: "exp" is experimental situation.

than are minorities (a mean of \$32,000 and standard deviation of \$40,000).[20] Using this basic setup of the EJ ABM, this chapter examines how different similarity preferences, levels of racial parity, and growth rates influence EJ outcomes. (See Table 3.6 for the model setup used in this chapter.)

### Model outcome

As adumbrated, this chapter focuses on analyzing three firm-siting scenarios, three resident similarity-preference scenarios, three racial-composition scenarios, and two growth-rate scenarios. We ran each scenario 200 times (with 70 time steps per run). For each of the scenarios (and sets of scenarios) we track the average environmental quality level, both overall and for each "race" group. Thus, we can compare average majority quality with minority quality in these different scenarios.

As in the previous chapter, the EJ outcome of interest is also the environmental quality *gap* between majority and minority groups. The quality gap is calculated by subtracting the average quality level of all minority agents from the average level of all majority agents. As before, a positive number indicates that the majority is relatively better off and by how much, while a negative number indicates that the minority is relatively better off and by how much. Zero indicates that there is no difference in the average quality level experienced by the two groups. In addition, we are interested in overall quality levels.

## The role of residential constraints in EJ outcomes

Figure 5.2 presents snapshots of the average quality levels for majorities and minorities at the last simulation step (time-step 70) under various combinations of growth rate, majority/minority proportion, and the minority similarity preference (all of these hold region size constant at 10,201 plots, and disamenity firm behavior is randomly distributed between the three different siting decision criteria detailed in Chapter 4). Each rectangular box in Figure 5.2[21] has a heading with three numerical values: the first number represents the growth rate, the second number indicates the starting percentage of majority residents in terms of racial composition, and the last number shows the minority residential similarity preference. In all cases, the majority similarity preference is fixed at 80%.

Using Figure 5.2, we can first compare the environmental quality level for majority and minority residents under two different growth-rate scenarios. Comparing the box plots in the top and bottom rows, the median quality level for both groups is noticeably lower with a 5% growth rate (bottom). The quality level remains around 60, whereas it stays around 65 when a 1% growth rate is used (top). On average, both resident groups are better off in a slowly growing region in terms of residential environmental quality. However, the variation in environmental quality, both within and between groups, is larger in the slowly growing region than in the rapidly growing region.

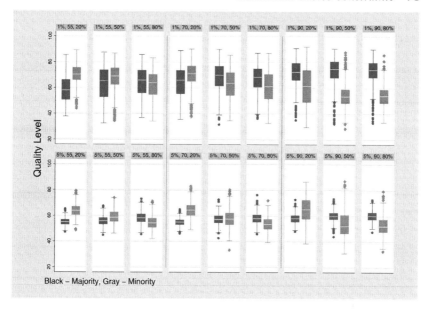

*Figure 5.2* Quality comparison between the majority and minority at *t*=70
Notes: For each box plot, the first number indicates the growth rate (e.g. 1% indicates a slow-growing region with net population growth at 1%), the second number indicates the percentage majority (e.g. 55 indicates 55% MA, 45% MI, and a relatively balanced population), and the third number indicates the minority resident's similarity preference (e.g. 20% indicates a 20% residential similarity preference, which is low compared with some empirical evidence). In all scenarios, the MA similarity preference is 80%.

Next we compare the environmental quality level under the three different racial-composition scenarios. The first six boxes, three each from the top and bottom rows on the left, show the quality levels when the racial composition is 55% and 45% for majority and minority residents, respectively. Here the numerical minority is close to parity with the majority. The six box plots in the top and bottom rows of the middle columns (columns 4, 5, and 6) show the environmental quality when the "racial" composition is 70% and 30%, respectively (the base case). The last six box plots on the right show the results with 90% majority and 10% minority. Thus, in the last set there is very high numerical disparity in terms of the racial composition. Overall, the environmental quality for minority residents in the disparity scenarios is relatively lower than that in the parity scenarios, holding constant the growth rate and similarity preferences.

In each scenario, three different numerical identifiers show the tightening of the minority similarity preference. For example, the first three box plots in the top row show the environmental quality levels with a similarity preference of 20%, 50%, or 80%. The minority group is better off when relaxing its residential similarity preference. In the near-parity scenarios (55%/45%), minority residents enjoy higher environmental quality by reducing the similarity preference to 50% or 20%. In the high-disparity scenario (90%/10%), the relaxation of the similarity preference to 20% improves the environmental quality level for minorities, but relaxing from 80% to 50% is estimated to have little effect on the median (though there is an effect on the spread). When minority residents hold a similarity preference of 80%, they are estimated to be worse off in every racial-composition and growth-rate scenario. These results support a hypothesis (mentioned above) that actual minority groups may have developed lower similarity preferences in order to increase their residential options along other dimensions.

We show in Figure 5.2 how the overall quality levels may vary when the similarity preference of the minority is relaxed (i.e., 50% or 20%) and the majority holds a strong similarity preference (i.e., 80%). In the analysis of the dynamics of environmental quality levels under differential similarity preferences, there are seven reported cases in which the median quality for minorities is at a higher level than that of majorities at the end of the simulation. In five of these cases, the minority similarity preference was at 20%. In the two other cases, minority similarity preference was at 50%. These results show that relaxing their similarity preferences always improves matters for the minority—but not necessarily enough to achieve environmental equality.

Figure 5.3 presents quality-gap dynamics under different racial composition scenarios and breaks out the effects of the disamenity firm's decision criteria. The lines represent the quality gap between majorities and minorities over the 70 time steps of each scenario. The solid lines show the scenario of 70% majority and 30% minority. Dashed lines show the quality gap under the racial near-parity scenario: 55% majority with 45% minority. Dotted lines show the high-disparity scenario: 90% majority and 10% minority. The three columns indicate whether disamenities decide where to locate based on finding the lowest price (a, d, and g), staying away from the majority (b, e, and h), or targeting the minority (c, f, and i) (see Chapter 4 for a more detailed discussion of these firm behaviors). The three rows indicate what level of similarity preference was assumed for minorities (20%, 50%, or 80%, respectively).

First, consider Figure 5.3(g)–(i), in the third row. Both groups hold strong similarity preferences (80%), but racial compositions differ across the lines. All three quality-gap lines end at greater than zero most of the time, showing that majorities are better off regardless of disamenities' (polluting firms') siting decision scenarios. Further, up to a point, relative racial composition does not matter much since quality gap lines remain at very similar levels in 55%/45% and 70%/30% scenarios. However, the extreme racial disparity scenario (90%/10%) significantly increases the quality gap. Majorities are generally much better off.

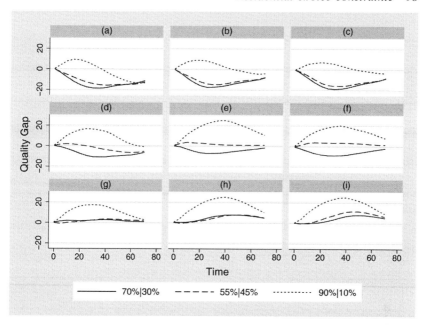

*Figure 5.3* Dynamics of quality gap under three firm choices
Note: In column 1 (a, d, and g) disamenity firms choose the lowest-price location; in column 2 (b, e, and h) disamenity firms choose to locate away from the majority; in column 3 (c, f, and i) disamenity firms target the minority. Figures in the first row (a, b, and c) assume 20% resident similarity preference. Figures in the second row (d, e, and f) assume a 50% resident similarity preference. Figures in the third row (g, h, and i) assume an 80% resident similarity preference.

Figure 5.3(a)–(f) (the top two rows) show the same experiment with the minority similarity preferences relaxed to 20% (top row) or 50% (second row). With 20% similarity preference (Figure 5.3(a)–(c)), the result is somewhat the opposite. Minority residents are actually better off as long as they are not a numerically extreme minority. Figure 5.3(a)–(c) also shows that there is a noticeable difference between the 90%/10% racial composition scenario and the other two scenarios. When they are a numerically extreme minority, minority residents are worse off at the beginning, but the gap is narrowed and neutralized at the end. Figure 5.3(d)–(f) clearly shows that when there is (close to) racial parity, the environmental quality gap is neutralized and, because of their reduced similarity preference, minorities may even be able to be better off (we see some lines ending below zero). With the 70%/30% scenario, minorities are better off. However, majorities can become quite better off when there is an extreme racial disparity in the community.

Across all graphs in Figure 5.3 (a)–(i), note that the behavior of the firm is not particularly important to these outcomes. Looking across each row, the results are surprisingly similar, with the shape of all curves similar from left to right within a single row—though when the disamenity firm is strictly economically rational (seeking only the minimum price), the outcomes are best for the minority.[22]

## Discussion

The focus of this chapter is on locational choice constraints on residents—due to residential similarity preferences, the proportion of the population represented by the numerical minority, or population growth rates—and their links to environmental disparities.

Overall the simulation experiments show that location choice constraints can help explain observed environmental quality variation. All else equal, when the minority agents lower their similarity preference (reducing their choice constraints), they usually enjoy environmental quality at a level similar to—or even greater than—the majority. This implies an important tradeoff: holding a higher similarity preference works against experiencing better environmental quality for minority residents, but might result in living in a neighborhood that is more comfortable in other ways. Racial composition and residential conditions (neither of which is controlled by minority preference) can also constrain or expand residential choice sets, contributing to different levels of exposure to environmental harm for majority and minority residents. In the simulation, combinations of these variables explain differences in environmental risk exposure between different social groups. Therefore, the findings suggest that these factors should be included in EJ analysis for specific locales, and whenever considering the pursuit of sustainable cities.

We found that even in the absence of any nefarious intent by firms, minorities tend to be worse off when:

- minority residents hold high similarity preferences;
- there is high racial disparity between the two social groups; or
- there is a high regional growth rate.

Holding constant the other factors, each of these situations reduces the ability of minorities to find plots that suit their preferences, and each generally results in worse environmental outcomes for minorities.

In the simulation, residential choice is ultimately made based on the utility of plots considered, which is a function of each plot's price, quality, and distance from the closest job. However, before the choice is made, residents consider a similarity preference in selecting potential alternatives. As Clark suggests, the degree of similarity preference may be different between majorities and minorities.[23] A racial minority population may have a lower residential similarity preference than the majority as a response to the fact that members are not only part of a socially constructed racial or ethnic minority, but a numerical minority as well. By reducing this residential similarity preference, minorities can increase the potential choice set of alternatives and thus find a relatively better plot in terms of environmental quality. With the increase in options, overall environmental injustice, measured as the quality gap, may decline.

A complication worth noting is that we may be confounding two different issues when we discuss similarity preferences. Similarity preferences are just one social structure that may lead to segregated communities, and may not be the most prominent structure. While we have expanded the minority choice set by decreasing the minority residents' similarity preference, we might also have modeled this dynamic as a lessening of exclusionary practices by majorities. In effect, the result should be the same end process—minority residents will have more choices available if they relax their similarity preference and/or exclusionary practices are reduced, but the difference in the underlying intent of these two processes is important. It is worth considering that if minority similarity preferences are lower than the ratio permitted by majority exclusionary practices, then we expect to find increased choices if majorities relax their exclusionary practices. It would seem that policy could more readily decrease exclusionary practices than it could alter minority similarity preferences.

The finding with respect to racial compositions also raises interesting questions for EJ and sustainable cities research. The basic premise of EJ studies is that minorities and environmental disamenities tend to be collocated together in space. As seen in Figure 5.2, the environmental quality gap may increase with the level of racial disparity.[24] In the simulations, as the percentage of the population made up of minorities increases (closer to the parity scenario), the quality gap between the majority and the minority generally closes. This raises an important question for empirical research and administrative practice: Should EJ policies pay attention to the relative percentages of minorities or the racial composition of residents in *regions*, in addition to those in Census blocks, etc?[25]

Also, an interesting empirical result in Campbell et al. is that, controlling for many other factors, the presence of Asian minority groups—one of the smallest measured groups in the region—is associated with increases in *new* TRIFs in Arizona's Maricopa County (which contains Phoenix, the United States' fifth largest city).[26] Given the history of this southwestern area, this seems surprising, but may be less so if the issue is locational constraints on this small minority group rather than firm-decision racism or discrimination explicitly directed against Asians. Some of the surprising findings with respect to certain minority groups' exposure to environmental risk may need to be reexamined along with the potential interdependency of residential similarity preferences and other minority choice constraints.

Environmental injustice occurs in the context of a dynamic social system. By modeling the problem via a dynamic simulation, we find that residential choice constraints—whether through residential preferences or other factors such as regional growth trends—also have a dynamic, interactive effect on EJ, which is one component of sustainability. Each of these processes was independently found to create the circumstances of environmental injustice.

An environmental quality gap can emerge between majority and minority residents whenever minority residents have a strong preference to live in communities with a high proportion of other minority residents, or when a region is growing rapidly so that better plots fill sooner, or when minorities are part of a very small minority group. However, these individual, independent effects are dwarfed by the dynamic combination of all effects occurring at the same time. When such is the case, the environmental injustice that occurs is considerably more than the sum of these component parts. Further, we must suspect that such interactions may play even larger unintended and unanticipated parts in more comprehensive elements of sustainability.

Through the simplified artificial environment, in a manner unavailable via empirical techniques, we see that each of these effects has its own impact on environmental justice outcomes. We are also able to analyze the cumulative effect of all of the processes interacting dynamically in a residential context (see Figure 5.2). Through this research, we are able to discern what may be important considerations for both studying and addressing environmental injustice—as well as glean some insight into some erstwhile puzzling empirical results.

As the hypotheses we propose are tested empirically, we may see a change in our understanding of environmental justice: rather than a phenomenon that is primarily the result of majority or firm decision making, it is a complex outcome due only in part to their decisions. Like overall urban sustainability, it is also a phenomenon that is affected by space and geographic constraints, by population growth or stagnation, and by the decisions that each of us makes about who we would like our neighbors to be.

In part, this complicates the issue—it is no longer sufficient to assign specific blame for environmental injustice. There may certainly be instances where lines of fault are clear, but the results of our simulations indicate that in contemporary circumstances the causes of EJ are likely to be much more complex than just inappropriate behavior by one actor type. These results enable us to look at the problem of race-based environmental injustice more holistically, and begin to think about holistic solutions that may finally address what has heretofore been an intractable social problem.

## Notes

1  The material in this chapter is based on the updated version of the EJ ABM, described in Chapter 3, but the analysis performed and discussed in this chapter is similar to that in Yushim Kim, Heather E. Campbell, and Adam Eckerd, "Residential Choice Constraints and Environmental Justice," *Social Science Quarterly* 95, no. 1 (2014). Any overlapping parts are used by permission. The model used in this chapter includes a more realistic distribution of US incomes

and housing prices. This enhances the realism of the model but can also influence EJ patterns reported in this chapter as compared with those in the *SSQ* article.

2 Dennis Epple, Radu Filimon and Thomas Romer, "Equilibrium Among Local Jurisdictions: Toward an Integrated Treatment of Voting and Residential Choice," *Journal of Public Economics* 24, no. 3 (1984): 281–308; H. Spencer Banzhaf and Randall P. Walsh, "Do People Vote with their Feet? An Empirical Test of Tiebout's Mechanism," *American Economic Review* 98, no. 3 (2008): 843–63.

3 William A.V. Clark, "Residential Preferences and Residential Choices in a Multiethnic Context," *Demography* 29, no. 3 (1992): 451–66; Maria Krysan and Reynolds Farley, "The Residential Preferences of Blacks: Do They Explain Persistent Segregation?" *Social Forces* 80, no. 3 (2002): 937–80.

4 Robert D. Bullard, "Environmental Justice: It's More than Waste Facility Siting," *Social Science Quarterly* 77 (1996): 493–99; Paul Mohai and Bunyan Bryant, "Is there a 'Race' Effect on Concern for Environmental Quality?" *Public Opinion Quarterly* 62 (1998): 475–505.

5 James T. Hamilton, "Testing for Environmental Racism: Prejudice, Profits, Political Power?" *Journal of Policy Analysis and Management* 14, no. 1 (1995): 107–32.

6 Ibid.

7 Thomas C. Schelling, *Micromotives and Macrobehavior* (New York: W.W. Norton & Company, 1978), 145, emphasis added.

8 Clark, "Residential Preferences and Residential Choices in a Multiethnic Context."

9 William A.V. Clark, "Residential Segregation in American Cities: A Review and Interpretation," *Population Research and Policy Review* 5 (1986): 95–117.

10 Clark, "Residential Preferences and Residential Choices in a Multiethnic Context."

11 Ibid., 454.

12 It's worth noting that the US white non-Hispanic racial percentage in 2010 was about 63%. Thus, a 70% similarity preference rate among white non-Hispanics is only slightly above their actual level in the population. "Detailed Tables – American FactFinder; T4-2008. Hispanic or Latino By Race [15]," *2008 Population Estimates*. US Census Bureau, as cited in Wikipedia.

13 Clark, "Residential Preferences and Residential Choices in a Multiethnic Context."

14 Reynolds Farley, Howard Schuman, Suzanne Bianchi, Diane Colasanto, and Shirley Hatchett, "'Chocolate City, Vanilla Suburbs': Will the Trend Toward Racially Separate Communities Continue?" *Social Science Research* 7, no. 4 (1978): 319–44.

15 Krysan and Farley, "The Residential Preferences of Blacks."

16 See NetLogo's Model Library, Sample Models, Social Science, Segregation, ccl. northwestern.edu/netlogo/models/Segregation.

17 This question is particularly relevant to the US Hispanic minority as it grows in some regions to become closer to parity with white non-Hispanics.

18 Seema Arora and Timothy N. Cason, "Do Community Characteristics Influence Environmental Outcomes? Evidence from the Toxics Release Inventory," *Journal of Applied Economics* 1, no. 2 (1998): 413–53; Heather E. Campbell, Laura R. Peck and Michael K. Tschudi, "Justice for All? A Cross-Time Analysis of Toxics Release Inventory Facility Location," *Review of Policy Research* 27, no. 1 (2010): 1–25.

19 In the United States the income distribution is right-skewed, and so is the gamma distribution.

20 These means and standard deviations are based on Census data.

98   *Heather E. Campbell, Yushim Kim, and Adam Eckerd*

21  The displayed box-and-whisker diagrams use median and percentile ranks (rather than mean and standard deviations).
22  These results may suggest that high levels of environmental injustice in communities that are close to racial parity indicate the presence of discrimination (cet. par.).
23  Clark, "Residential Preferences and Residential Choices in a Multiethnic Context."
24  These results are rather different from those reported by Arora and Cason, who indicate that "a larger percentage of non-white residents may be associated with a higher level of releases in the southeastern states." In their study, for example, the mean percentage of non-white residents was 10.56% within zip codes with no release vs. 15.90% within zip codes with releases, both of which are similar to our racial composition scenario of 90% MAs and 10% MIs. Arora and Cason, "Do Community Characteristics Influence Environmental Outcomes?" 415–16.
25  Of course the real world has more than two races/ethnicities. Some EJ research that is interested in collective action does look at the percentage of minorities.
26  Campbell et al., "Justice for All?"

# References

Arora, Seema and Timothy N. Cason. "Do Community Characteristics Influence Environmental Outcomes? Evidence from the Toxics Release Inventory." *Journal of Applied Economics* 1, no. 2 (1998): 413–453.
Banzhaf, H. Spencer and Randall P. Walsh. "Do People Vote with their Feet? An Empirical Test of Tiebout's Mechanism." *American Economic Review* 98, no. 3 (2008): 843–863.
Bullard, Robert D. "Environmental Justice: It's More than Waste Facility Siting." *Social Science Quarterly* 77, no. 3 (1996): 493–499.
Campbell, Heather E., Laura R. Peck and Michael K. Tschudi. "Justice for All? A Cross-time Analysis of Toxics Release Inventory Facility Location." *Review of Policy Research* 27, no. 1 (2010): 1–25.
Clark, William A.V. "Residential Segregation in American Cities: A Review and Interpretation." *Population Research and Policy Review* 5 (1986): 95–117.
Clark, William A.V. "Residential Preferences and Residential Choices in a Multi-ethnic Context." *Demography* 29, no. 3 (1992): 451–466.
Epple, Dennis, Radu Filimon and Thomas Romer. "Equilibrium Among Local Jurisdictions: Toward an Integrated Treatment of Voting and Residential Choice." *Journal of Public Economics* 24, no. 3 (1984): 281–308.
Farley, Reynolds, Howard Schuman, Suzanne Bianchi, Diane Colasanto and Shirley Hatchett. "'Chocolate City, Vanilla Suburbs': Will the Trend Toward Racially Separate Communities Continue?" *Social Science Research* 7, no. 4 (1978): 319–344.
Hamilton, James T. "Testing for Environmental Racism: Prejudice, Profits, Political Power?" *Journal of Policy Analysis and Management* 14, no. 1 (1995): 107–132.
Kim, Yushim, Heather E. Campbell and Adam Eckerd. "Residential Choice Constraints and Environmental Justice." *Social Science Quarterly* 95, no. 1 (2014).
Krysan, Maria and Reynolds Farley. "The Residential Preferences of Blacks: Do they Explain Persistent Segregation?" *Social Forces* 80, no. 3 (2002): 937–980.
Mohai, Paul and Bunyan Bryant. "Is there a 'Race' Effect on Concern for Environmental Quality?" *Public Opinion Quarterly* 62, no. 4 (1998): 475–505.

Schelling, Thomas C. *Micromotives and Macrobehavior.* New York: W.W. Norton & Company, 1978.

US Census Bureau. "Mover Rate Reaches Record Low, Census Bureau Reports." November 15, 2011. Newsroom. www.census.gov/newsroom/releases/archives/mobility_of_the_population/cb11-193.html (accessed February 16, 2012).

# 6 Race, class, and environmental disparities

Among environmental policy and urban sustainability questions, consideration of environmental justice (EJ) is viewed as increasingly important. As mentioned in Chapter 2, empirical evidence indicates that environmental injustice exists in some circumstances, but there is heated debate as to why. A classic and continuing debate is on the degree to which EJ is a function of racial effects versus income-based market dynamics that happen to be correlated. To the extent they exist, proponents' views of sustainable cities are also comprised accordingly.

Chapter 4 reports that a purely neoclassical world in which both firms and residents behaved economically rationally did not lead to environmentally unjust outcomes; only when either firms or residents (or both) were modeled as caring about "race" (belonging to the majority or the minority) did we observe appreciably environmentally unjust outcomes. However, the model described in Chapter 4 is very simple, especially in terms of representing the role of resident agents' characteristics. Minority and majority agents were identical to each other except for their assigned "races." Yet, there are a variety of ways that we know dominant groups and minority groups may be different. In the EJ literature, one of the most frequently considered is income variation.

This chapter tackles the dynamic effects of income and its relationship to EJ and race. We compare two different scenarios: 1 majorities are richer than minorities; and 2 minorities are richer than majorities. This chapter also indicates the results of each scenario outcome under two different levels of residential similarity preference: none versus high (80%). The scenarios help us analyze under what conditions each factor seems more important than the other and how they interact.

## The "race versus class" debate

In Chapter 2, we introduced several methodological issues in EJ research. Along with the question of "which comes first," Mohai, Pellow and Roberts point out that there are significant methodological questions around another major issue in EJ research: What is the relative amount of environmental inequity based on economic class differences versus race?[1]

Recall that there are a number of analyses that examine the question of race and economic class from an EJ perspective (reviewed in earlier chapters). Considering their mixed outcomes and ongoing debates, the question arises as to whether the problem should really be framed as "race *or* class," or if we should consider the combined effects of the two. Downey argues that we need to pay further attention to how existing theories may conceptualize explanations of racially disparate environmental outcomes.[2] In other words, are race and class competing explanatory variables or interdependent variables in environmental injustice? According to Downey, there are at least two competing models of EJ, given how environmental racism has been defined in the literature: the intentional model and the institutional model.[3]

The intentional model of EJ is a simple cause-and-effect conception that observed environmental injustice is "discriminatory only if inequity arises from racist intent in the siting process itself."[4] The institutional model of EJ conceptualizes environmental discrimination relatively broadly, including "any policy, practice, or directive that differentially affects or disadvantages individuals, groups, or communities based on race or color."[5] As Downey puts it:

> The institutional formulation does not require evidence that more people of color than whites are affected by pollution, only that a disproportionate number are so affected. Nor does it imply that race or ethnicity will in all, or even the majority of cases, be more strongly correlated than income with the incidence of environmental hazards— even when environmental hazards are distributed in a racially biased manner. Therefore, charges of environmental racism cannot automatically be construed as claims that a) nonminority communities are not severely affected by environmental hazards or b) environmental hazards are not also differentially distributed by income or class.[6]

Because race continues to be identified as a significant explanatory variable even when income-based class variables are controlled, the institutional perspective urges us to pay attention to specific social mechanisms (e.g., residential similarity preferences, zoning) that relate race to environmental inequality in society, even if unintentionally.[7]

On the other hand, while the magnitude may be smaller than that for race, findings of environmental inequity due to economic class persist when race is controlled. This invites further investigation of socioeconomic characteristics and environmental inequity.[8] In fact, in some countries, such as the United Kingdom, the focus on class-based environmental injustice may be viewed as more important than the race-based focus in the United States.[9]

The institutional model of EJ opens up the possibility of examining environmental injustice from different angles than those implied by the intentional model, supporting that a more fruitful question may be "how factors interplay with each other through what mechanisms," rather than "which factor is key." Downey, in fact, concludes, "it would be more fruitful to take institutional models seriously and investigate how race and income are both implicated in the distribution of environmental hazards."[10] Continuing, Downey notes that "[i]nstitutional models provide a theoretical basis for expecting that race and income will be highly correlated. However, if income and race are highly correlated, statistical models may have difficulty separating out the effects of each."[11] An agent-based modeling approach makes it possible to experiment with different combinations of race and income, and thus to tease out the separate and interacting effects of each.

## Considering income class of residents

As mentioned, the EJ ABM includes two types of agents: firms—polluting or non-polluting—and residents—of majority or minority "race." As before, these agents follow decision rules described in detail in Chapter 3. Here we focus on income variability as an attribute of resident agents (see Table 3.6 to see the basic setup of the EJ ABM for this chapter). Below we reiterate and elaborate key aspects of the model that are relevant for the current chapter.

### Residents

In the scenarios used for this chapter, each agent's income is drawn from one of two different distributions depending on each agent's defined "race" (minority or majority). Each resident agent in each racial group is randomly assigned an income from a distribution that roughly approximates 2010 US Census averages for whites or for African Americans. For our initial set of scenarios, this means that majority residents are assigned an income from a distribution with mean US$54,000 and standard deviation of $41,000. Minority residents are assigned an income from a distribution with mean $32,000 and standard deviation of $40,000 (with both constrained to be no less than zero).

Because income distributions tend to be skewed, with more people on the poorer end and fewer wealthy individuals distributed over a wide range of high incomes, in the model resident income is randomly drawn from a right-skewed distribution.[12] That is, we draw income from gamma distributions, with shape and scale parameters calculated using the means and standard deviations mentioned above.[13] When new resident agents enter the region, either at the initial setup of the simulation or due to regional population growth, a random value drawn from the appropriate income distribution (given the new resident's race) is assigned to that resident.

We categorize agents into three income classes—poor, middle, and rich—based on the value of the randomly assigned income. Since we derive income variables from data at the national level in the United States, we classify residents based upon US federal government indicators of relative wealth and poverty. An income level greater than $100,000, roughly corresponding to the income level at which an individual would be in at least the second-highest federal income-tax bracket, is defined as "rich."[14] We categorized agents with incomes less than $28,000 as "poor," corresponding to an income that is, at most, 150% of the defined poverty level for a family of three.[15] According to the 2010 Census Briefs, US average household sizes are 2.58, and average family sizes are 3.14, so the use of 3 as the assumed household size is reasonable.[16] All other resident agents are categorized as "middle class." For simplicity, residents' income classes do not change during the simulation.[17]

By assigning an income variable to agents who are also assigned a race, we can use the EJ ABM to examine the roles of race and class in explaining environmental injustice. To unpack the race-class relationship further beyond discussions in the literature, in some experiments we vary the means and standard deviations for each racial group from this US empirical base, as described below (see Table 6.1).

*Firm siting*

In Chapter 4, we noted that the absence of racial similarity preferences muted, and in some cases eliminated, environmental injustice, particularly when polluting firms selected locations based solely on price, rather than on a particular preference for being near minorities. Even when polluting firms specifically chose to locate in minority communities, but resident agents had no similarity preferences, the environmental quality gap was of very small magnitude. This distinction—between intentional targeting of minorities and unintended outcomes of residential similarity preferences—is important because it gets to the heart of the difference between the intentional view of environmental justice, embodied by work such as the United Church of Christ (UCC) report and Bullard's 1996 piece in *Social Science Quarterly*, and the institutional view expressed by Been and Gupta, and Banzhaf and Walsh.[18]

For the experiments described in this chapter, we assume all firms to be economically rational—i.e., firms seek to site on the lowest-priced plots of land, and seek to agglomerate by locating near other similar firms (we expect that agglomeration goals are consistent with economic rationality because they indicate otherwise unobservable cost factors). Thus, these experiments let us control for the effects of firm behavior by assuming that firms all make economically rational choices, and focus on the interactions of residential race and income characteristics.

We add further realism to the model by including a real-estate market in this chapter. As described in detail in Chapter 3, plot prices rise or fall based on environmental quality and how much demand there is in the plots nearby. The higher the quality and the higher the income levels of residents nearby, the higher a plot's price will be (and vice versa). Thus, as in real-world housing markets, residents with lower income levels may be constrained from locating on plots that have high levels of quality.

*Scenarios*

Our first scenario mirrors the US population, with majority incomes assumed to be similar to the distribution for white Americans, and minority incomes assumed to be similar to the distribution for African Americans (based on US Census data). We assess this scenario in two ways: with no similarity preferences and also with 80% similarity preferences for both groups. Then, in order specifically to get at the issue of race versus class, we flip the income distributions and analyze situations in which the ABM minority is richer on average, with minority income distributed like the majority income really is in the United States, while the ABM majority's income is distributed as the US minority income actually is. This exhibits one of the advantages of ABM—it lets us directly explore a counterfactual of analytic interest whether real-world data allow such an analysis or not. As shown in Table 6.1, this results in four distinct scenarios.

*Model outcomes*

For each of the scenarios (and sets of scenarios) we track the average environmental quality level, both overall and for each race and class set. We ran each scenario 200 times (with 70 time steps per trial, as before). Thus, we can compare average majority quality with minority quality in these different scenarios, as well as the averages for all poor, middle-class, and wealthy residents, and for each of the six subgroups (e.g., rich minority, rich majority, through poor majority).

## Race, income, similarity preferences, and their dynamics

The base EJ ABM shows some mechanisms by which environmental injustice can emerge in a two-race world, particularly when those two races have a tendency to aggregate themselves in choosing where to live. Here our focus is on how this result is altered by the introduction of different income

*Table 6.1* Income distribution and similarity preference scenarios

| | | Income distributions | |
|---|---|---|---|
| | | a) Majorities are wealthier than minorities (MA>MI) | b) Minorities are wealthier than majorities (MA<MI) |
| Similarity preferences (both groups) | No similarity preference | Scenario a | Scenario b |
| | 80% similarity preference | Scenario c | Scenario d |

Note: a) Average income for majorities $54,000 (standard deviation $41,000), whereas average income for minorities $32,000 (standard deviation $40,000); b) income distributions were reversed.

structures. Therefore, we begin by examining environmental quality dynamics by income-based class only, and then investigate the dynamics when income and race are simultaneously considered.

## Income class only

In the income-class-only scenario, there is one type of resident (i.e., there is no racial difference) whose mean income is $54,000 and whose standard deviation is $41,000. The simulation starts with 200 residents whose incomes are drawn from the gamma distribution, and the number of residents grows at the rate of 5%.

In this scenario (not illustrated), the poor experience the lowest environmental quality over time. The rich enjoy a higher quality than the poor and the highest quality at the beginning for a short time period. However, it is the middle class that is estimated to enjoy the highest environmental quality throughout most of the simulation. At the end of the simulation, the rich catch up to the middle class in terms of environmental quality.

We experimented with two additional income scenarios. When a smaller standard deviation ($20,000) is set for income, this limits the sizes of both the rich class and the poor class relative to the middle class. Here the rich experience higher quality compared with the other two classes. When a larger standard deviation ($60,000) is set, which ensures more balance between the sizes of the three classes (albeit with the middle class still being the largest), the middle class is again the one that experiences the highest quality.

Thus, the examination of income alone already presents surprises. Though most who argue that income interacting with housing market dynamics is the underlying determinant of what appear to be race-based inequities would expect that the rich would have the best outcomes and the poor the worst, in this simulation the middle class often come out the best. The rich enjoy the highest environmental quality only when income among residents is narrowly distributed around the mean. These results, along with those in the base EJ ABM, suggest that within a dynamic interactive structure, there may be something about being in a minority that causes differential impact, for the rich are a numerical minority in this case.

## Income and race

Illustrating the four scenarios listed in Table 6.1, Figure 6.1 shows a result different from previous work and somewhat contrary to expectations. Absent income variability, Chapter 4 showed that minorities tended to see lower levels of quality, most importantly if residents had a similarity preference. In the experiment with income variability between "races," as Figure 6.1 shows, the story appears to be simply an income one: when the majority is richer, it is better off on average, and when the minority is

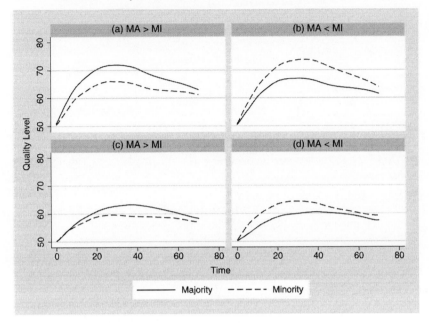

*Figure 6.1* Overall majority and minority quality, with different incomes
Note: Letters match scenarios as listed in Table 6.1; "MA>MI" indicates that the mean majority income exceeds the mean minority income, while "MA<MI" indicates that mean minority income is greater. The graphs in the top row represent scenarios run with no similarity preference (resident agents pay no attention to "race" of neighbors when deciding where to live), while the two graphs below represent scenarios for which all residents have an 80% similarity preference when seeking a residential plot.

richer, the minority is better off on average. It should be noted that Figure 6.1 collapses all majorities and minorities together, regardless of whether low, middle, or upper class. Also note that overall quality levels are higher for both groups when there is no similarity preference (compare quality levels in Figure 6.1(a) to (c), and (b) to (d)).

Figure 6.2 collapses all three income classes together regardless of race. The results with no similarity preference are similar to our race-free base case, discussed above. Across all scenarios, the poor class lives with the lowest level of environmental quality, a result that is consistent with both the institutional model of EJ and the economic explanation. However, while an economic perspective would expect that the rich would live with higher quality over all times and all scenarios, the rich tend to do best when residents have a racial similarity preference regardless of whether minorities or majorities are richer (Figure 6.2(c) and (d)). In Figure 6.2(a) and (b), where there is no similarity preference, the middle class sees the highest levels of overall quality most of the time. However, the middle class experiences the

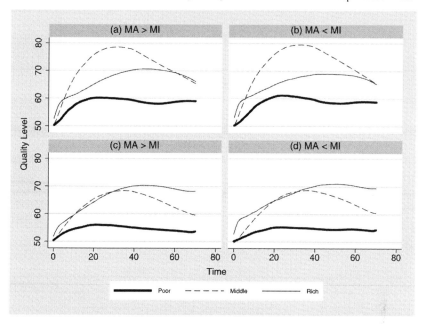

*Figure 6.2* Rich, poor, and middle-class quality, regardless of race
Note: Letters match scenarios as listed in Table 6.1; "MA>MI" indicates that the mean majority income exceeds the mean minority income, while "MA<MI" indicates that mean minority income is greater. The two graphs in the top row present scenarios run with no similarity preference (resident agents pay no attention to "race" of neighbors when deciding where to live), while the two graphs below present scenarios in which all residents have an 80% similarity preference when seeking a residential plot.

highest environmental quality only for a very short period in Figure 6.2(c) and (d). Again, these results show the importance of interacting factors—and of the racial similarity preference.

Figure 6.3 displays the separation of residents into six different subgroups based on all combinations of wealth and race. In all of the images shown in Figure 6.3, the poor, whether minority or majority, are about equally poorly off, bumping along the bottom in environmental quality. In Figure 6.3(a) and (b), without a similarity preference, racial variation seems to make little difference, and what matters is income, since minority and majority groups of the same income class are grouped together. The respective racial groups follow nearly the same trajectory, with middle-class groups usually the most well off and the poor the least well off. In the scenarios with a similarity preference (Figure 6.3(c) and (d)), regardless of whether the minority group is, on average, wealthier or poorer than the majority group, rich minority residents tend to live with higher quality than the other subgroups and,

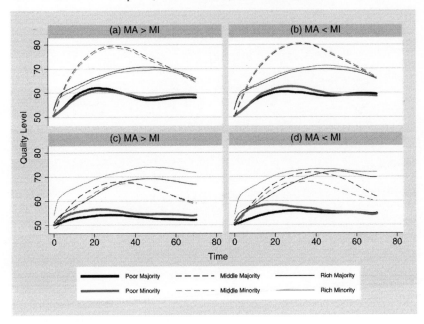

*Figure 6.3* Quality for all six subgroups

Note: Letters match scenarios as listed in Table 6.1; "MA>MI" indicates that the mean majority income exceeds the mean minority income, while "MA<MI" indicates that mean minority income is greater. The two graphs in the top row display scenarios run with no similarity preference (resident agents pay no attention to "race" of neighbors when deciding where to live), while the two graphs below represent scenarios for which all residents have an 80% similarity preference when seeking a residential plot.

unexpectedly, with much higher quality when the rich minority group is the smallest of the subgroups.

In the similarity preference scenarios, rich majorities tend to start off with rather low quality that rises throughout the trial, while middle-class minorities soon gain fairly high quality that slowly declines. These results corroborate our earlier chapters (Chapters 4–5), emphasizing the importance of residential similarity preferences to environmental justice outcomes: without a residential similarity preference the middle class is relatively better off, while with a preference the rich are relatively better off; the latter more closely approximates observed outcomes.[19] We also know from empirical research that modeling residents as having similarity preferences is more realistic than modeling them as not.[20]

It is worth noting that one reason to expect that income must matter more than race is that basic neoclassical microeconomic models imply that racism is inconsistent with free markets. Here, the results with a world modeled as race-blind—neither firms nor residents paying attention to race—imply that income is the key determinant of environmental quality.

However, once residents are race-conscious—even though all firms are economically rational—as with Schelling's model of residential segregation, race does matter, and interacts with income in sometimes unexpected ways.

### Nearness to *disamenities* and *amenities*

Another insight emerges from this analysis. Looking systematically at the scenario using Census-based income information with residents preferring 80% of neighbors to be racially similar (scenario c from Table 6.1)—which we think is a scenario reasonably reflecting current reality—we see evidence of clustering of minority residents around disamenities. Clustering of minorities near disamenities is what is usually measured in the empirical EJ literature, which generally looks at disproportionate collocation, not overall quality levels. Yet, we also notice evidence of clustering of minorities around *amenities*.

Figure 6.4 reveals this pattern of clustering by residents. Figure 6.4(a) shows the average distance away that majority and minority residents locate from both disamenities and amenities. The thick solid line shows average distance to disamenities for majorities and the thick dashes for minorities. The thinner lines (solid and dashed) similarly show nearness to amenities for each group. Minorities are, on average, about five plots closer to both disamenities and amenities than are majority residents over the entire analysis. This pattern barely changes during the simulation.

Figure 6.4(b) changes the focus to the firms and looks at the proportions of resident types near firms—the common question in EJ research. As shown in Figure 6.4(b), each type of firm sees a larger proportion of minority residents clustering nearby. Keeping in mind that minorities constitute about 30% of the total resident population, within a small radius of two plots from each type of firm, minorities often make up more than 50% of the local population. While the trends show a regression to the population proportions of 70% / 30% as the model steps forward, throughout the simulation trials the population clusters around both amenities and disamenities show an overrepresentation of minority residents, never dropping to 30%, or even 40% for amenities.

As mentioned, EJ studies tend to focus on finding the disamenity and seeing who lives nearby. This result suggests that such an approach may lead to limited understanding.

### Discussion

This chapter focuses on analyzing the effect of "income" vs. "race" on EJ outcomes. With the results of the model yielding some unexpected outcomes, we sought to understand why, on average, simulated rich minorities often lived with better environmental quality than majorities, in contrast to previous results that did not include income variation.

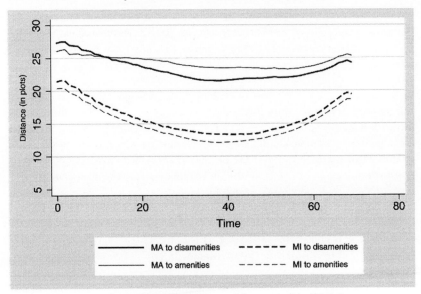

(a) Average Distance (Measured in Plots)

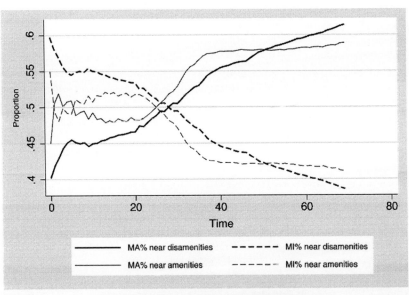

(b) Proportion of Types of Residents

*Figure 6.4* Do the EJ ABM outcomes match observed EJ patterns?

First, we had been conceiving of an American context wherein the majority tends to be the advantaged group, but as noted earlier there are contexts in which the minority is the advantaged group, such as in South Africa, and in those cases the result of the minority rich being better off would be expected.

Second, in reviewing extant environmental justice literature, it came to our attention that virtually all research (including our own empirical EJ work) has focused on either: 1 demographics in proximity to a disamenity; or 2 demographics in proximity to an amenity. While there has been a stream of research in the hedonic modeling tradition aimed at determining price equilibrium given proximity to *both* amenities and disamenities (for example, see Greenwood et al.[21]), we are aware of no EJ-focused research that does the same—although there are some works that investigate good and poor air quality, such as Seig et al.[22] However, through the ABM simulation and analysis process, we realized that this narrowed focus may be very important in affecting what is found.

In Figure 6.4 we see disproportionate numbers of minorities near dis-amenities, but also disproportionate numbers of minorities near amenities. In our aggregate, the picture looks much less bleak for the minority group as a whole than it would if we had only investigated who lives near dis-amenities—and relatively worse for the poor, regardless of race, than some studies indicate. Bearing in mind that often minorities, amenities, and dis-amenities are all more prevalent in urban areas than in rural or suburban areas,[23] environmental justice studies may only be seeing part of the picture.

To truly understand the phenomenon, we suggest that future empirical studies should not just focus on the location of a disamenity type and the surrounding populations, but should also investigate the aggregate trends for groups overall. We should note that in the model these trends are not noticeable without a similarity preference in place, but similarity preferences are supported by empirical evidence and even with low modeled similarity preferences of 20% (which are below empirical findings for similarity pre-ferences), we tended to see minority residents clustering near both types of firms (amenity and disamenity) and majority residents much more spread out.

We suggest that these findings are not terribly different from observed urban patterns, with white residents often living with longer commutes and homes far from work locations and minority residents tending to cluster near the urban core (which includes both amenities and disamenities).[24] Might the frequent focus on disamenities alone in environmental justice studies have skewed, or at least limited, EJ conclusions? This calls for empirical examination. Further, if amenities and disamenities both tend to cluster together in multi-ethnic urban cores, this suggests that urban sus-tainability may need to be examined on a regional rather than city-by-city basis. For example, it might be easier for an outlying mostly well-off and white city to appear sustainable because it relies on the urban center for both amenities and disamenities.

Third, our results are interesting in speaking to the economic hypothesis of environmental justice.[25] In instances without a residential similarity preference (i.e., scenarios most in line with economic assumptions, especially given that all firms behave economically rationally in the Chapter 6 experiments), we see an expected result of income mattering more than race, but an unexpected result of middle classes usually living with higher quality than the wealthy. This unexpected result suggests that even in a neoclassically economic world, the constraints of space must be taken into consideration in understanding environmental justice outcomes.

The results nonetheless suggest that even in a race-blind world the ability of the wealthy to acquire all highly valued land is limited. Moreover, while the poor live with the lowest levels of environmental quality, there is very little variation in the quality level for the two poor residential groups. Both the minority poor and majority poor see similar levels of comparatively low environmental quality under all of the scenarios, including those with similarity preferences. Thus, with strictly economically rational firms, there is little to suggest that poor minorities will be worse off than poor majorities, even with residential awareness of racial difference.

Taken together, the results in this chapter point to a conclusion that is, perhaps, not surprising: environmental injustice is not a function of race *or* class, but is a function of race *and* class among race-aware residents. Our results suggest that despite the EJ race–income debate's prominence as a topic of research for nearly two decades, we have much to learn about the form of that function.

As noted at the beginning of this work, although for 20 years each federal agency has been required to "make achieving environmental justice part of its mission,"[26] statistical analysis since then indicates that environmental justice has not yet been achieved in the United States. The complexity of the race–income interactions presented here suggests that this may not be surprising because EJ outcomes are so race–income context dependent that a federal approach is unlikely to be successful; instead, this complexity implies that environmental injustice must be tackled based on locale-specific data and deeper understanding of unintended outcomes in a race-conscious world. Similarly, it suggests that urban sustainability must be examined based on locale-specific, but region-wide, information, also keeping in mind unanticipated interactions.

## Notes

1 Paul Mohai, David Pellow, and J. Timmons Roberts, "Environmental Justice," *Annual Review of Environment and Resources* 34 (2009): 410.
2 Liam Downey, "Environmental Injustice: Is Race or Income a Better Predictor?" *Social Science Quarterly* 79, no. 4 (1998): 766–78.
3 These differences, by the way, may explain the heated disagreements about whether the EJ literature demonstrates "racism" or not.
4 Downey, "Environmental Injustice," 769.

5  Robert Bullard, "Environmental Justice: It's more than Waste Facility Siting," *Social Science Quarterly* 77, no. 3 (1996): 497.
6  Downey, "Environmental Injustice," 774.
7  Mohai et al., "Environmental Justice."
8  Ibid.
9  See *Environmental Justice: Rights and Means to a Healthy Environment for All*, Economic and Social Research Council (ESRC) Special Briefing 7, November 2001. The introduction clearly focuses on the poor and elderly, rather than racial and ethnic minorities, www.foe.co.uk/sites/default/files/downloads/environmental_justice. pdf. See also Capacity Global's (2007) definition of diversity relevant to EJ, in which the young and poor are mentioned before "Black, Asian, Minority and Ethnic communities," www.capacity.org.uk/policyandadvocacy/diversity.html.
10  Downey, "Environmental Injustice," 775.
11  Ibid., 775.
12  We performed the same analysis based on a normal distribution of income in a separate analysis. We find that the simulation results based on the two different income distribution assumptions—a normal distribution and a distribution skewed to the right—were not very different from each other throughout the analysis. While the right-skewed distribution may reflect reality better, similar results from both distributional forms give us assurance of robustness. This type of simplification of the underlying probability distribution is one of the types of adaptations often made in an ABM.
13  In NetLogo *random-gamma* function, *alpha* is calculated as (mean * mean) / variance and *lamda* is calculated as 1 / (variance / mean). Using 2010 US Census data, *alpha* and *lamda* for majorities and minorities are separately calculated.
14  We define the second-highest tax bracket as the cutoff because we otherwise would have had very few "rich" residents in our region, especially for the minority group, given the comparatively low mean income for the distribution from which the income variable is drawn.
15  Heather E. Campbell, Laura R. Peck and Michael K. Tschudi, "Justice for All? A Cross-Time Analysis of Toxics Release Inventory Facility Location," *Review of Policy Research* 27, no. 1 (2010): 1–25.
16  See www.census.gov/prod/cen2010/briefs/c2010br-14.pdf.
17  Though an analyst who is interested in income mobility rather than EJ could set up the model so that an agent's income can change during the course of the analysis.
18  United Church of Christ, Commission for Racial Justice, *Toxic Wastes and Race: A National Report on the Racial and Socioeconomic Characteristics of Communities with Hazardous Wastes Sites* (New York: United Church of Christ, 1987); Robert Bullard, "Environmental Justice: It's More than Waste Facility Siting," *Social Science Quarterly* 77, no. 3 (1996): 493–99; Vicki Been and Francis Gupta, "Coming to the Nuisance or Going to the Barrios?" *Ecology Law Quarterly* 24, no. 1 (1997): 1–56; H. Spencer Banzhaf and Randall P. Walsh, "Do People Vote with their Feet? An Empirical Test of Tiebout's Mechanism," *American Economic Review* 98, no. 3 (2008): 843–63.
19  Banzhaf and Walsh, "Do People Vote with their Feet?" 846–63.
20  William A.V. Clark, "Residential Preferences and Residential Choices in a Multiethnic Context," *Demography* 29, no. 3 (1992): 451–66; Michael O. Emerson, George Yancey, and Karen J. Chai, "Does Race Matter in Residential Segregation? Exploring the Preferences of White Americans," *American Sociological Review* 66, no. 6 (2001): 922–35.
21  Michael J. Greenwood, Gary L. Hunt, Dan S. Rickman, and George I. Treyz, "Migration, Regional Equilibrium, and the Estimation of Compensating Differentials," *American Economic Review* 81, no. 5 (1991): 1382–90.

22  Holger Seig, V. Kerry Smith, H. Spencer Banzhaf and Randall P. Walsh, "Estimating the General Equilibrium Benefits of Large Changes in Spatially Delineated Public Goods," *International Economic Review* 45, no. 4 (2004): 1047–77.

23  This pattern seems to match the situation in San Diego's "Barrio Logan," which is exposed to high levels of pollution and near disamenities, but also near amenities and jobs.

24  Michael A. Stoll, Harry J. Holzer and Keith R. Ihlanfeldt, "Within Cities and Suburbs: Racial Residential Concentration and the Spatial Distribution of Employment Opportunities Across Sub-Metropolitan Areas," *Journal of Policy Analysis and Management* 19, no. 2 (2000): 207–31; Bernadette Hanlon and Thomas J. Vicino, "The Fate of Inner Suburbs: Evidence from Metropolitan Baltimore," *Urban Geography* 28, no. 3 (2007): 249–75.

25  For example, James T. Hamilton, "Testing for Environmental Racism: Prejudice, Profits, Political Power?" *Journal of Policy Analysis and Management* 14, no. 1 (1995): 107–32; Been and Gupta, "Coming to the Nuisance or Going to the Barrios?"

26  William J. Clinton, "Executive Order No. 12898," *Federal Register* 59, no. 32 (2/11/1994), 1, www.archives.gov/federal-register/executive-orders/pdf/12898.pdf.

# References

Banzhaf, H. Spencer and Randall P. Walsh. "Do People Vote with their Feet? An Empirical Test of Tiebout's Mechanism." *American Economic Review* 98, no. 3 (2008): 843–863.

Been, Vicki and Francis Gupta. "Coming to the Nuisance or Going to the Barrios?" *Ecology Law Quarterly* 24, no. 1 (1997): 1–56.

Brown, Phil. "Race, Class, and Environmental Health: A Review and Systematization of the Literature." *Environmental Research*, no. 69 (1995): 15–30.

Bullard, Robert. "Environmental Justice: It's More than Waste Facility Siting." *Social Science Quarterly* 77, no. 3 (1996): 493–499.

Campbell, Heather E., Laura R. Peck and Michael K. Tschudi. "Justice for All? A Cross-Time Analysis of Toxics Release Inventory Facility Location." *Review of Policy Research* 27, no. 1 (2010): 1–25.

Capacity Global. "Diversity." 2007. www.capacity.org.uk/policyandadvocacy/diversity.html (accessed June 2013).

Clark, William A.V. "Residential Preferences and Residential Choices in a Multi-ethnic Context." *Demography* 29, no. 3 (1992): 451–466.

Clinton, William J. "Executive Order No. 12898." *Federal Register* 59, no. 32 (February 11, 1994.)

Downey, Liam. "Environmental Injustice: Is Race or Income a Better Predictor?" *Social Science Quarterly* 79, no. 4 (1998): 766–778.

Emerson, Michael O., George Yancey and Karen J. Chai. "Does Race Matter in Residential Segregation? Exploring the Preferences of White Americans." *American Sociological Review* 66, no. 6 (2001): 922–935.

ESRC (Economic and Social Research Council). *Environmental Justice: Rights and Means to a Healthy Environment for All.* ESRC Special Briefing 7, November 2001. www.foe.co.uk/resource/reports/environmental_justice.pdf (accessed June 2013).

Greenwood, Michael J., Gary L. Hunt, Dan S. Rickman and George I. Treyz. "Migration, Regional Equilibrium, and the Estimation of Compensating Differentials." *American Economic Review* 81, no. 5 (1991): 1382–1390.

Hamilton, James T. "Testing for Environmental Racism: Prejudice, Profits, Political Power?" *Journal of Policy Analysis and Management* 14, no. 1 (1995): 107–132.

Hanlon, Bernadette and Thomas J. Vicino. "The Fate of Inner Suburbs: Evidence from Metropolitan Baltimore." *Urban Geography* 28, no. 3 (2007): 249–275.

Mohai, Paul and Bunyan Bryant. "Environmental Injustice: Weighing Race and Class as Factors in the Distribution of Environmental Hazards." *University of Colorado Law Review* 63, no. 1 (1992): 921–932.

Mohai, Paul, David Pellow and J. Timmons Roberts. "Environmental Justice." *Annual Review of Environment and Resources* 34 (2009): 405–430.

Seig, Holger, V. Kerry Smith, H. Spencer Banzhaf and Randall P. Walsh. "Estimating the General Equilibrium Benefits of Large Changes in Spatially Delineated Public Goods." *International Economic Review* 45, no. 4 (2004): 1047–1077.

Stoll, Michael A., Harry J. Holzer and Keith R. Ihlanfeldt. "Within Cities and Suburbs: Racial Residential Concentration and the Spatial Distribution of Employment Opportunities Across Sub-metropolitan Areas." *Journal of Policy Analysis and Management* 19, no. 2 (2000): 207–231.

United Church of Christ, Commission for Racial Justice, *Toxic Wastes and Race: A National Report on the Racial and Socioeconomic Characteristics of Communities with Hazardous Wastes Sites.* New York: United Church of Christ, 1987.

US Census. *2010 Census Briefs, Households and Families.* Issued April 2012. www.census.gov/prod/cen2010/briefs/c2010br-14.pdf (accessed June 2013).

# 7 Residential mobility

Environmental quality and urban sustainability are pure public goods.[1] Therefore, residents cannot directly pay for them. In general, one challenge with looking at environmental justice from an economic perspective is the inability *directly* to measure the prices that residents are willing to pay for such public goods. Absent a direct measure, scholars have used different perspectives to assess how much residents value environmental quality, and many of these assessments are based on one assumption: that residents can reveal their preference for environmental quality by choosing a home. An important factor underlying such models is residential mobility—the ability of residents readily to move in order to select locations with desired bundles of attributes.

In the previous chapters, we considered how firm and resident location choice and residential income variability affected environmental justice, but in those scenarios once settled residents could not move. In this chapter we consider how outcomes are affected when residents are able better to reveal environmental preferences by having the mobility to relocate.

## Settlement patterns

Economists have been considering urban settlement patterns and their relationship with public goods for a long time. In the 1820s, Johann Heinrich von Thünen, an amateur economist, first described why and how settlement occurs around an urban core.[2] In the von Thünen model, specialization allowed a city to form. Resources for the city were provided from the hinterlands surrounding it, with a close-in ring providing agricultural goods, the next ring providing timber resources for fuel, a third ring with livestock, and then finally a sparsely populated outer ring, consisting mostly of natural resources.

The key to the model and understanding of the urban form was the cost of transporting various goods back into the city for sale. It was necessary for agriculture to locate close to prevent spoilage as goods went into the city. Timber would be located next, for transportation would be expensive, but risk of spoilage was much lower than for produce. Livestock would be in the third ring because animals could transport themselves to the city before being used.

Over 100 years later, Alonso described a 20th-century version of von Thünen's monocentric city, this time with the concentric rings made up of various layers of residential development.[3] In Alonso's model, jobs resided in the central business district (CBD). Because all workers were assumed to commute to the CBD, houses would be valued in diminishing circles from the CBD. The further from the CBD a home was located, the higher the commuting costs would be to arrive at the CBD. Thus, comparing the prices of identical homes, say the price of one in the first ring around the CBD to one in the fourth ring, we could arrive at a way to calculate the cost of the commute. There would be a premium on the value of the home in the first ring due to the minimal commuting costs, and the difference in housing prices (cet. par.) would reflect the cost residents placed on the commute.

Around the same time, Edwin Mills was describing the rationale for why a CBD began in the first place, and what encouraged further business growth in a CBD.[4] All else equal, firms would locate close to the resources required for production (this could include natural resources or labor), ideally in a location with access to cheap transportation to facilitate trade of goods produced. Once established, firms that were vertically related would want to locate close to the focal firm in order to minimize the shipping/transportation costs between the firms.[5] Workers would follow, as would businesses catering to those workers, such that a city would form. The city would grow until such time as the advantageous transportation costs began to increase. At that point, land would have to be dedicated to transportation, which would raise rents on all other land, and the city would reach its maximum size.

Both Alonso and Mills, however, assumed that these regions would be homogeneous with respect to all social and environmental conditions, and would be grouped under a single jurisdiction. The same set of institutions would govern all portions of the CBD and residential areas, and there would be no variation of amenities between different places. Historical settlement patterns, widely varying amenities between neighborhoods within cities, and varying governmental systems within metropolitan regions demonstrate that such a pattern was not likely.[6]

More likely, an urban region would be made up of various jurisdictions with different rules, different amenities, and different provisions of public goods. With different communities within one region offering a variety of different public goods and environmental and social conditions, residents would surely choose locations based on more than commuting costs. This realization complicated the assessment of commuting costs, but also opened the possibility of observing the preferences of residents for public goods like environmental quality.

Tiebout's landmark 1956 paper was the first to suggest that residential mobility in a region of multiple cities created a "competitive market" that enabled policymakers to observe how much residents were willing to pay for public goods. Under the Tiebout model, residents of a region did not consider only the distance to the CBD in deciding where to live, but also amenities including the basket of public goods, like environmental quality and social stability, provided by each jurisdiction.[7] People could "vote with their feet" and decide to live in whichever community best met their preferences for public goods, and reveal their willingness to pay for such public goods through local taxes. If a clean environment was important to people, they might opt to pay higher taxes to live in a cleaner community rather than a dirtier one with lower taxes. Or, if low costs were important, people could opt to deal with high crime in order to have lower rents and taxes.

Specifically with respect to environmental quality, Ridker and Henning suggested that, not only can mobility and willingness to pay taxes reveal preferences, but that real-estate prices can as well.[8] The model they propose measures the variations between housing prices in areas with higher levels of air pollution and those with lower levels of pollution. Controlling for other exogenous variables, such as school quality, access to highways and shopping, taxes, and crime rates, Ridker and Henning find that air pollution differences can relate to substantial variation in home prices. Such analyses are typically called "hedonic" because they focus on pleasant and unpleasant factors of houses and location rather than market structures.[9]

These hedonic methods have been used to analyze value incorporated into real-estate prices in proximity to environmental amenities, such as open space,[10] forested areas,[11] and waterfront areas,[12] and also in proximity to environmental disamenities, like Superfund sites,[13] hazardous waste facilities,[14] and swamplands.[15] Hedonic models have also been extensively used to measure how housing prices incorporate air pollution. Smith and Huang conducted a meta-analysis of 37 hedonic property value studies related to air quality, published over a 20-year span.[16] They found relative agreement that the wealthy tend to be more willing to pay for air quality (as is expected for all normal goods), and the hedonic models they reviewed consistently showed that home prices tend to be higher in areas with better air quality. These results suggest that more sustainable cities will be more wealthy cities.

## Residential mobility

However, for any of these hedonic models for pricing environmental quality to function, residents need to be mobile. Residents can only reveal their preferences to the extent that they are able to move to new locations. Yet, it is on this point that the Tiebout model has been most criticized, for Tiebout's mobility assumptions are quite strict. He assumed that people could move at any time, without incurring relocation expenses; that residents were fully aware of the full set of public goods provided in each potential relocation community; that there was, essentially, a full range of possible choices in public goods provisions within a region; and that there was no spillover of public goods from one jurisdiction to another.[17] It is worth noting explicitly that although Tiebout's conception required a region within which cities could compete, he did not consider the possibility that some cities within regions could free ride on other cities within the same region, a possibility raised in Chapter 6. Most problematically, an assumption of full and costless mobility is clearly at odds with observed patterns of settlement—residents have some level of mobility, but moving is costly, and ability to move is affected by wealth (and, as mentioned before, other constraints).

Nevertheless, Tiebout-type model predictions have been shown to be relevant when considering the effect of environmental quality on settlement patterns. Been and Gupta found that when environmental hazards were sited in a community those with the ability to shoulder the costs of relocation tended to move away.[18] Conversely, Banzhaf and Walsh found that when the environment in a community improved, real-estate prices also tended to rise, signaling that new residents were willing to pay more to live in a community that possessed less environmental disamenity.[19]

Thus, the Tiebout model is not off-base, but it is not contextualized. People may be immobile for a variety of reasons. They may not have the resources to manage relocation expenses, or they may live close to family and therefore feel it necessary to remain in neighborhoods that do not have high levels of environmental quality.[20] In addition, since it has been shown that people are willing to pay more for environmental quality, some may not have the income or wealth to afford to live in communities with high levels of environmental quality or high levels of sustainability more broadly. There are, therefore, at least two key constraints on mobility—first, some are constrained from moving to communities with additional public goods because they either cannot afford to move or cannot afford to move to a community that would better satisfy their individual preferences; and second, some may have other living preferences or constraints that dominate those having to do with public goods like environmental quality.

Neither full mobility (as Tiebout assumed in 1956) nor full immobility (as assumed in our EJ ABM up until now) is a realistic assumption; do these assumptions damage the value of these models? Fortunately, there is some empirical guidance with respect to how frequently people move.[21] Lee and Waddell found that in the Seattle metro area, about 35% of households moved within a five-year period.[22] Using data from California and Texas, Ferreira noted that mobility varies by age, with younger residents more likely to relocate in a given year.[23] In their sample, homeownership had an even greater effect on mobility: only 7% of homeowners in their sample moved in a given year, while about 25% of renters moved. This is similar to Dieleman's 2001 findings.[24] Using a national sample, Dieleman found that the young, and especially renters, are more likely to relocate, and that the larger the household, the less likely is relocation. Dieleman also found variability by region, noting that about 20% of residents relocated in the South in a given year, while only about 10% of residents in the Pacific Northwest did so.

Adding more granularity across time, Strassmann assessed home turnover rates from each US Decennial Census from 1970 to 1990.[25] In 1970, 18.8% of US residents had moved in the previous year; in 1980, 18.9%; and in 1990, 17.4%. Strassmann also found wide variability in mobility by city in the 1990 Census, ranging from low-mobility regions like New York, Cleveland, and Philadelphia (where respectively 11.3%, 12.0%, and 12.2% of residents had relocated in the previous year), to high-mobility regions like Houston, Seattle and Miami (23.1%, 21.7%, and 20% respectively had relocated). Unfortunately, aside from some consensus that renters move more frequently as a result of escalating rents, there is little definitive evidence for why most people move—most likely, people move for a wide variety of different reasons.

## Modeling residential mobility

As presented, the EJ ABM includes two types of agents: firms (polluting or non-polluting); and residents (of majority or minority "race," and with their economic-class status). These agents basically follow the decision rules described in Chapter 3, except that we implement residential mobility for analysis in this chapter. Because there are so many reasons why people move, in our EJ ABM we modeled the decision to search for a better location as random.

Although we note in other chapters that firms may choose to locate for a variety of different reasons, throughout this chapter we simplify firm decisions and model all firms as selecting the plot within their choice set that has the lowest price. This allows us to focus attention on the residential choice, which some EJ analysts consider key to observed environmentally unjust outcomes.

### Residents' mobility assumptions

Both initial residential choice and the relocation behavior of resident agents in the mobility model function just as initial residential choice was described in Chapter 3. The mobility difference is that at each time step some proportion of already located resident agents are randomly selected to consider relocation. At each time step, depending upon the proportion selected, the appropriate number of resident agents is assigned a variable indicating that they are potential movers, and these potential movers then reenter the residential choice process described in Chapter 3.

As in other chapters, we implement a regional population growth rate of 5%. This implies that there will be two categories of residents seeking locations: Those who entered in a previous time and are considering relocating (i.e., existing residents), and those who are newly introduced to the simulation and looking for an initial location (i.e., new residents). New residents are seeking locations based on the residential choice rule in Chapter 3, and they are not part of the calculation regarding potential relocation.

Existing residents who are selected to consider relocation will only relocate if they find an affordable plot with a higher utility score than the plot upon which they are currently residing.

As an example, if the assumption is that 25% of residents consider relocating at each time step, then 25% of both types of existing resident agents (minority and majority) will be chosen at random to reenter the residential choice location function. The selected residents then scan the environment for open plots that satisfy their price and similarity preferences. If any of the potential plots that the resident considers have a higher utility score than its current plot (see Chapter 3, Equation 3.1), residents move to the plot that has the highest utility score within their choice set. If none of the plots in their choice set has a higher utility score than the plot upon which they currently reside, they do not relocate. In the 25% residential mobility scenario, the 75% of residents not randomly chosen remain in their current locations. This relocation procedure occurs at each time step throughout the simulation. Relocation is implemented afresh at each time step forward; residents who were selected previously for relocation can be reselected for relocation during the simulation because the selection of residents to consider moving is random.

### Scenarios

We ran a total of 14 different scenarios to test the effect of residential mobility along with similarity preferences. The first model was, essentially, a pure Tiebout world. At each time step, 100% of the residents considered relocation and there were no racial similarity preferences. The only constraint on moving was the price constraint. The rest of the scenarios, as shown in Table 7.1, vary mobility roughly according to the regional extremes noted by Strassmann, at 12% and 25%,[26] sometimes using each value for both sets of residents and sometimes making one group more mobile than the other. We also varied similarity preferences. We ran a set of scenarios with no similarity preferences, with both groups choosing based on an 80% similarity preference, and a set of scenarios with majorities using an 80% similarity preference and minorities using a 50% similarity preference.[27] Table 7.1 summarizes experimental scenarios and associated scenario numbers used in this chapter.

### Model outcomes

For each of the scenarios we track the average environmental quality level, both overall and for each race group. We ran each scenario 200 times (with 70 time steps per trial, as before). Thus, we can compare average majority quality with minority quality in these different scenarios. We also calculated a quality gap by subtracting average minority quality level from average majority quality level (especially see Table 7.2).

Table 7.1 Mobility scenarios

| Similarity preferences | Mobility | | | | | |
| --- | --- | --- | --- | --- | --- | --- |
| | No difference between MA and MI | | | | Difference between MA and MI | |
| | 100% for both | No mobility for both | 12% for both | 25% for both | 12% for MA; 25% for MI | 25% for MA; 12% for MI |
| No similarity preference | Scenario 1 | Scenario 2 | Scenario 3 | Scenario 4 | | |
| Both groups hold 80% | | Scenario 5 | Scenario 6 | Scenario 7 | Scenario 8 | Scenario 9 |
| Majorities hold 80%, minorities hold 50% | | Scenario 10 | Scenario 11 | Scenario 12 | Scenario 13 | Scenario 14 |

## Impact of residential mobility on EJ outcomes

As has generally been the case throughout this modeling enterprise (and in the empirical literature), we commonly see an environmental quality gap, with minorities usually living with worse environmental quality than majorities. As can be seen in the figures below, in each scenario minority residents live with worse environmental quality most of the time.

However, mobility has a complicated effect, especially in conjunction with similarity preferences. Two important outcomes:

- When minorities have a lower similarity preference than majorities (50% for minorities, and 80% for majorities), higher mobility tends to result in a decreased environmental quality gap and higher overall quality for minorities.
- When both have a high similarity preference, any level of mobility seems to improve average minority quality relative to no mobility, but the same is true for majorities, and thus with high similarity preferences mobility does not alter the environmental quality gap very much.

Figure 7.1 shows the results of the four trials with no similarity preferences. The top left figure is the closest approximation of the Tiebout model, in which residents have no similarity preference and are fully mobile when there is a better plot for them (and, as in all simulations in this chapter, all firms choose locations to minimize costs). This is contrasted with no mobility on the top right (scenario 2), and 12% (scenario 3) and 25% (scenario 4) mobility along the bottom. In each case, the environmental quality gap is approximately the same; however, overall quality levels for both groups are higher when there is mobility than when there is no mobility.

With the no-mobility assumption, environmental quality levels never reach 70 for either majorities or minorities during the simulation. Thus, although mobility does not change the quality *gap* much with no similarity preferences, mobility appears to improve overall quality for residents, but only to a point. With 25% mobility, overall quality for both groups is slightly higher than with 12% mobility, but also higher than with 100% mobility. While complete stability is not ideal for quality, there appears to be some point of mobility where more stability is relatively advantageous.

Figure 7.2 compares scenarios for the three mobility assumptions (0%, 12%, and 25%) between cases with both groups at 80% similarity preference, and cases with minorities relaxing their similarity preference to 50% while majorities maintain an 80% preference. Overall, regardless of ethnicity/race, residents seem to enjoy higher environmental quality with either mobility assumption than in the scenario without mobility. However, when residents hold 80% similarity preferences, mobility improves majorities' environmental quality quite a bit more than that of minorities (scenarios 5, 6, and 7). The gap becomes bigger with 25% mobility than with 12%

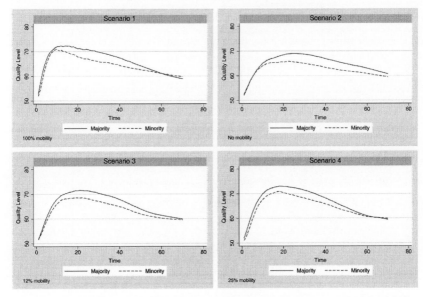

*Figure 7.1* Mobility experiments with no similarity preferences

Note: In all scenarios, there are no residential similarity preferences. In scenario 1 there is complete mobility (similar to a Tiebout, 1956, model). In scenario 2 there is no mobility (consistent with the previous chapters). In scenario 3 mobility is randomly assigned to 12% of residents each time step, and in scenario 4 to 25% each step. Scenario numbers in this figure correspond to scenario numbers in Table 7.1.

mobility (compare scenarios 6 and 7). Thus, majorities are the ones who are appreciably advantaged by mobility.

A significant contrast is found when minorities relax their similarity preferences to 50% while majorities hold an 80% similarity preference (scenarios 10, 11, and 12). In this case, mobility leads both groups to enjoy higher environmental quality than in the scenario without mobility,[28] and the EJ gap is significantly reduced—with some periods during which there is no gap.

Figure 7.3 contrasts using the same similarity preferences as in Figure 7.2, but with mobility varying between the two groups—with minorities being more mobile than majorities (25% to 12%), or with minorities being less mobile than majorities (12% to 25%).[29] Here we find quite similar patterns to those observed in Figure 7.2 (outcomes for scenarios 8, 9, 13, and 14 are very similar to 6, 7, 11, and 12). Differential mobility for each racial group does not bring much difference in environmental quality between majorities and minorities.

These results suggest strongly that it is—again—racial similarity preference that is a more important driver of environmental quality gaps. Mobility can improve the situation for both groups, but relaxation of the similarity preference is much more important to the quality gap than either the level of mobility or which group is more mobile.

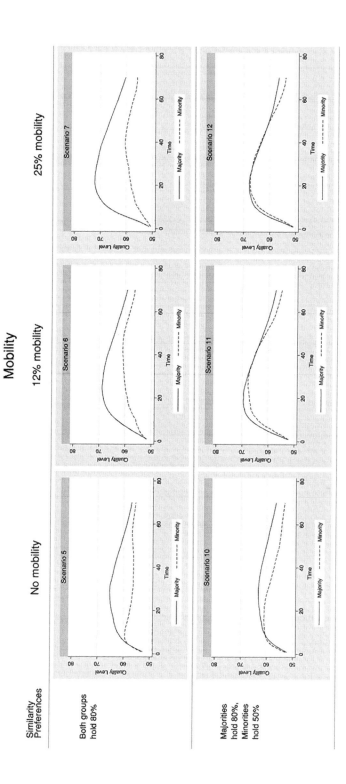

*Figure 7.2* Scenarios varying mobility, holding similarity preference constant across rows
Note: Each labeled proportion of residential mobility applies for both groups.

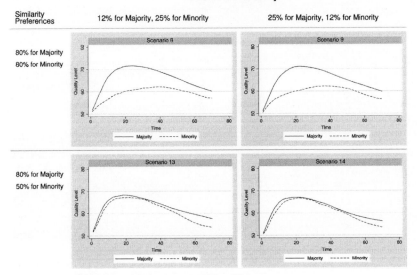

*Figure 7.3* Scenarios varying both similarity preferences and mobility across minorities and majorities

Finally, in Table 7.2 we show the size of the environmental quality gap (average majority quality minus average minority quality) every 10 time steps from time steps 20 to 70. The larger the number in each cell in this table, the greater the quality advantage that majority residents have, and the smaller (larger in magnitude) a negative value is, the greater the quality advantage for minorities. Regardless of mobility scenarios, quality gaps become significantly larger when both types of resident hold an 80% similarity preference (scenarios 5–9).

Looking at the complete set of scenarios, the results point to several key trends. Mobility appears to have at most a marginal effect on the environmental quality *gap*, but residents may live with higher *overall* quality when they are mobile, particularly if there are no similarity preferences (scenarios 3 and 4). The latter outcome supports Tiebout-type models, but the former tends to contradict the assumption that minority mobility is a key to environmental justice outcomes.

In fact, when both sets of residents hold equally high similarity preferences, increased mobility appears actually to increase the size of the environmental quality gap. In all of the scenarios where both groups chose locations based on 80% similarity preferences (scenarios 5–9), the gap started quite large, though it gradually lessened as time stepped forward. Further, in these scenarios, mobility did not have much of an effect on the overall level of minority quality, but majority quality was much higher overall than when residents were immobile.

The environmental quality *gap* was largest throughout the trials with high similarity preferences whenever both sets of residents had high mobility (25%) and lowest when both sets of residents were immobile. This latter point indicates that the assumption of no mobility, which has been maintained in the preceding chapters, does not magnify the extent of the environmental quality gap in the scenarios analyzed therein. In contrast, in the scenarios where minorities had a 50% similarity preference (scenarios 10–14), mobility tended both to decrease the extent of the quality gap and—perhaps more importantly—improve overall levels of minority quality.

Through the large majority of all scenarios, including the Tiebout model (with no similarity preference and 100% mobility for each group), we see an environmental quality gap. At various points in some scenarios (e.g., scenario 11), minorities have slightly higher quality levels than majorities, but it is much more common to observe majorities with higher quality levels, and often much higher levels (of the 84 results reported in Table 7.2, only six are negative and all of these are small in magnitude, ranging between -0.03 and -0.82).

That we see an environmental quality gap even with 100% mobility for both groups *and no similarity preference* is an important result.[30] It suggests that even when residents "vote with their feet," at least for on-average-poorer minorities those votes are constrained and likely result in suboptimal social outcomes.

*Table 7.2* Quality gaps by scenario and time step

| | | Quality gap over time | | | | | |
|---|---|---|---|---|---|---|---|
| | | *t = 20* | *t = 30* | *t = 40* | *t = 50* | *t = 60* | *t = 70* |
| Similarity preference 0% | Scenario 1 | 3.36 | 3.90 | 3.03 | 1.62 | -0.03 | -0.82 |
| | Scenario 2 | 2.90 | 3.71 | 3.55 | 2.88 | 2.10 | 1.29 |
| | Scenario 3 | 2.89 | 3.29 | 2.93 | 1.96 | 1.10 | 0.37 |
| | Scenario 4 | 2.49 | 3.09 | 2.42 | 1.42 | 0.35 | -0.43 |
| Similarity preference 80% for both groups | Scenario 5 | 6.93 | 8.74 | 7.24 | 4.65 | 2.28 | 1.53 |
| | Scenario 6 | 9.22 | 8.02 | 5.83 | 3.56 | 3.28 | 2.79 |
| | Scenario 7 | 13.89 | 11.95 | 8.87 | 7.04 | 5.85 | 4.32 |
| | Scenario 8 | 11.14 | 9.44 | 6.72 | 5.01 | 3.69 | 3.09 |
| | Scenario 9 | 10.88 | 8.63 | 5.72 | 3.80 | 4.00 | 3.40 |
| Similarity preference 80% majority 50% minority | Scenario 10 | 1.77 | 3.77 | 4.92 | 4.99 | 4.08 | 3.36 |
| | Scenario 11 | 2.25 | 0.43 | -0.10 | 0.93 | 2.18 | 2.35 |
| | Scenario 12 | 0.38 | -0.14 | -0.30 | 0.23 | 2.00 | 2.62 |
| | Scenario 13 | 1.16 | 0.35 | 0.99 | 1.78 | 3.78 | 3.88 |
| | Scenario 14 | 0.48 | 0.31 | 0.77 | 0.80 | 2.20 | 2.81 |

Note: See Table 7.1 for scenario descriptions. Positive values indicate that majority quality is greater than minority quality. Negative values indicate that minority quality is greater than majority quality.

## Discussion

In this chapter, residential mobility has been posited as a way to assess the value of public goods, and potentially as a way to ameliorate the EJ problem. However, our results imply that residential mobility is not the key to the environmental injustice problem. Considering Figure 7.1, the level of mobility is essentially irrelevant.

Been and Gupta, for example, argue that residential mobility explains the gap when the minority is poorer on average, because when a hazard is sited nearby, wealthy residents will leave.[31] Property values will decline and poorer residents will move in, and those poor residents will be disproportionately minority (since minorities are disproportionately poor). Under our approximation of a Tiebout model, with residents having complete mobility and no similarity preference, but with minority incomes drawn from a poorer distribution, we do see the emergence of an environmental quality gap. However, this gap is generally quite small, only reaching a meaningful difference from about time steps 20 to 50. The gap that emerges under this scenario is dwarfed by gaps that emerge when minorities have a high similarity preference, regardless of how mobile they are, though *overall* quality levels are much higher when residents are mobile than when they are not, particularly when there are no similarity preferences. However, the effect of mobility changes when residents have similarity preferences: at a comparatively lower similarity preference, mobility appears both to close the gap and allow minorities to live with higher quality than without mobility; however, some results indicate that at some interactions between similarity preferences and mobility, mobility may actually exacerbate the environmental quality gap.

These results complicate efforts both to hedonically estimate the value of public goods like environmental quality, and also to consider how to ameliorate the EJ problem. That we see very different effects of mobility, depending upon the level of the minority similarity preference, suggests that the effect of mobility might not be easily understood independently of other preferences. These results imply complex interactions. That mobility has different effects depending on the level of minority similarity preference also provides a good justification for the use of ABMs to understand complex social processes.

The results imply that the market value of public goods likely cannot be assessed simply by noting the relative prices of residences in neighborhoods with different public goods baskets. Unless also controlling for racial and ethnic composition of the neighborhood, comparing relative prices could be problematic, for the price differences might be reflecting segregative preferences, and not public goods provision. This could mean we overestimate—and underestimate—the value of certain public goods because we are actually including segregation as a confound in our calculations.

These results also call into question the extent to which encouraging mobility could address the EJ problem. If minorities hold high similarity preferences or, more problematically, if majority neighborhoods exclude minority residents, then more mobility could actually exacerbate the environmental quality gap. However, if communities overall are less race aware, and/or minorities are more open to living in more racially balanced communities, then a more mobile population might decrease the environmental quality gap.

This latter result suggests both an empirical hypothesis and a potential policy implication. For empirical research, our results suggest that in areas where similarity preferences are comparatively low (perhaps observable as areas where there is comparatively less segregation) and where residents are more mobile, we would expect to see a much smaller environmental quality gap than in areas with high similarity preferences (perhaps evidenced by high levels of observed segregation) where residents are not especially mobile. Thus, for example, we might expect a low aggregate environmental quality gap in a region like the Seattle area (with high mobility and low levels of segregation), and a larger gap in a city like Cleveland, which has low mobility and relatively high levels of segregation.

If this result is empirically validated, there would be policy implications for EJ and sustainability analyses. Most clearly, some cities and regions might find it beneficial to try to increase residential mobility, particularly if segregation is not a particular problem in the area. This could be done through tax breaks for moving costs, or even subsidization of moving expenses to encourage a more mobile population. If segregation is high, these policy tools may not work, but as previous chapters have also indicated, if similarity preferences are lowered, then the environmental quality gap is likely to decline (at which point increasing mobility may be helpful). While we do not know of a solution to the segregation problem, cities may be able to take steps to ensure that exclusion is not the root cause of the EJ problem by ensuring minority access to communities though housing assistance and by discouraging housing discrimination.

The results reported in this chapter suggest that mobility may be an important factor to understand in explaining and addressing levels of environmental injustice, levels of environmental quality, and urban sustainability. However, they also indicate that mobility can only be understood in the context of the broader social preferences of a community and perhaps even a region.

## Notes

1 Generally speaking, public goods exhibit either non-rivalry in consumption (more than one person can consume the same unit of the good without degrading its benefit to other consumers, up to the point of congestion), or non-excludability (given that a public good is provided within an area, those within the area cannot

be excluded from its consumption), or both. Either of these characteristics makes it difficult for a market to reveal the value of the public good. Also, it should be noted that "public goods" can also be bad, as long as they are non-rival and/or non-excludable.

2 Johann Heinrich von Thünen, *Der Isolierte Staat*, trans. Peter Hall (Oxford: Pergamon Press, 1966).

3 William Alonso, *Location and Land Use: Toward a General Theory of Land Rent* (Cambridge, MA: Harvard University Press, 1964).

4 Edwin S. Mills, "An Aggregative Model of Resource Allocation in a Metropolitan Area," *The American Economic Review* 57, no. 2 (1967): 197–210.

5 For firms, a vertical relation exists if one set of firms provides inputs to another. For example, companies that makes car seats are vertically related to a company that makes cars.

6 Gordon H. Hanson, "Scale Economies and the Geographic Concentration of Industry," *Journal of Economic Geography* 1, no. 3 (2001): 255–76.

7 Charles Tiebout, "A Pure Theory of Local Expenditure," *Journal of Political Economy* 64, no. 5 (1956): 416–24, www.jstor.org/stable/1826343.

8 Ronald G. Ridker and John A. Henning, "The Determinants of Residential Property Values with Special Reference to Air Pollution," *The Review of Economics and Statistics* 49, no. 2 (1967): 246–57.

9 The root word for "hedonic" is the Greek word for "pleasure."

10 Elena Irwin, "The Effects of Open Space on Residential Property Values," *Land Economics* 78, no. 4 (2002): 465–80.

11 G. Garrod and K. Willis, "Valuing Goods' Characteristics: An Application of the Hedonic Price Method to Environmental Attributes," *Journal of Environmental Management* 34, no. 1 (1992): 59–76.

12 Christopher G. Leggett and Nancy E. Bockstael, "Evidence of the Effects of Water Quality on Residential Land Prices," *Journal of Environmental Economics and Management* 39, no. 2 (2000): 121–44.

13 John A. Hird, "Environmental Policy and Equity: The Case of Superfund," *Journal of Policy Analysis and Management* 12, no. 2 (1993): 323–43.

14 Janet E. Kohlhase, "The Impact of Toxic Waste Sites on Housing Values," *Journal of Urban Economics* 30, no. 1 (1991): 1–26.

15 Garrod and Willis, "Valuing Goods' Characteristics."

16 V. Kerry Smith and Ju-Chin Huang, "Can Markets Value Air Quality? A Meta-Analysis of Hedonic Property Value Models," *Journal of Political Economy* 103, no. 1 (1995): 209–27.

17 Tiebout, "A Pure Theory of Local Expenditure."

18 Vicki Been and Francis Gupta, "Coming to the Nuisance or Going to the Barrios? A Longitudinal Analysis of Environmental Justice Claims," *Ecology Law Quarterly* 24, no. 1 (1997): 1–56.

19 H. Spencer Banzhaf and Randall P. Walsh, "Do People Vote with their Feet? An Empirical Test of Tiebout's Mechanism," *American Economic Review* 98, no. 3 (2008): 843–63.

20 Gwen Ottinger, *Refining Expertise: How Responsible Engineers Subvert Environmental Justice Challenges* (New York: NYU Press, 2013).

21 Here we limit this discussion to observed mobility trends in the United States. In some countries mobility is much more constrained, and the earlier versions of the model may be more relevant.

22 Brian H.Y. Lee and Paul Waddell, "Residential Mobility and Location Choice: A Nested Logit Model with Sampling of Alternatives," *Transportation* 37, no. 4 (2010): 587–601.

23 Fernando Ferreira, "You Can Take it with You: Proposition 13 Tax Benefits, Residential Mobility, and Willingness to Pay for Housing Amenities," *Journal of Public Economics* 94 (2010): 661–73.

24 Frans M. Dieleman, "Modelling Residential Mobility: A Review of Recent Trends in Research," *Journal of Housing and the Built Environment* 16, no. 3–4 (2001): 249–65.

25 W. Paul Strassmann, "Mobility and Affordability in US Housing," *Urban Studies* 37, no. 1 (2000): 113–26.

26 Ibid.

27 William A.V. Clark, "Residential Preferences and Residential Choices in a Multiethnic Context," *Demography* 29, no. 3 (1992): 451–66.

28 Quality for both groups follows a downward trend in the latter time periods due to the constrained choice sets—as more residents exist in the world, there are fewer plots available and thus there are more residents located on plots with lower quality, bringing down the average overall quality level.

29 Since minorities, being poorer, are more likely to be renters, greater mobility among minorities may be more realistic.

30 It is possible that these results are caused or exacerbated by the fact that minorities are poorer, but we cannot know that for sure without testing. One lesson of nonlinear dynamics is that it is hard to sort out specific causes without estimation.

31 Been and Gupta, "Coming to the Nuisance or Going to the Barrios?"

# References

Alonso, William. *Location and Land Use: Toward a General Theory of Land Rent.* Cambridge, MA: Harvard University Press, 1964.

Banzhaf, H. Spencer and Randall P. Walsh. "Do People Vote with their Feet? An Empirical Test of Tiebout's Mechanism." *American Economic Review* 98, no. 3 (2008): 843–863.

Been, Vicki and Francis Gupta. "Coming to the Nuisance or Going to the Barrios? A Longitudinal Analysis of Environmental Justice Claims." *Ecology Law Quarterly* 24, no. 1 (1997): 1–56.

Clark, William A.V. "Residential Preferences and Residential Choices in a Multiethnic Context." *Demography* 29, no. 3 (1992): 451–466.

Dieleman, Frans M. "Modelling Residential Mobility: A Review of Recent Trends in Research." *Journal of Housing and the Built Environment* 16, no. 3–4 (2001): 249–265.

Ferreira, Fernando. "You Can Take it with You: Proposition 13 Tax Benefits, Residential Mobility, and Willingness to Pay for Housing Amenities." *Journal of Public Economics* 94, (2010): 661–673.

Garrod, G. and K. Willis. "Valuing Goods' Characteristics: An Application of the Hedonic Price Method to Environmental Attributes." *Journal of Environmental Management* 34, no. 1 (1992): 59–76.

Hanson, Gordon H. "Scale Economies and the Geographic Concentration of Industry." *Journal of Economic Geography* 1, no. 3 (2001): 255–276.

Hird, John A. "Environmental Policy and Equity: The Case of Superfund." *Journal of Policy Analysis and Management* 12, no. 2 (1993): 323–343.

Irwin, Elena. "The Effects of Open Space on Residential Property Values." *Land Economics* 78, no. 4 (2002): 465–480.

Kohlhase, Janet E. "The Impact of Toxic Waste Sites on Housing Values." *Journal of Urban Economics* 30, no. 1 (1991): 1–26.

Lee, Brian H.Y. and Paul Waddell. "Residential Mobility and Location Choice: A Nested Logit Model with Sampling of Alternatives." *Transportation* 37, no. 4 (2010): 587–601.

Legget, Christopher G. and Nancy E. Bockstael. "Evidence of the Effects of Water Quality on Residential Land Prices." *Journal of Environmental Economics and Management* 39, no. 2 (2000): 121–144.

Mills, Edwin S. "An Aggregative Model of Resource Allocation in a Metropolitan Area." *The American Economic Review* 57, no. 2 (1967): 197–210.

Ottinger, Gwen. *Refining Expertise: How Responsible Engineers Subvert Environmental Justice Challenges*. New York: NYU Press, 2013.

Ridker, Ronald G. and John A. Henning. "The Determinants of Residential Property Values with Special Reference to Air Pollution." *The Review of Economics and Statistics* 49, no. 2 (1967): 246–257.

Smith, V. Kerry and Ju-Chin Huang. "Can Markets Value Air Quality? A Meta-analysis of Hedonic Property Value Models." *Journal of Political Economy* 103, no. 1 (1995): 209–227.

Strassmann, W. Paul. "Mobility and Affordability in US Housing." *Urban Studies* 37, no. 1 (2000): 113–126.

Thünen, Johann Heinrich von. *Der Isolierte Staat*, translated by Peter Hall. First edn. Oxford: Pergamon Press, 1966.

Tiebout, Charles. "A Pure Theory of Local Expenditure." *Journal of Political Economy* 64, no. 5 (1956): 416–424. www.jstor.org/stable/1826343.

US Census Bureau. *Mover Rate Reaches Record Low, Census Bureau Reports*. Newsroom. November 15, 2011. www.census.gov/newsroom/releases/archives/mobility_of_the_population/cb11-193.html (accessed February 16, 2012).

# 8 Local zoning[1]

Besides a vicious intention by decision makers in siting polluting facilities (the intentional model of environmental justice, or EJ),[2] at least three other competing but non-exclusive explanations of EJ outcomes have been discussed: market dynamics, political power, and local land-use policies. In this chapter we focus on local land-use policies by adding zoning models to the EJ ABM. Zoning not only has the potential to correct or prevent environmental injustice, but to enhance urban sustainability overall.

As we noted earlier, local zoning affects siting decisions of firms and residents in cities. So, its relation to EJ outcomes requires further attention. There are some studies that investigate the link between collective action and local land-use *decisions*, usually focusing on NIMBY (not in my back yard) action, and the potential of powerful actors to keep undesirable land uses out of high-status communities.[3] However, previous EJ research has been relatively silent on the role of local land-use *policies* themselves,[4] despite the importance they may have for EJ outcomes, both as causal factors and potentially as mitigators for existing problems.[5] This is quite surprising considering that efforts to address the EJ problem have been developed by considering the spatial distribution and collocation of environmental disamenities and low socioeconomic status,[6] and that zoning policies result in inherently spatial land-use structures. Further, most American cities utilize some set of zoning mechanisms for local land use, and they will surely be a key component of initiatives toward creating sustainable cities.

Here we modify the base EJ ABM to include two simplified governmental zoning structures. As before, we model an artificial city in which residents and firms dynamically interact during their siting decisions, and we explore the environmental consequences, especially for the minority compared to the majority. Through this effort, we can assess the difference, if any, that well-intentioned zoning policies can have on EJ outcomes, especially in providing a policy tool to decrease disparities, and pose hypotheses for future empirical assessments of local land-use policies and EJ outcomes. These analyses should also provide early insight into the use of zoning for other sustainability goals. We focus on two primary contrasts: 1 EJ outcomes *without* versus *with* zoning, and 2 EJ outcomes using a *proactive* versus a *reactive* zoning policy.

## Why local zoning in EJ research?

In the United States, local zoning is a common tool of land-use policy.[7] It has been used for various purposes such as promoting economic development and sheltering residential populations from industrial disamenities. Thus, it is sometimes intended to affect residential environmental quality, and it may have consequences for EJ and sustainable cities.

In the next subsection we provide a brief sketch of typical zoning practices (for a more detailed discussion, see e.g., Fischel[8]).

### Local zoning in the United States

Zoning restrictions can be articulated in two ways: 1 when certain uses are omitted from the description of a particular zone, such a use is prohibited in that zone; or 2 a zone's description can explicitly prohibit a particular use. For example, "R-zones" refer to residential zones, and R-zone codes can include details of permitted uses such as single-family residences, height limits, lot sizes, and so on. R-zones can be further classified as R-1, R-2, R-3, and so forth, with different permitted residential uses, and the lower-number zones can be logically nested within higher ones. In other words, R-2 can include permitted uses for R-1 zones plus additional uses. R-3 includes R-2 uses and additional uses, etc. Similarly, "C-zones" specify commercial uses, and some uses permitted in R-zones can also be nested within C-zones. "M-zones" specify manufacturing or industrial uses. They may explicitly say that residential uses are not permitted. See Woodworth, Gump, and Forrester for simplified zoning-code examples.[9]

While zoning is one of the most widely used local land-use regulations, there are localities that have no explicit zoning regulations. With a strong free-market predilection, for example, Houston, Texas, is the largest US city without zoning.[10] Even in Houston, however, rather than a fully unfettered land market, other land-use control structures such as homeowner associations and deed restrictions are used to segment land uses.[11]

Zoning regulation is exercised within what is called the "police power" of the state, meaning the state's ability to regulate to protect the public's health, safety, and welfare.[12] However, it is not straightforward to pinpoint which segment of "the public" zoning intends to protect, nor to define exactly what the public's "health, safety, and welfare" imply. Also, zoning laws have evolved and have been open to different interpretations by decision makers and planners at different times.

For example, with the rise of the smart-growth movement and new urbanism, the traditional zoning system has been criticized via the claim that it does not properly reflect demographic changes—such as urban sprawl—that have exposed shortcomings of the old system.[13] Recent zoning reform proposals (e.g., the smart-growth and form-based[14] approaches) share a common understanding that traditional land-development policies can prohibit more compact and mixed-use neighborhoods that can promote physically active communities.[15]

Next we explain two distinct possible motives for zoning in order to gain some insight into its integration with environmental policy and environmental justice.

### Competing motives for zoning

#### Exclusionary motives

Some argue that zoning is used for the malicious purpose of segregation—or at least historically was, which could create path dependencies that explain some current inequities. The *exclusionary* rationale for zoning refers to "a deliberate desire to exclude lower-income and/or minority households from the jurisdiction."[16] Exclusion can be based on pure racial prejudice or the use of race as a proxy for neighborhood quality—for example, for fiscal purposes.

Two very early examples that illustrate this zoning idea date from 1885, when San Francisco prohibited laundries in residential areas, and 1916, with New York City's Zoning Resolution.[17] It is argued that both had an exclusionary intent to segregate certain social groups: the former attempted to restrict Chinese people from living in white neighborhoods, and the latter created an exclusive zone to "keep the immigrant factory workers out of sight of the wealthy women shopping on Fifth Avenue."[18]

#### Fiscal motives

Zoning can be created solely for a fiscal purpose,[19] but some argue such use inevitably has an exclusionary implication for certain social groups. That is, fiscal zoning may attract property owners with high tax-to-service ratios, and thus exclude the poor or the racial minorities who might reduce property values in exclusive residential areas.[20] Such considerations may also be relevant to zoning for sustainability.

#### Protective motives

Others argue that zoning can be beneficent, intended to separate citizens from negative externalities of production, with an unintended consequence of housing markets responding accordingly, which causes segregation by economic status (note the clear links between this argument and the economic rationales for environmentally unjust outcomes discussed in earlier chapters).

The rationale of *externality* zoning policies is to minimize the impact of production externalities on residents by separating arguably incompatible land uses (e.g., residential, commercial, and industrial). For example, waste-related facilities can be sited in areas designated as M-zones, intended to buffer residents from harm. However, Maantay argues that somehow noxious uses tend to be concentrated in poor and minority areas, "due to the re-zoning of more affluent and less minority industrial neighborhoods to other uses."[21]

### Evidence regarding motives for zoning

In a review of empirical studies that examine these rationales,[22] Ihlanfeldt concludes that while there is a paucity of evidence on the motive for zoning, "there is consensus across studies that fiscal considerations frequently motivate restrictive land-use regulations. Evidence on the externality and exclusionary motives, on the other hand, is mixed across studies."[23] It is not easy to separate these motives of local planners or localities as they make zoning decisions, and they most likely are intertwined to some degree.

### Effects of zoning

As early as 1968, though critical of what it saw as emerging misuses of zoning, the American Society of Planning Officials stated, "zoning has done much more good than harm."[24] Schilling and Linton argue:

> The exclusion of intensive industrial and commercial uses has undoubtedly improved the quality of life in many communities. ... [However, z]oning is still subject to considerable tensions involving social and environmental justice, such as the disproportionate number of waste production and waste-disposal uses in districts bordering or including poor residential populations.[25]

Relatedly, in the urban literature zoning has gained much scholarly attention due to the argument that it results in exclusion of lower-income households from suburban communities by artificially inflating the cost of housing.[26] A large number of studies thus have examined the consequence of urban zoning regulations on housing market inflation,[27] income and racial segregation,[28] or labor-market imbalance.[29]

While limited, there is some research that explicitly analyzes the connection between land-use control through zoning and EJ outcomes.[30] For example, Maantay argues that zoning policy has an inevitable connection to environmental injustice, but the underlying zoning designations and subsequent changes have not been properly factored into EJ analysis.[31] Since zoning policy regulates land-use types and densities, intentionally or not it also governs potential environmental impacts on populations in zoned areas, and thus impacts urban sustainability. As suggested above, zoning may specify the siting of noxious uses within certain areas, but, depending on where those areas are, it can also contribute to the disproportionate burden of environmental and health impacts on certain social groups.[32]

Even now, Mantaay's critique remains valid except for a few studies (e.g., Pastor et al.[33]) that explicitly include land-use variables in EJ research. Further, it is important to keep in mind that the *motives* and *consequences* of zoning may be separate, and zoning's effect on EJ outcomes and sustainability is still not clear, partially because it has been little studied. Zoning, whether done for beneficent or malicious purposes, can create both negative and positive externalities within complex urban systems.

## Introducing local zoning scenarios

For this chapter, our EJ ABM is extended to add zoning scenarios. Among many types of zoning that have been used, here we focus on modeling zoning that internalizes negative externalities of noxious facilities. By doing this, we test a potential policy tool for its effects on EJ directly, and indirectly on sustainability (though results may not be generalizable to other types of zoning).

Given the paucity of existing empirical studies on the matter, we do not have specific expectations with regard to the relationship between zoning and environmental outcomes. A case could be made that zoning contributes to environmental injustice by establishing the institutional rules whereby lower socioeconomic status groups tend to cluster near noxious facilities, but a case could also be made that one of the original intents of zoning was to protect residents from noxious facilities and that zoning ought thus to alleviate environmental injustice. Using the EJ ABM, we aim to draw some insight into previously unconsidered hypotheses for empirical testing on zoning policies and environmental injustice in US cities and municipalities.

As described in previous chapters, the EJ model includes two types of agents: firms (polluting or non-polluting), and residents (of majority or minority "race," with their economic-class status given through assigned income at the beginning of the simulation). Firm and resident agents follow decision rules described in Chapter 3. Following Chapter 5, residents' income distribution in the society is assumed to be right-skewed. Here, an implicit local government plans its strategy to prevent or reduce environmental injustice using zoning.

### Zoning rules

All experiments in the previous chapters were done without zoning—no land was off limits to any type of firm. Here, we introduce two zoning scenarios as types of local government action: proactive zoning and reactive zoning.

### Proactive zoning

When a city is in the process of developing, planners can think of ordering land use via zones. Zones can be designed for various purposes, and protecting citizens from environmental risk and annoyance can be one rationale. We assume that such a case is proactive, and we can experiment to determine its effect on EJ.

While we could have utilized a set of planning-oriented decision rules, we decided to rely on a stochastic procedure for the proactive zoning rule. This was done mainly to assess the proactive zoning scenario across a set of heterogeneous contexts, rather than with any particular city or region in mind. Thus, for the proactive zoning scenario, the following procedure is used. At the beginning of the simulation, approximately 10 patches are randomly selected to be zoned. Half of them are defined as industrial zones (M-zones) and the other half as commercial zones (C-zones). Using a stochastic distance function that selects plots near the 10 randomly selected patches, the zones are then expanded outward from each of these blocks, with the end result consisting of randomly sized clusters of zoned plots, usually between 2 and 5 blocks, but potentially clusters as large as 10 blocks.

At the start of a trial, this means a set of approximately 12–15 random blocks designated as M-zones and another 12–15 random blocks designated as C-zones. Because of the stochastic distance procedure, the zoned areas will tend to be contiguous areas of 2–5 blocks in a row, similar to how actual zones tend to be located along major transportation routes. The rest of the plots are then open to residential settlement (similar to R-zones).

Once the M- or C-zones are set, new polluting firms must locate in industrial zones, and new non-polluting firms must locate in commercial zones.[34] Residents cannot locate in either industrial or commercial zones. Though in real cities sometimes land is designated as mixed use (such as in cities where commercial and residential buildings can be collocated),[35] for this set of simulations we made an assumption of no mixed use of land in order to approximate how most cities were zoned during the period when environmental justice issues began to emerge. Once proactive zones are set, they do not change during the simulation.

*Reactive zoning*

In the second set of experiments, zones are created throughout the simulation trial as a reaction to the location choices of each type of firm. Whereas the proactive zoning mechanism represents the intent to keep residents away from harmful land uses before harmful uses are established, the basic idea of reactive zoning is that firms choose locations (based on the procedures described in Chapter 3), and the local government responds to these location choices retroactively, attempting to separate residents from undesirable uses as they become apparent. When a block has two or more polluting firms, the entire block becomes M-zoned. If resident agents already occupy plots in the zone just created, they must relocate to other, non-zoned plots (in accordance with the standard residential location decisions as described in Chapter 3). The same logic is applied for non-polluting firms and the creation of C-zones.

After an iterative trial-and-error process, we set maximum firm capacity on any zoned block at five. This was chosen because higher capacities tended to result in most firms sited on just one zoned block, owing to the price advantages (since pollution affects prices, and firms seek low prices, the lowest-priced and thus preferred locations would be near polluting firms without this constraint), and smaller capacities resulted in zoned areas quickly becoming saturated and eliminating the utility of having zoning in the first place.

Once commercial or industrial zones are created, new firms must locate in an appropriate zone, as long as the zones have not reached their maximum capacity of firms (five firms per zoned block), while still maximizing utility from amongst allowed sites within the zones based on the firms' siting decision criteria described in Chapter 3. If there are no zoned spaces available, firms may locate on any plot that is not occupied (potentially leading to new reactive zones). Polluting firms cannot locate in C-zones, and non-polluting firms cannot locate in M-zones, although neither type of firm is forced to move if its plot subsequently gets designated a non-conforming zone.

### Scenarios

We ran three sets of simulations with the three zoning possibilities: no zoning, proactive zoning, and reactive zoning. Within each of these sets, we examined three different sets of scenarios varying polluting firms' location choice preferences: low price, siting away from majority concentrations, and siting near minority concentrations. As shown in Table 8.1, this results in nine distinct scenarios (throughout maintaining the assumption of no mixed use of land).

### Model outcomes

For each of the scenarios, we track the average environmental quality levels, both overall and for each race group. Using the quality level for each group, we can calculate the gap between majorities and minorities and use this gap

*Table 8.1* Zoning and polluting firms' siting scenarios

| | | Polluting firms' siting decision criteria | | |
| --- | --- | --- | --- | --- |
| | | *Lowest price* | *Locate away from majorities* | *Locate near minorities* |
| Government's zoning scenarios | No zoning | Scenario 1 | Scenario 2 | Scenario 3 |
| | Proactive zoning | Scenario 4 | Scenario 5 | Scenario 6 |
| | Reactive zoning | Scenario 7 | Scenario 8 | Scenario 9 |

Notes: No mixed-use of C-zones is assumed; Non-polluting firms always site on the lowest-priced plot; Residents are assumed to have an 80% similarity preference.

as an EJ outcome. We ran each scenario 200 times (with 60 time steps per trial rather than the standard 70).[36] Thus, we can compare average majority quality with minority quality in these different scenarios. Analytical procedures are consistent with those in previous chapters.

## The effect of zoning to internalize negative externalities of noxious facilities

As can be seen in the figures presented, across our scenarios, zoning, however deployed, tended to reduce and in some cases mitigate environmental injustice for the minority residents by the end of the simulation. If all scenarios are aggregated together, as in Figure 8.1, the quality gap—measured as average majority quality minus average minority quality—became wider when no zoning mechanism was used.

In Figure 8.1, the quality gap under proactive zoning is consistently lower than when there is no zoning. Under the reactive zoning scenarios, while the gap is quite large at the beginning, it tended to close much more quickly than under no zoning and even dips below proactive zoning at the end. Whereas under proactive zoning the quality gap was smaller through most of the time steps, reactive zoning resulted in more equitable distributions of pollution at the end (a gap closer to zero), catching up to and improving on the quality gap between majorities and minorities.[37]

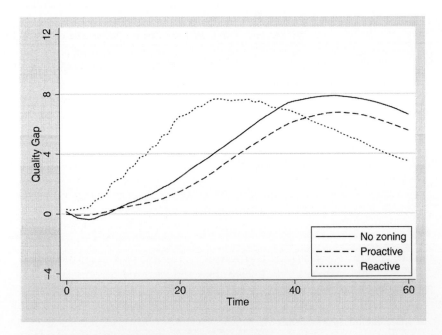

*Figure 8.1* Overall quality gaps by zoning strategies

However, aggregating all polluting firm location scenarios together, as in Figure 8.1, may miss important trends if different polluting firm location criteria cause different outcomes. As can be seen in Figure 8.2, the polluting firm location criteria do affect the results. When disamenity firms choose the lowest-priced plot, while an environmental quality gap does emerge, the extent of that gap is much smaller than when polluting firms either avoid majority populations or target minority populations (i.e., the gap stays closer to zero during the simulation). Also, when polluting firms choose plots based on low price, in the end no zoning and reactive zoning have about the same effect, and no zoning usually dominates reactive; with proactive zoning the gap emerges much more slowly, but ends up worse.

The trends when polluting firms locate away from majorities and when they locate near minorities are similar to the overall trends as shown in Figure 8.1. Reactive zoning starts out the worst, but eventually ends up the best. The no-zoning scenario starts reasonably well at first, but the quality gap ends up the largest. Across the scenarios, the size of the gap reaches its peak somewhere between time-steps 20 and 50, depending upon the zoning mechanism, and begins to decline through the rest of the simulation. By the end of the simulation, each gap is below its peak, with the best results for reactive zoning.

Thus, in each of the cases, the quality gaps separate during about the first 20 time steps, peak around 40 or 50, and then begin to decline. Figure 8.2 shows that there is an explicit tradeoff between proactive and reactive zoning, with proactive working best in the shorter term and reactive working best in the longer run. No zoning is a high-risk strategy, performing well in some scenarios and during some time periods, but also exhibiting the largest gaps of all. As part of this pattern, when disamenity firms target minority communities, no zoning actually results in better quality for minorities than for majorities over about the first 18 time steps—though that no-zoning scenario ends up with a large quality gap.

We should note that the size of the gap tells little about the levels of environmental quality for the two groups and society overall. The gap can be closing in one of three ways: majority quality decreases, or minority quality increases, or a combination of the two. Figure 8.3 shows the levels for both average majority quality and average minority quality over the different polluting firm location and zoning scenarios. It is important to note that across all scenarios majority quality tends to follow a similar trend regardless of the polluting firms' choice or type of zoning used. It tends to be somewhat higher when proactive zoning is used, and the trend is similar across all scenarios: majority quality rises rapidly through about time-step 30 or 40, and declines after that through the end. Thus, Figure 8.3 makes it clear that differences in the environmental quality gap are mostly reflections of the trends for overall minority quality levels.

Not surprisingly given the purpose of proactive zoning, minority quality, as well as majority quality, tends to be consistently higher in proactive

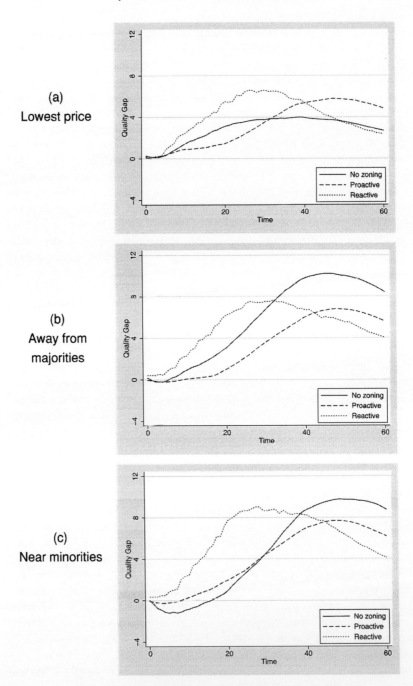

*Figure 8.2* Quality gap trends by zoning and disamenity decision criteria

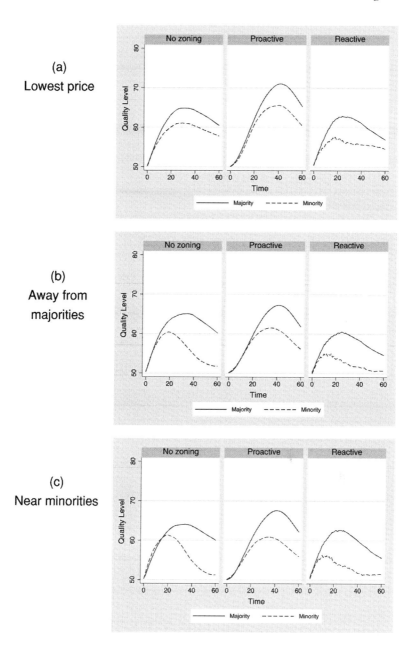

(a)
Lowest price

(b)
Away from
majorities

(c)
Near minorities

*Figure 8.3* Quality trends for majority and minority by zoning and firm decision criteria

zoning scenarios. Though reactive zoning may appear to be better from a purely environmental *equity* perspective—ensuring that minorities are not much worse off than minorities—both groups are worse off at each time step of the reactive zoning simulation than at the matching time step of the other two types of scenarios. Thus, here we see a fairly explicit tradeoff between equity and efficiency, with reactive zoning dominating on equity in the long run, but proactive dominating on overall quality throughout the duration of the simulations. This suggests that proactive zoning may be efficacious as a tool of urban sustainability, but that reactive zoning must be used with care.

## Discussion

In Chapter 4, we show that environmental justice problems are more likely to emerge as serious problems when there is some level of "racial" awareness in a social system. In that chapter, once racial awareness existed among residents, environmental justice problems were more likely to emerge as serious problems when polluting firms made conscious decisions to locate either near clusters of minority agents or away from clusters of majority agents. In these cases the quality gap between majority and minority was consistently larger than if polluting firms selected locations based on low prices.

In this chapter our interest is less in investigating the circumstances under which environmental justice problems emerge than in exploring how policy might address problems when they emerge—or even prevent them from emerging. We investigate one of the key policies through which local governments might be able to confront these problems: zoning.

The results imply that, for addressing EJ concerns, using some sort of zoning is better than having no zoning system in place, all else equal. Unless all polluting firms always chose the lowest-priced plot, in the long run we found smaller gaps in environmental quality whenever some zoning mechanism was deployed. Smaller environmental quality gaps emerged, and minority quality tended to reach comparatively high points, whenever zones were created proactively. When zones were set up in reaction to firm location choices, the environmental quality gap between the majorities and minorities was somewhat larger than under proactive scenarios, but subsequent zoning tended to close the gap. Looking only at the gap (Figures 8.1 and 8.2) makes reactive zoning look like a good policy, but looking at quality levels shows that reactive zoning is generally worse for both groups and particularly suppresses quality for minorities. In reactive zoning, the benefit of the closing quality *gap* is purchased at the price of relatively low *quality* for both groups. These results imply that while reactive zoning may improve some measures of justice, it does not improve sustainability.

A simulation taking place in a generalized artificial world cannot adequately tell us what will happen in actual cities, but our results suggest that while zoning has often been criticized as a tool of segregation it may also be a tool to address environmental justice problems associated with segregation—if it is deployed correctly. However, the simulation also indicates that zoning systems would likely work best to improve resident quality when they are planned in advance, and work best to increase equity when they are flexible to changing local conditions.

We assessed two types of zoning as ideal cases: once deployed, the zoning mechanisms in our model followed strict rules.[38] In the case of proactive zoning, once the zones were established, there were no adjustments of the zones during the simulation trials. As a result, environmental degradation problems were mostly held in check. In the reactive zoning scenario, firms were not restricted at the start, but only became restricted after a sufficient number of proximate firms had been sited. In this case, the quality gap declined, but only at the cost of lower overall quality for all—a result antithetical to concern with urban sustainability overall.

If we take addressing environmental justice to be an effort to decrease the environmental quality gap by increasing the environmental quality levels for lower-status populations (rather than by decreasing the environmental quality level for higher-status populations), then perhaps some combination of zoning mechanisms may work best. Local policymakers may thus be able to use proactive zoning to keep residential environmental quality relatively high, and use reactive zoning to solve EJ problems that emerge. However, if such a policy is followed, it is important to keep track of quality levels for all, and especially for minorities.

While these results should be taken with the appropriate amount of caution, they raise some interesting hypotheses that may be worth exploring further. Consider that while most zoning systems across the United States share commonalities, there is much variation in how zoning is implemented and managed. Some states and localities have flexible zoning rules, like much of the Sun Belt, while others have long-established zones that do not tend to change, like the spatially constrained northeastern corridor cities. Some new cities are created with zoning structures in place. Others, like the aforementioned Houston and some other smaller cities, do not have zoning at all.

While earlier chapters underline that additional contextual variables relating to these jurisdictions must also be taken into account, studying environmental justice outcomes comparatively across different types of cities with different zoning systems could show interesting trends with respect to the relative amount and equity of environmental quality and thus sustainability; all else equal, our results suggest that land-use regulation may have an effect on EJ, and that outcomes are likely the least equitable where no zoning rules have been in place for quite some time, and more equitable where zones have been planned ahead with the goal of separating residents from polluting facilities. These are empirically testable hypotheses that can be used to validate the insights of the EJ ABM presented here.

Taken all together, the findings of this simulation may suggest one reason why some EJ studies find injustice while others do not: The simulation indicates that the extent of environmental injustice is an interactive factor not only of firm decisions, but also of residential choices and local government policy. Taking a step back, it is not surprising that a broadly observed social trend has roots in the combination of decisions that individuals, organizations, and governments make. Nevertheless, to this point EJ has largely been treated as a problem of firm decision making, and policies to address the problem have largely flowed from this assumption.[39]

This chapter suggests that, while regulating firm decision making can help in addressing EJ problems, it is not a complete response. To respond fully may require more action, but the framework for acting need not be radically different from how governments regulate firm location decisions today. Even when all polluting firms were modeled as overtly nefarious in our simulation (seeking minority neighborhoods), even a simple proactive zoning requirement tended to lessen the environmental quality gap via an improvement in average minority quality. Such a policy thus has great promise for urban sustainability.

## Notes

1  The analysis of zoning reported in Heather E. Campbell, Yushim Kim and Adam Eckerd, "Local Zoning and Environmental Justice: An Agent-Based Model Analysis," *Urban Affairs Review* 50, no. 4 (2014): 521–52, is based on a distribution of residents' income drawn from the 2010 US Census but simplified by fit to a normal distribution. The revision to a right-skewed distribution of income in this chapter slightly changed the result of the simulation; the primary difference is in magnitudes.

2  Liam Downey, "Environmental Injustice: Is Race or Income a Better Predictor?" *Social Science Quarterly* 79, no. 4 (1998): 766–78.

3  Michael Kraft and Bruce Clary, "Citizen Participation and the NIMBY Syndrome: Public Response to Radioactive Waste Disposal," *Political Research Quarterly* 44, no. 2 (1991): 299–328; Michael Dear, "Understanding and Overcoming the NIMBY Syndrome," *Journal of the American Planning Association* 58, no. 3 (1992): 288–300; Gregory McAvoy, "Partisan Probing and Democratic Decisionmaking: Rethinking the NIMBY Syndrome," *Policy Studies Journal* 26, no. 2 (1998): 274–92.

4  Juliana Maantay, "Zoning Law, Health, and Environmental Justice: What's the Connection?" *Journal of Law, Medicine & Ethics* 30 (2002): 572–93.

5  Douglas S. Noonan, "Evidence of Environmental Justice: A Critical Perspective on the Practice of EJ Research and Lessons for Policy Design," *Social Science Quarterly* 89, no. 5 (2008): 1153–74.

6  Vicki Been and Francis Gupta, "Coming to the Nuisance or Going to the Barrios?" *Ecology Law Quarterly* 24, no. 1 (1997): 1–56.

7  Willam A. Fischel, *The Economics of Zoning Laws: A Property Rights Approach to American Land Use Controls* (Baltimore, MD: Johns Hopkins University Press, 1987).

8  Ibid.

9  James R. Woodworth, W. Robert Gump and James R. Forrester, *Camelot: A Role-Playing Simulation of Political Decision Making*, fifth edn (Belmont, CA: Thomson, 2006), 116–70.

10  Zou (Joe) Qian, "Shaping Urban Form Without Zoning: Investigating Three Neighborhoods in Houston," *Planning Practice and Research* 261, no. 1 (2011): 21–42.

11  Ibid.

12 Maantay, "Zoning Law, Health, and Environmental Justice."

13 Moira L. Zellner, Rick L. Riolo, William Rand, Daniel G. Brown, Scott E. Page and Luis E. Fernandez, "The Problem with Zoning: Nonlinear Effects of Inter-action between Location Preferences and Externalities on Land Use and Utility," *Environment and Planning B* 37 (2010): 408–28.

14 For a discussion of form-based approaches, and approaches in Miami, see Kaid Benfield, "Miami 21 Leads the Way on Zoning Reform," *Switchboard: National Resources Defense Council Staff Blog*, January 7, 2010.

15 Joseph Schilling and Leslie S. Linton, "The Public Health Roots of Zoning: In Search of Active Living's Legal Genealogy," *American Journal of Preventive Medicine* 28, no. 2S2 (2005): 96–104.

16 Keith R. Ihlanfeldt, "Exclusionary Land-Use Regulations within Suburban Com-munities: A Review of the Evidence and Policy Prescriptions," *Urban Studies* 41, no. 2 (2004): 273.

17 Sacoby Wilson, Malo Hutson and Mahasin S. Mujahid, "How Planning and Zoning Contribute to Inequitable Development, Neighborhood Health, and Environmental Injustice," *Environmental Justice* 1, no. 4 (2008): 211–16.

18 Maantay, "Zoning Law, Health, and Environmental Justice," 577.

19 Willam A. Fischel, "Property Taxation and the Tiebout Model: Evidence for the Benefit View from Zoning and Voting," *Journal of Economic Literature* 30, no. 1 (1992): 171–77.

20 J.M. Pogodzinski and Tim R. Sass, "Measuring the Effects of Municipal Zoning Regulations: A Survey," *Urban Studies* 28, no. 4 (1991): 597–621.

21 Maantay, "Zoning Law, Health, and Environmental Justice," 583.

22 Depending upon the literature, the motives are categorized in two or three groups. Some consider fiscal and exclusionary motives in the same group: Pogodzinski and Sass, "Measuring the Effects of Municipal Zoning Regulations." Others such as Ihlanfeldt, "Exclusionary Land-Use Regulations within Suburban Communities," examine them as separate categories.

23 Ihlanfeldt, "Exclusionary Land-Use Regulations within Suburban Communities," 275.

24 Arthur S. Lazerow, "Discriminatory Zoning: Legal Battleground of the Seven-ties," *The American University Law Review* 21 (1971): 160, www.wcl.american. edu/journal/lawrev/21/lazerow.pdf?rd=1 (accessed August 6, 2011).

25 Schilling and Linton, "The Public Health Roots of Zoning," 100–1.

26 Ihlanfeldt, "Exclusionary Land-Use Regulations within Suburban Communities."

27 Pogodzinski and Sass, "Measuring the Effects of Municipal Zoning Regulations."

28 Rolf Pendall, "Local Land Use Regulation and the Chain of Exclusion," *Journal of the American Planning Association* 66, no. 2 (2000): 125–42; Jonathan Rothwell and Douglas S. Massey, "The Effect of Density Zoning on Racial Seg-regation in U.S. Urban Areas," *Urban Affairs Review* 44, no. 6 (2009): 779–806.

29 Harry W. Richardson, Peter Gordon, M.J. Jun and M.H. Kimm, "PRIDE and Prejudice: The Economic Impacts of Growth Controls in Pasadena," *Environ-ment and Planning* 25, no. 7 (1993): 987–1002.

30 Maantay, "Zoning Law, Health, and Environmental Justice"; Sacoby Wilson, M. Hutson and Mahasin S. Mujahid, "How Planning and Zoning Contribute to Inequitable Development, Neighborhood Health, and Environmental Injustice," *Environmental Justice* 1, no. 4 (2008): 211–16.

31 Maantay, "Zoning Law, Health, and Environmental Justice," 572.

32 Ibid.; Schilling and Linton, "The Public Health Roots of Zoning."

33 Manuel Pastor, Rachel Morello-Frosch and James L. Sadd, "The Air is Always Cleaner on the Other Side: Race, Space, and Ambient Air Toxics Exposures in California," *Journal of Urban Affairs* 27, no. 2 (2005): 127–48.

34  In most trials, there were sufficient proactively set zones for all firms to find locations in the proper zone. In the rare outcome of no space being available on existing zoned land, non-polluting firms select a location in an M-zone, and polluting firms were allowed to exceed the five firms per block constraint.

35  To see the result of relaxing the no mixed use assumption for C-zones, check Campbell et al., "Local Zoning and Environmental Justice," Figure 2.

36  In previous chapters, we ran the trials until time-step 70, but here we stopped the simulation at time-step 60 mainly because, due to the creation of zones, the land is quickly filled and no more plots are available for residential choice.

37  Our previous study, Campbell et al., "Local Zoning and Environmental Justice," modeled the income distribution as normal. Comparing the results here (with a right-skewed gamma income distribution), the effect of the no-zoning scenario is consistent with Figure 8.1. However, the quality gap under reactive zoning scenarios emerges more quickly at the beginning in Figure 8.1, but it nonetheless ends up with similar trends as the simulation time progresses. Also, considering the proactive zoning scenario, the quality gap in Figure 8.1 is larger than that with a normal distribution of income (see Campbell et al., op cit., Figure 2).

38  As pointed out by an anonymous reviewer, in real cities zoning regimes may be very changeable—responsive to local pressure for variances.

39  William M. Bowen and Michael V. Wells, "The Politics and Reality of Environmental Justice: A History and Considerations for Administrators and Policy Makers," *Public Administration Review* 62, no. 6 (2002): 688–99.

# References

Been, Vicki and Francis Gupta. "Coming to the Nuisance or Going to the Barrios? A Longitudinal Analysis of Environment Justice Claims." *Ecology Law Quarterly* 24, no. 1 (1997): 1–56.

Benfield, Kaid. "Miami 21 Leads the Way on Zoning Reform." *Switchboard: National Resources Defense Council Staff Blog.* January 7, 2010. Switchboard. nrdc.org/blogs/kbenfield/miami_21_leads_the_way_on_zoni.html.

Bowen, William M. and Michael V. Wells. "The Politics and Reality of Environmental Justice: A History and Considerations for Administrators and Policy Makers." *Public Administration Review* 62, no. 6 (2002): 688–699.

Campbell, Heather E., Yushim Kim and Adam Eckerd. "Local Zoning and Environmental Justice: An Agent-Based Model Analysis." *Urban Affairs Review* 50, no. 4 (2014): 521–552.

Dear, Michael. "Understanding and Overcoming the NIMBY Syndrome." *Journal of the American Planning Association* 58, no. 3 (1992): 288–300.

Downey, Liam. "Environmental Injustice: Is Race or Income a Better Predictor?" *Social Science Quarterly* 79, no. 4 (1998): 766–778.

Fischel, William A. *The Economics of Zoning Laws: A Property Rights Approach to American Land Use Controls.* Baltimore, MD: Johns Hopkins University Press, 1987.

Fischel, William A. "Property Taxation and the Tiebout Model: Evidence for the Benefit View from Zoning and Voting." *Journal of Economic Literature* 30, no. 1 (1992): 171–177.

Ihlanfeldt, Keith R. "Exclusionary Land-Use Regulations within Suburban Communities: A Review of the Evidence and Policy Prescriptions." *Urban Studies* 41, no. 2 (2004): 261–283.

Kraft, Michael and Bruce Clary. "Citizen Participation and the NIMBY Syndrome: Public Response to Radioactive Waste Disposal." *Political Research Quarterly* 44, no. 2 (1991): 299–328.

Lazerow, Arthur S. "Discriminatory Zoning: Legal Battleground of the Seventies." *The American University Law Review* 21 (1971): 157–183. www.wcl.american. edu/journal/lawrev/21/lazerow.pdf?rd=1 (accessed August 6, 2011).

Maantay, Juliana. "Zoning Law, Health, and Environmental Justice: What's the Connection?" *Journal of Law, Medicine & Ethics* 30 (2002): 572–593.

McAvoy, Gregory. "Partisan Probing and Democratic Decisionmaking: Rethinking the NIMBY Syndrome." *Policy Studies Journal* 26, no. 2 (1998): 274–292.

Noonan, Douglas S. "Evidence of Environmental Justice: A Critical Perspective on the Practice of EJ Research and Lessons for Policy Design." *Social Science Quarterly* 89, no. 5 (2008): 1153–1174.

Pastor, Manuel, Rachel Morello-Frosch and James L. Sadd. "The Air is Always Cleaner on the Other Side: Race, Space, and Ambient Air Toxics Exposures in California." *Journal of Urban Affairs* 27, no. 2 (2005): 127–148.

Pendall, Rolf. "Local Land Use Regulation and the Chain of Exclusion." *Journal of the American Planning Association* 66, no. 2 (2000): 125–142.

Pogodzinski, J.M. and Tim R. Sass. "Measuring the Effects of Municipal Zoning Regulations: A Survey." *Urban Studies* 28, no. 4 (1991): 597–621.

Qian, Zou (Joe). "Shaping Urban Form Without Zoning: Investigating Three Neighborhoods in Houston." *Planning Practice and Research* 261, no. 1 (2011): 21–42.

Richardson, Harry W., Peter Gordon, M.J. Jun and M.H. Kimm. "PRIDE and Prejudice: The Economic Impacts of Growth Controls in Pasadena." *Environment and Planning* 25, no. 7 (1993): 987–1002.

Rothwell, Jonathan and Douglas S. Massey. "The Effect of Density Zoning on Racial Segregation in U.S. Urban Areas." *Urban Affairs Review* 44, no. 6 (2009): 779–806.

Schilling, Joseph and Leslie S. Linton. "The Public Health Roots of Zoning: In Search of Active Living's Legal Genealogy." *American Journal of Preventive Medicine* 28, no. 2S2 (2005): 96–104.

Wilson, Sacoby, Malo Hutson and Mahasin S. Mujahid. "How Planning and Zoning Contribute to Inequitable Development, Neighborhood Health, and Environmental Injustice." *Environmental Justice* 1, no. 4 (2008): 211–216.

Woodworth, James R., W. Robert Gump and James R. Forrester. *Camelot: A Role Playing Simulation of Political Decision Making.* Fifth edn. Belmont, CA: Thomson, 2006.

Zellner, Moira L., Rick L. Riolo, William Rand, Daniel G. Brown, Scott E. Page and Luis E. Fernandez. "The Problem with Zoning: Nonlinear Effects of Interaction between Location Preferences and Externalities on Land Use and Utility." *Environment and Planning B* 37, no. 3 (2010): 408–428.

# 9    Polluted-site remediation[1]

Perhaps the most direct way to alter the locational impacts of polluted facilities is either to remediate and redevelop an existing hazardous site, or to move polluting facilities elsewhere. For instance, if a hazardous site is located in a predominantly minority area, the site could be remediated, thereby perhaps eliminating the cause of an environmental disparity in that area. Such actions should also improve the sustainability of an area.

However, a policy targeting cleanup efforts to minority communities may only behave as expected if the demographic makeup of those communities is relatively unchanging. That is, if a community's population composition changes over time, then cleanup benefits may predominantly accrue to new residents moving into a community, in which case environmental justice may not be improved. Therefore, if a regional residential market is dynamic, prioritizing the remediation of sites near the largest concentration of minority residents might not actually be the best approach to addressing the environmental quality gap. As earlier chapters have shown, the effects of dynamic interactions can be hard to predict off the cuff.

This chapter analyzes the effect on the environmental quality gap of different hazardous-site remediation policies. We compare potential consequences for the environmental quality gap of prioritizing the cleanup of those sites that: 1 have the highest land values; 2 pollute the most; or 3 have the most minority residents in their proximity. The last seems the most directly to address the EJ problem, but 1 is often suggested as the most economically efficient approach; and 2 is suggested as improving environmental quality (and thus health and sustainability) overall.

Below, we discuss why different prioritizations might matter and why targeting the sites in minority communities may not necessarily lead to better environmental outcomes for minorities.

## Hazardous site remediation

### Dynamic neighborhoods

Much existing brownfields[2] remediation policy is premised on the idea that targeting cleanup to those communities with high poverty and large minority populations will address the environmental quality gap by ensuring that policy benefits flow directly to these intended beneficiaries.[3] This premise, however, is implicitly based on an assumption that communities are largely static with respect to relevant characteristics. As explained above, for benefits of cleanup to improve the environmental lot of minorities, minority residents must remain in the targeted community after the cleanup.[4] In a dynamic market for land, this is a doubtful premise.[5]

At least in the United States, there is ample evidence that communities are dynamic—that the character and characteristics of neighborhoods are constantly in flux as old residents leave and new residents move in.[6] If neighborhoods are dynamic, then policies targeting neighborhoods will affect whomever happens to be in the neighborhood after the cleanup, whether those individuals are the intended beneficiaries or not. This largely depends upon who will be attracted to cleaned-up communities, whether rising land values will force out intended beneficiaries, and who will be able to move to the communities. As a result, environmental justice outcomes of such a direct approach are unknown. Outcomes may not follow policymakers' assumptions.

## The logic

Both the environmental quality gap and environmental gentrification[7] have been investigated through the residential sorting lens.[8] This work has investigated how both degradation of and improvement in environmental quality alter the economic and demographic makeup of communities. When the environmental quality in a community degrades, for example after the siting of a hazardous facility, we may expect that demand for housing in the community will fall, lowering real-estate values, and encouraging those who have invested in real estate in the community to leave.[9] As demand falls and the supply of available homes increases, prices fall, making the community more affordable for the poor. Worsening environmental conditions may have the effect of decreasing demand for and increasing the supply of available land. Those who can afford to leave the community will tend to do so, reducing the general level of prices for the housing stock nearby, and appealing to potential residents unable to afford the premium for higher environmental quality.[10]

As mentioned in earlier chapters, according to this line of reasoning, we tend to see a collocation between environmental hazards and poor residents due not necessarily to discrimination, but to neighborhood dynamics and residential sorting. Regardless of who predominantly bears the costs of environmental degradation initially, the poor are most likely to end up bearing most of the costs. If racial and ethnic minorities are disproportionately poor, they will disproportionately end up in such neighborhoods.[11]

Conversely, when the environment in a community improves, it is plausible that the opposite set of circumstances occurs. The remediation of a hazardous facility and subsequent redevelopment of the site can improve environmental conditions in the community in a salient way.[12] This improvement may appeal to residents from outside the neighborhood, who might now consider moving to the community, driving up demand for housing and increasing land prices.[13] This increase in prices may raise rents beyond what current residents can afford, and current renters may be forced to move elsewhere for affordable housing. In such cases, the benefits of environmental improvement could be reaped by incoming residents who were not the intended targets of the benefits (but who will pay extra for the new improvements), while the original residents (who were the intended targets) not only do not receive the benefits, but are faced with the personal costs associated with relocation.[14]

In short, it is possible that environmental changes can subsequently change the economic and demographic makeup of the surrounding area. Thus, while it might seem clear that cleaning up polluted sites will benefit urban sustainability overall, if it does not also improve environmental equity, weakness may remain in the crucial social pillar of sustainability. Yet, most existing policy approaches to addressing environmental disparities do not take this possibility into account.[15] EJ-informed policies regarding the siting of environmental hazards tend to provide incentives to keep hazards away from minority areas, or place restrictions on considering such areas as potential sites.[16] Cleanup policies specifically target funds to projects that are based in low-socioeconomic-status communities.[17] However, for these policies to be effective at addressing environmental disparities, it seems that the affected neighborhoods would have to be relatively static.

### The evidence

What happens in communities after environmental hazards have been cleaned up is therefore an important consideration in crafting a policy to address environmental injustice, and the results of the few empirical studies conducted so far are mixed. For instance, Dale et al. looked at land values pre- and post-cleanup of Superfund sites and found that after sites have been cleaned up the value of land nearby tends to increase.[18] McCluskey and Rausser used a time-series analysis to look at value trends near Superfund sites, finding that land values nearby have a tendency to decrease while a site is being cleaned, but increase once the cleanup is complete[19]—although these changes may be mitigated when there is substantial negative publicity association with a site, in which case values nearby may continue to decline even after the cleanup.[20] For hazardous facilities that are less salient than Superfund sites, closing down the site may be the critical factor in the subsequent increase in land values, whether a cleanup has occurred or not.[21] Beyond land-value changes, Seig et al. found that demographic shifts consistent with gentrification tend to occur in school districts after environmental improvements take place.[22] However, using resident-demarcated neighborhoods as the unit of analysis, Eckerd found economic change but did not find much demographic change in neighborhoods where hazardous sites are cleaned up (though given the necessary use of Census data, it is unclear whether residents remained in the communities and benefited, or if the residents who moved in were similar demographically to the residents who were displaced).[23] At minimum, it is clear that there is a relationship between hazardous sites and local real-estate markets, but data limitations make it difficult to find suitable causal evidence about whether cleanups foster gentrification, have little overall impact, or provide benefits to existing community members.

This question is important, because assumptions of subsequent land-value increases and changes in land use tend to be a major focus for both those requesting funds for cleanup and the organizations, including governments, that provide cleanup funding.[24] In a detailed case study of 20 brownfield sites that have been redeveloped as parks or open spaces, De Sousa found that economic development and reduction of urban blight were two of the primary reasons for redevelopment, and were subsequently cited as benefits of the projects by environmental regulators, and as commonly portrayed as benefits in the media and by developers seeking grant support.[25]

*Calculating risk from environmental hazards*

A second issue in designing an effective hazardous-site remediation plan to improve environmental quality within (minority) communities resides in the difficulty of assessing the levels of risk posed by environmental hazards. As mentioned earlier, for the most part previous empirical research has treated risk homogeneously—all hazardous sites are treated as equally hazardous, with the risk calculation consisting entirely of relative closeness to the hazardous site. Thus, environmental quality tends to be measured only through proximity to hazardous sites, rather than through an assessment of the nature and state of the contamination at a site and the subsequent risk posed by the site, of which proximity is only part of the risk calculation.[26]

This level of detail is not necessarily a limitation of the research design, but a limitation of available data; with a preponderance of hazardous sites, most of which are privately owned, self-reporting and enforcement are somewhat haphazard, and data are often unreliable.[27] Lacking quality information regarding the nature of the pollutants at a site, and the manner in which those pollutants are stored and handled, it is extremely difficult to assess the risk posed by a site. Even among those sites that have been targeted for cleanup and therefore assessed in detail, determining the level of risk posed can quickly become complicated due to the large number of factors that affect risk, and the uncertainty regarding the nature of the relationships amongst those factors with one another, and with resulting risk.[28]

This focus on proximity in research has engendered a similar focus by policymakers. To the extent that public agencies consider environmental justice implications, they do so via the proximity of the site to certain populations, for example by investigating if a site is located in a community with high poverty or with a large minority population, or with large numbers of children (who are more susceptible to many pollutants). As reviewed earlier, the environmental justice literature leaves little doubt that hazardous sites tend to be clustered in lower-status areas,[29] and surely this on average translates to increased risk for nearby populations. However, it is difficult to discern whether those clustered sites constitute a relatively higher risk to the local population than one highly contaminated site a little further away. For instance, how many nearby gas stations does it take to be more risky than one slightly more distant nuclear facility? Is a closed chemical plant one mile away riskier than an in-use city dump three miles away? Using agent-based modeling, it would be possible to model lower and higher levels of risk from closer and nearer facilities, allowing policymakers more directly to address such questions.

Further complicating the assessment of the value of remediating a particular hazard on the environmental quality gap is that, while the cleanup of one site surely does reduce risk pertaining to that site, it may have little impact on the overall risk to nearby targeted populations. An explicit prioritization of sites located in minority neighborhoods only appreciably improves overall environmental quality for the residents of that neighborhood if the targeted neighborhood sites are comparatively riskier than other sites in other locations near enough to impose pollution on the focal neighborhood.

Thus, the direct-approach policy aimed at targeting for remediation sites in poor and/or minority areas may be tenuous. It is not clear that cleaning up a larger number of sites in such neighborhoods necessarily decreases environmental risk more for residents than would a policy with a specific focus on the most environmentally hazardous sites, regardless of their location, for the effects of the most hazardous sites may spread much beyond their "neighborhood" locations.

## Modeling hazardous-site remediation plans

This chapter continues to use the EJ ABM presented in earlier chapters and, as before, the model includes two types of agent: firms (polluting or non-polluting), and residents (of majority or minority "race," with their economic-class status assigned via income distributions, as described in Chapter 3, with majorities wealthier on average than minorities). Given the potential importance of mobility and residential sorting around both amenities and disamenities, both groups are mobile at the 12% level (as described in detail in Chapter 7).

Within the artificial world, this chapter simulates possible government policy choices to address environmental injustice. An implicit government agent chooses strategies to remedy environmental harm caused by hazardous sites. The question is *which hazardous-site remediation strategy* is likely to have greater effects on EJ. Also, would the policy outcome differ in communities with different levels of severity of the environmental justice problem?

As in Chapter 8 on zoning, rather than focusing on social processes that may lead to societal environmental injustice, this chapter aims to assess the effect of potential government policy. Here the focus is on policy to address already existing environmental injustice. Therefore, unlike in the other chapters, in which we begin each analysis from a de novo world in which a city grows, here we use what we have learned about resident and firm behavior and its relationship with environmental disparities to set up starting conditions—partially developed cities—with different amounts of environmental injustice. We test policy options in a community with a severe EJ problem and one with a moderate EJ problem. Thus, the simulations are separated into two different phases: Phase I, a setup period (before time-step 35); and Phase II, a cleanup period (after time-step 35).

### Designing communities with EJ problems

First, we engineer a community with a severe EJ problem. During the setup period, both types of firms are sited and residents sort according to the decision rules explained previously. Using what we learned from the previous chapters, we alter our typical approach and purposely create a community with a serious environmental equity problem during this setup period. During the setup phase, as with most simulations, the minority group is poorer on average than the majority group, but we also ensure an environmental quality gap by using high (80%) similarity preferences for each group and, further, having polluting firms select locations based solely on finding the largest concentrations of minority residents (and of course there is no zoning). With these extreme settings we are not aiming for a realistic model of behavior, but instead we are simply aiming to create a situation where the EJ problem is severe and, indeed, the setup phase (the first 35 time steps) under these conditions results in a significant environmental quality gap.

In the cleanup phase (after time-step 35) we revert similarity preferences to the 80% for majorities and 50% for minorities that we use in Chapters 5 and 7 (based on empirical findings on residential similarity preferences),[30] and also revert polluting firms to select locations based on price, not discrimination. Our reasoning is that it would be unlikely that a cleanup policy intending to address environmental injustice would be implemented without also restricting where new hazardous sites may locate. Further, having hazardous firms continue to site during the cleanup phase is a conservative way to assess the effect of cleaning up, while still recognizing that hazardous land uses are necessary—even when remediating existing hazardous sites, undesirable land uses are a necessary feature of modern life. However, as we know from scenarios in other chapters, even if there is no remediation policy, this lowering of similarity preferences and altering how polluting firms locate will alter the environmental quality gap between majorities and minorities. We would expect a slight improvement of environmental quality for minorities since new firms are no longer sited in areas where minorities are clustered, and the minority group has decreased its similarity preference. We call this scenario without any remediation the "no cleanup" scenario.

For a second set of scenarios, because the efficacy of policy action can be different in different community contexts, we engineered a second type of community, which has a more moderate environmental justice problem. To create moderate EJ problems, again given what we learned in previous chapters, we set a much lower similarity preference (20%) for both racial groups. The setup period (the first 35 time steps) was otherwise the same as for the scenario described above, with polluting firms purposely selecting locations near minority populations. After time-step 35, polluting firms again shift to select locations based on low prices, and similarity preferences remain at 20%. As expected, this change resulted in a much less severe, but still present, environmental justice problem than under the 80% similarity preference scenario described above.

Table 9.1 summarizes key aspects of community conditions and agents' behaviors during different phases of the simulation.

### Modeling remediation scenarios

Policy contrasts are made with regard to the process through which polluting firms are prioritized for remediation during the cleanup phase. After the setup phase, the environmental justice problem is clearly evident in both the severe case and the moderate case. Then the cleanup phase begins, and a remediation policy is implemented such that one existing polluting firm begins to be eliminated each time step, according to one of three prioritization policies: 1 cleaning up the firm that is on the highest-priced plot; 2 the firm that has the highest pollution score; or 3 the firm that has the highest

*Table 9.1* Community conditions and simulation phases

| | | Simulation phases | |
|---|---|---|---|
| | | Setup phase (before time-step 35) | Cleanup phase (after time-step 35) |
| Severe EJ problem | Polluting firms | Site on a plot with the largest cluster of minorities | Site on the lowest-priced plot |
| | Residents | Similarity preference: 80% for both groups | Similarity preference: 80% for majorities/ 50% for minorities |
| Moderate EJ problem | Polluting firms | Site on a plot with the largest cluster of minorities | Site on the lowest-priced plot |
| | Residents | Similarity preference: 20% for both groups | Similarity preference: 20% for both groups |

Note: Mobility of residents is set at 12% during the simulation regardless of the phase.

proportion of minority residents on the surrounding eight patches. The four scenario sets are thus following:

- No cleanup (base scenario): no cleanup policy action is taken during the simulation.
- Economic pressure (*EP policy*): the firm that begins remediation is that which is located on the highest-priced plot of land.
- Eliminating risk (*ER policy*): the firm that begins remediation is that which emits the largest amount of pollution.
- Environmental justice (*EJ policy*): the firm that begins remediation is that which is located on the plot of land with the largest concentration of minority residents nearby.

While these three priorities represent ideal cases and we recognize that no city would exclusively use one criterion, they are not unlike the balancing of choices that governments must regularly make, and our aim here is to assess the relative efficacy of each approach rather than any particular mix of approaches (which is often the more realistic assumption).[31]

That said, there are good examples of these strategies being utilized in relative isolation from one another. The Superfund program is a good example of the ER policy. The Environmental Protection Agency (EPA) has long focused on the remediation of sites it deems the most potentially risky to nearby populations.[32] There are many instances of policies similar to our EP policy, which suggests that governments focus on taking advantage of development pressures and remediate sites that appear more likely to be on land worth redeveloping;[33] examples abound, from recent cleanup activity near the Washington, DC, Navy Yard,[34] to the Nine Mile Run efforts in Pittsburgh.[35] Finally, although specifically focusing on equity considerations and environmental justice, as in our EJ policy, is less common, there are some notable examples.[36] The Green Impact Zone, in Kansas City,[37] emphasizes the need to be inclusive and eliminate the chances of environmental gentrification in the area that is being cleaned up, and the cleanup and redevelopment of sites in the Weinland Park neighborhood of Columbus, Ohio,[38] is focused on using environmental remediation as a tool to stave off encroaching gentrification and ensure that beneficiaries of the cleanup are the existing poor, mainly African-American, residents. It is important for practitioners to know if one of these approaches dominates—or if all are useless, or all are beneficial.

The time it actually takes to remediate sites is highly variable and depends on a number of different factors. In order to approximate the added complexity of cleaning up dirtier sites, modeled remediation takes a variable number of time steps to be completed, based on the pollution level of the firm (the pollution variable as described in Chapter 3), with high-polluting facilities taking more time to clean up. The number of time steps a remediation takes is determined by the pollution variable of the firm. If a firm's pollution level is 9, the site is not remediated until nine steps after it was selected for remediation. Since hazardous sites are nonetheless necessary for society (for example, we need garbage incinerators and recycling centers), despite the remediation of existing polluting firms, new polluting firms continue to be sited after time-step 35.

## Model outcomes

As previously, differences in the average levels of environmental quality for majorities and minorities are compared as a key outcome. Because we are interested in exploring how effective each of these policy alternatives is at addressing race-based gaps in environmental quality, we tabulate the average environmental quality for both sets of resident agents over each time step for each policy option, and compare the trends of the changes in those average quality levels over time. We also calculate the size of the environmental quality gap at various points throughout the simulation to assess the relative effectiveness of each policy at closing the gap.

For each of the policy scenarios, varying each of the three policy options and, as a base comparison, the no cleanup scenario, 200 trials were conducted, resulting in 800 simulation trials in each of the community conditions. Because we experiment with two different community conditions (severe and moderate EJ conditions), the total number of simulation trials is 1,600.

## Which alternative reduces the EJ problem more effectively?

### Community with a severe EJ problem

As described in Chapter 3, environmental quality is measured as a value between 0 and 100, with a starting (neutral) point of 50. As can be seen in Figure 9.1, in every scenario average majority quality declines over the 35 time steps that constitute the cleanup phase. However, average minority quality improves except when no sites are being cleaned up. Each of the policy alternatives that cleans up sites is clearly better for minority quality and has little effect on majority quality—though all three cleanup policies result in better quality outcomes for the majority than does no cleanup. In each case, since majority quality continues to decline after time-step 35 while minority quality improves, the environmental quality gap is actually reversed by about time-step 60. However, at that point, minority quality stops rising and begins to decline at a similar rate to majority quality. For minorities, the primary difference between the cleanup policies is in the steepness of improvement.

In Table 9.2, we show the general trends of both majority and minority quality and the environmental quality gap at three points during the cleanup phase. At each time point, minority quality is lowest when there is no cleanup (except at time-step 40), and is generally about the same regardless of the cleanup policy selected, but is usually the highest when the EJ policy

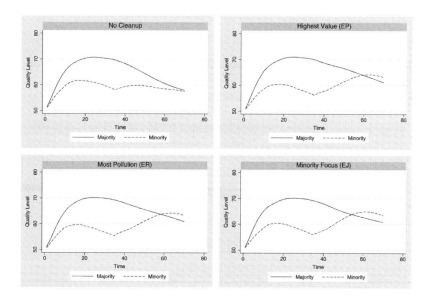

*Figure 9.1* Environmental quality gaps in a region with a severe EJ problem
Note: There is a slight improvement "bump" for minorities in the no cleanup scenario; this occurs when polluting firms stop targeting minority communities and switch to choosing the lowest-priced plot during the cleanup phase (time-step 35). Also, resident similarity preference is set at 80% for majorities and 50% for minorities after time-step 35 (both are set at 80% prior to time-step 35). Resident mobility is set at 12% throughout.

*Table 9.2* Quality results at various points during the cleanup phase

| | Quality level over time | | | | | |
|---|---|---|---|---|---|---|
| | t = 40 | | t = 50 | | t = 60 | |
| | Majority quality | Minority quality | Majority quality | Minority quality | Majority quality | Minority quality |
| No cleanup | 68.32 | 59.38 | 64.43 | 59.63 | 60.62 | 58.51 |
| EP policy | 68.76 | 57.75 | 66.64 | 61.55 | 64.02 | 64.11 |
| ER policy | 68.16 | 57.34 | 65.63 | 61.07 | 63.37 | 64.07 |
| EJ policy | 68.07 | 57.71 | 64.94 | 62.32 | 62.82 | 64.97 |

Note: EP is economic pressure, focusing on the most valuable polluted sites; ER is eliminating risk, focusing on the most polluted sites; and EJ is environmental justice, focusing on the polluted sites with the most minorities nearby.

is chosen and remediated sites are those with the largest concentrations of minority residents nearby. Conversely, while majority quality is also generally about the same across policies, it is most consistently the highest when the EP policy is followed and the sites targeted for remediation are those on the highest-valued land.

These results suggest that any policy of cleaning up sites will tend to benefit minority residents, and can be used as a tool to address environmental injustice. It is also worth noting that all three approaches to environmental cleanup benefit majorities too. While the trend in majority quality is generally about the same regardless of the cleanup policy (trending downward as available locations become more constrained), majority quality is still at a higher level when there is any cleanup policy rather than none.

As depicted in Figure 9.1, a policy cleaning up hazardous sites in a region with a significant environmental justice problem is a policy that can address, and perhaps even solve, this problem, and not at the majority's expense. There are two ways to close an environmental quality *gap*—by improving quality for the lower group, or by degrading quality for the other. As illustrated, these policies close the gap by improving quality for the lower group, and not by degrading quality for the other.

The policies compared here are ideal states—no government agency targets sites for cleanup based on a single criterion. However, these three policy options seem to represent the factors that the EPA balances when deciding where to invest cleanup dollars, for it tries to reduce risk; have sites not just cleaned up, but also redeveloped; and address environmental inequalities.[39] Excitingly, the results presented here suggest that it might be possible to accomplish more than one goal with one policy approach. In the idealized state of the model, and in scenarios for which the environmental justice problem was severe, environmental justice was addressed whether it was a specific policy goal or not. Thus, these policies combine improving urban sustainability overall through environmental improvement, and also improve EJ and thereby the social pillar of sustainability. These are strong policies.

A reason for these results may be because, in a region with a severe EJ problem, hazardous sites are so overrepresented in minority areas that any cleanup policy will be effective at improving outcomes for minorities. Given this possibility, we wondered whether the same would hold in a region with a less severe EJ problem.

### Community with a moderate EJ problem

As expected, in Figure 9.2 overall environmental quality for majorities and minorities during the simulation is higher (peaking at well above 70 for majorities) than we saw for a community with a severe EJ problem in Figure 9.1, and the environmental quality gap is not as significant. However, there is still an environmental justice problem and in this case there is a noticeable difference in the efficacy of policy actions.

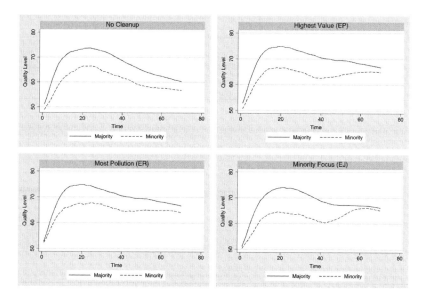

*Figure 9.2* Environmental quality gaps in a region with a moderate EJ problem
Note: Polluting firms target minority communities during the setup phase and switch
to choosing the lowest-priced plot during the cleanup phase (after time-step 35).
Also, resident similarity preference is set at 20% for both groups during the simulation
regardless of phase. Resident mobility is set at 12% throughout.

In this community condition, when there is no cleanup policy, quality for
both groups declines throughout the trial. Once again, majority quality follows a very similar trend regardless of the policy option, but any cleanup
option results in better outcomes for majorities than no cleanup. In this case,
however, minority quality varies more according to the policy. Under the EP
and ER policies, minority quality stopped declining and evened out, and even
increased a bit under the highest-value (EP) policy, but there is a steeper
upward trend in minority quality that significantly closes the environmental
quality gap in the EJ policy.

## Discussion

Our results suggest that, while policies need to be considered in context,
cleaning up existing hazardous sites can be a useful strategy for practitioners
seeking to address environmental injustice. We considered two contexts. In
the case of a region with a significant environmental justice problem (Figure
9.1), any cleanup policy resulted in substantial improvement in minority
environmental quality—and also raised majority quality compared to no
cleanup. Addressing the gap takes time; in the best case it took 20 time steps
to close the environmental quality gap, but any cleanup policy was effective

at addressing the gap, given the distribution of hazardous sites and minority residents in a region with a significant environmental justice problem.

In the second case, in a region with a smaller (but still important) environmental justice gap (Figure 9.2), there were variations in the efficacy of policy options. In this case, while any cleanup policy was better than none, a policy specifically aimed at addressing the environmental quality gap did so the most effectively. If the highest-risk sites or sites on the most valuable land were selected (ER or EP, respectively), the environmental quality gap became smaller, but whether it would continue closing was unclear. Another, unmeasured, potential benefit of the EJ approach is that it may enhance government–minority relations and thus strengthen sustainability's social pillar even more.

The results for this chapter present new types of conclusions. While we note that the *causes* of the environmental quality gap are complex and difficult to disaggregate, here our model suggests that *directly improving* the problem may be less complex, depending upon the regional context. If the EJ problem is significant, any cleanup policy is effective at multiple goals of urban sustainability. If the EJ problem is less severe, a more specific focus on amelioration of environmental injustice would be better. Each cleanup policy decreased the gap, but the specifically focused policy did so at a quicker rate. These results are particularly encouraging because they may represent potential Pareto[40] improvement. Improving both the lot of minorities and the gap between minorities and majorities also reduces quality declines for majorities and improves both macro and social sustainability.

It is worth noting a few caveats. Given the importance of similarity preferences in previous chapters, in the higher-injustice scenarios we opted to use an 80% majority, 50% minority similarity-preference structure, which is the most empirically supported. However, we also assumed that this preference structure does not change over time. It might be reasonable to assume that as the region moves forward in time, and as sites are remediated, these similarity preferences might also decrease, potentially improving minority quality further. Second, while residents were mobile (at 12% each),[41] we did not take into account any burdens of relocation, such as moving costs or loss of community. Yet, the latter factor is probably important to overall urban sustainability.

Also, given the pricing function of the model, when a polluting firm is cleaned up, the prices of the plots nearby rise in price, perhaps pricing out poor residents and becoming more attractive locations to wealthier residents. We did not track the extent of the environmental gentrification process, focusing instead on aggregate environmental quality for both groups rather than the also important outcomes related to displacement.[42] Urban practitioners might want to revise the model outputs to allow measurement of gentrification outcomes, as well.[43]

In this chapter, as with the chapter on zoning, we moved beyond consideration of the causes of the environmental justice problem and looked at a set of policies intended to fix the problem. We analyzed how different hazardous-site remediation policy priorities changed both the level of majority and minority environmental quality, and the gap that exists between these two "racial" groups. We specifically set up the model to create environmental justice problems, and then compared policies that remediated polluted sites on: 1 the highest-priced land; 2 the site with the highest level of pollution; and 3 the site located near the most minority residents.

We found that the context of the environmental justice problem certainly has an effect, but that hazardous-site remediation is promising as an important policy tool to address environmental justice problems. In the case of a severe problem, any policy was effective, but with a less severe problem, a specific focus on environmental justice addressed the EJ problem most quickly and significantly and thus contributed best to sustainability. As long as the context of implementation is understood, these results suggest that it might be possible for any approach to brownfields cleanup to achieve multiple policy goals—and without the political and organizational complexity so difficult for practitioners when they try to balance multiple objectives of competing groups.

## Notes

1 Material in this chapter is based on the more complicated version of the EJ ABM described in Chapter 3, but the analysis performed is similar to that in Adam Eckerd, "Policy Alternatives in Adaptive Communities: Simulating the Environmental Justice Consequences of Hazardous Site Remediation Strategies," *Review of Policy Research* 30, no. 3 (2013): 281–301. Any overlapping material is used by permission.
2 "Brownfields" are (generally urban) land sites that previously had development that left pollution behind (or is believed to have left pollution behind), which should be cleaned up before redevelopment can occur.
3 H. Spencer Banzhaf and Eleanor McCormick, "Moving Beyond Cleanup: Identifying the Crucibles of Environmental Gentrification," *Andrew Young School of Policy Studies Research Paper Series*, Working Paper 07-29 (2007).
4 H. Spencer Banzhaf and Randall P. Walsh, "Do People Vote with their Feet? An Empirical Test of Tiebout's Mechanism," *American Economic Review* 98, no. 3 (2008): 843–63.
5 Vicki Been and Francis Gupta, "Coming to the Nuisance or Going to the Barrios? A Longitudinal Analysis of Environmental Justice Claims," *Ecology Law Quarterly* 24, no. 1 (1997): 1–56.
6 David Ley, "Alternative Explanations for Inner-city Gentrification: A Canadian Assessment," *Annals of the Association of American Geographers* 76, no. 4 (1986): 521–35; Neil Smith, "Toward a Theory of Gentrification: A Back to the City Movement by Capital, not People," *Journal of the American Planning Association* 45, no. 4 (1979): 538–48.
7 "Environmental gentrification" is a specific type of gentrification, where environmental improvement in a community is expected to make nearby properties more attractive to potential buyers, thereby raising prices, potentially pricing out poor renters who will be replaced by wealthier incoming residents.
8 Holger Seig, V. Kerry Smith, H. Spencer Banzhaf and Randall Walsh, "Estimating the General Equilibrium Benefits of Large Changes in Spatially Delineated Public Goods," *International Economic Review* 45, no. 4 (2004): 1047–77; Adam

Eckerd, "Cleaning Up without Clearing Out? An Assessment of Environmental Gentrification," *Urban Affairs Review* 47, no. 1 (2011): 31–59.

9  Been and Gupta, "Coming to the Nuisance or Going to the Barrios?"

10  Warren Kriesel, Terence J. Centner and Andrew G. Keeler, "Neighborhood Exposure to Toxic Releases: Are there Racial Inequities?" *Growth and Change* 27, no. 4 (1996): 479–99.

11  However, note that though such residential sorting undoubtedly occurs in the US context, Pastor, Sadd and Hipp have found evidence that minorities are more likely to move from disamenities than to them, and Campbell, Peck and Tschudi have found evidence of imposition of new hazardous sites onto *Asian* communities, even though in the United States Asians are on average the richest US Census race/ethnicity group—richer than white non-Hispanics. Manuel Pastor, James Sadd and John Hipp, "Which Came First? Toxic Facilities, Minority Move-in, and Environmental Justice," *Journal of Urban Affairs* 23, no. 1 (2001): 1–21; Heather E. Campbell, Laura R. Peck and Michael K. Tschudi, "Justice for All? A Cross-time Analysis of Toxics Release Inventory Facility Location," *Review of Policy Research* 27, no. 1 (2010): 1–25.

12  Banzhaf and Walsh, "Do People Vote with their Feet?"

13  Seig et al., "Estimating the General Equilibrium Benefits of Large Changes in Spatially Delineated Public Goods."

14  Hamil Pearsall, "From Brown to Green? Assessing Social Vulnerability to Environmental Gentrification in New York City," *Environment and Planning C: Government and Policy* 28, no. 5 (2010): 872–86.

15  Steven Bonorris, *Environmental Justice for All: A Fifty-State Survey of Legislation, Policies, and Initiatives*, fourth edn, Joint Report, Hastings College of Law and American Bar Association (2010).

16  James T. Hamilton, "Environmental Equity and the Siting of Hazardous Waste Facilities in OECD Countries: Evidence and Policies," Presented at the National Policies Division, OECD Environmental Directorate, March 4–5, 2003.

17  Matthew Dull and Kris Wernstedt, "Land Recycling, Community Revitalization, and Distributive Politics: An Analysis of EPA Brownfields Program Support," *Policy Studies Journal* 38, no. 1 (2010): 119–41.

18  Larry Dale, James Murdoch, Mark Thayer and Paul Waddell, "Do Property Values Rebound from Environmental Stigmas?" *Land Economics* 75 (1999): 311–26.

19  Jill McCluskey and Gordon Rausser, "Stigmatized Asset Value: Is it Temporary or Long-term?" *Review of Economics and Statistics* 85, no. 2 (2003): 276–85.

20  Kent Messer, William Schulze, Katherine Hackett, Trudy Cameron and Gary McClelland, "Can Stigma Explain Large Property Value Losses? The Psychology and Economics of Superfund," *Environment and Resource Economics* 33 (2006): 299–324.

21  Daniel McMillen and Paul Thorsnes, "The Aroma of Tacoma: Time-Varying Average Derivatives and the Effect of a Superfund Site on House Prices," *Journal of Business & Economic Statistics* 21, no. 2 (2003): 237–46.

22  Seig et al., "Estimating the General Equilibrium Benefits of Large Changes in Spatially Delineated Public Goods."

23  Eckerd, "Cleaning Up Without Clearing Out?"

24  Matthew Dull and Kris Wernstedt, "Land Recycling, Community Revitalization and Distributive Politics: An Analysis of EPA Brownfields Program Support"; Adam Eckerd and Andrew Keeler, "Going Green Together? Environmental Justice and Environmental Remediation," *Policy Sciences* 45, no. 4 (2012): 293–314.

25  Christopher De Sousa, "The Greening of Brownfields in American Cities," *Journal of Environmental Planning and Management* 47, no. 4 (2004): 579–600.

26  Seig et al., "Estimating the General Equilibrium Benefits of Large Changes in Spatially Delineated Public Goods."

27  David Konisky, "Inequities in Enforcement? Environmental Justice and Government Performance," *Journal of Policy Analysis and Management* 28, no. 1 (2009): 102–21.
28  William Freudenberg, "Perceived Risk, Real Risk: Social Science and the Art of Probabilistic Risk Assessment," *Science* 242, no. 4875 (1988): 44–49.
29  Evan Ringquist, "Assessing Evidence of Environmental Inequities: A Meta-Analysis," *Journal of Policy Analysis and Management* 24, no. 2 (2005): 223–47.
30  William A.V. Clark, "Residential Preferences and Residential Choices in a Multiethnic Context," *Demography* 29, no. 3 (1992): 451–66.
31  Arthur Okun, *Equality and Efficiency: The Big Tradeoff* (Washington, DC: Brookings Institution Press, 1975).
32  Christopher De Sousa, *Brownfields Redevelopment and the Quest for Sustainability* (Oxford: Elsevier, 2008).
33  Dorothy Daley and David Layton, "Policy Implementation and the Environmental Protection Agency: What Factors Influence Remediation at Superfund Sites?" *Policy Studies Journal* 32, no. 3 (2004): 375–92.
34  See www.gsa.gov/graphics/regions/The_Yards_Final_EA_7_16_10.pdf.
35  See www.ninemilerun.org.
36  Michelle DePass, "Brownfields as a Tool for the Rejuvenation of Land and Community," *Local Environment* 11, no. 5 (2006): 601–6.
37  See www.greenimpactzone.org/Plan/vision.aspx.
38  See assets.columbus.gov/development/planning/WeinlandParkPlan.pdf.
39  Eckerd and Keeler, "Going Green Together?"
40  Pareto improvement makes some better off without making any worse off.
41  See Chapter 7 for empirical evidence on residential moving rates.
42  Eckerd, "Cleaning Up without Clearing Out?"
43  See ibid.

# References

Banzhaf, H. Spencer and Eleanor McCormick. "Moving Beyond Cleanup: Identifying the Crucibles of Environmental Gentrification." Andrew Young School of Policy Studies Research Paper Series, Working Paper 07–29 (2007).

Banzhaf, H. Spencer and Randall P. Walsh. "Do People Vote with their Feet? An Empirical Test of Tiebout's Mechanism." *American Economic Review* 98, no. 3 (2008): 843–863.

Been, Vicki and Francis Gupta. "Coming to the Nuisance or Going to the Barrios? A Longitudinal Analysis of Environmental Justice Claims." *Ecology Law Quarterly* 24, no. 1 (1997): 1–56.

Bonorris, Steven. *Environmental Justice for All: A Fifty-state Survey of Legislation, Policies and Initiatives, fourth edn.* San Francisco, CA: American Bar Association and Hastings College of Law, 2010.

Campbell, Heather E., Laura R. Peck and Michael K. Tschudi. "Justice for All? A Cross-time Analysis of Toxics Release Inventory Facility Location." *Review of Policy Research* 27, no. 1 (2010): 1–25.

Clark, William A.V. "Residential Preferences and Residential Choices in a Multiethnic Context." *Demography* 29, no. 3 (1992): 451–466.

Dale, Larry, James Murdoch, Mark Thayer and Paul Waddell. "Do Property Values Rebound from Environmental Stigmas?" *Land Economics* 75 (1999): 311–326.

Daley, Dorothy and David Layton. "Policy Implementation and the Environmental Protection Agency: What Factors Influence Remediation at Superfund Sites?" *Policy Studies Journal* 32, no. 3 (2004): 375–392.

DePass, Michelle. "Brownfields as a Tool for the Rejuvenation of Land and Community." *Local Environment* 11, no. 5 (2006): 601–606.

De Sousa, Christopher. "The Greening of Brownfields in American Cities." *Journal of Environmental Planning and Management* 47, no. 4 (2004): 579–600.

De Sousa, Christopher. *Brownfields Redevelopment and the Quest for Sustainability.* Oxford: Elsevier, 2008.

Dull, Matthew and Kris Wernstedt. "Land Recycling, Community Revitalization, and Distributive Politics: An Analysis of EPA Brownfields Program Support." *Policy Studies Journal* 38, no. 1 (2010): 119–141.

Eckerd, Adam. "Cleaning Up without Clearing Out? An Assessment of Environmental Gentrification." *Urban Affairs Review* 47, no. 1 (2011): 31–59.

Eckerd, Adam. "Policy Alternatives in Adaptive Communities: Simulating the Environmental Justice Consequences of Hazardous Site Remediation Strategies." *Review of Policy Research* 30, no. 3 (2013): 281–301.

Eckerd, Adam and Andrew Keeler. "Going Green Together? Environmental Justice and Environmental Remediation." *Policy Sciences* 45, no. 4 (2012): 293–314.

Freudenberg, William. "Perceived Risk, Real Risk: Social Science and the Art of Probabilistic Risk Assessment." *Science* 242, no. 4875 (1988): 44–49.

Hamilton, James T. "Environmental Equity and the Siting of Hazardous Waste Facilities in OECD Countries: Evidence and Policies." Presented at the National Policies Division, OECD Environmental Directorate, March 4–5, 2003.

Konisky, David. "Inequities in Enforcement? Environmental Justice and Government Performance." *Journal of Policy Analysis and Management* 28, no. 1 (2009): 102–121.

Kriesel, Warren, Terence J. Centner and Andrew G. Keeler. "Neighborhood Exposure to Toxic Releases: Are there Racial Inequities?" *Growth and Change* 27, no. 4 (1996): 479–499.

Ley, David. "Alternative Explanations for Inner-city Gentrification: A Canadian Assessment." *Annals of the Association of American Geographers* 76, no. 4 (1986): 521–535.

McCluskey, Jill and Gordon Rausser. "Stigmatized Asset Value: Is it Temporary or Long-term?" *Review of Economics and Statistics* 85, no. 2 (2003): 276–285.

McMillen, Daniel and Paul Thorsnes. "The Aroma of Tacoma: Time-Varying Average Derivatives and the Effect of a Superfund Site on House Prices." *Journal of Business & Economic Statistics* 21, no. 2 (2003): 237–246.

Messer, Kent, William Schulze, Katherine Hackett, Trudy Cameron and Gary McClelland. "Can Stigma Explain Large Property Value Losses? The Psychology and Economics of Superfund." *Environment and Resource Economics* 33, no. 3 (2006): 299–324.

Okun, Arthur. *Equality and Efficiency: The Big Tradeoff.* Washington, DC: Brookings Institution Press, 1975.

Pastor, Manuel, James Sadd and John Hipp. "Which Came First? Toxic Facilities, Minority Move-in, and Environmental Justice." *Journal of Urban Affairs* 23, no. 1 (2001): 1–21.

Pearsall, Hamil. "From Brown to Green? Assessing Social Vulnerability to Environmental Gentrification in New York City." *Environment and Planning C: Government and Policy* 28, no. 5 (2010): 872–886.

Ringquist, Evan. "Assessing Evidence of Environmental Inequities: A Meta-Analysis." *Journal of Policy Analysis and Management* 24, no. 2 (2005): 223–247.

Seig, Holger, V. Kerry Smith, H. Spencer Banzhaf and Randall Walsh. "Estimating the General Equilibrium Benefits of Large Changes in Spatially Delineated Public Goods." *International Economic Review* 45, no. 4 (2004): 1047–1077.

Smith, Neil. "Toward a Theory of Gentrification: A Back to the City Movement by Capital, not People." *Journal of the American Planning Association* 45, no. 4 (1979): 538–548.

# 10 All politics is spatial

## Integrating an agent-based model with spatially explicit landscape data

*Hal T. Nelson, Nicholas L. Cain, and Zining Yang*

"All politics is local."

(O'Neill and Hymel[1])

Tip O'Neill's famous quote is a pithy way to introduce the topic of integrating real-world data into agent-based modeling research.[2] O'Neill's truism stresses that politicians have to know their constituents in order to win elections, and that these constituents are primarily concerned about local issues. For example, what matters to a person in Cambridge, Massachusetts, home to Harvard and MIT, often is very different from what matters to a resident in blue-collar south Boston, where up to 75% of households earn less than US$30,000 per year.

If one accepts the premise that local issues are defined in large measure by local institutions, demographics, and economic conditions—all of which vary from place to place—then the implication is that all politics is *spatial*. Seen this way, "local" is just a synonym for "spatial," and this is especially the case when it comes to issues of environmental justice (EJ), for which geospatial factors influence both the location of pollution and the "social geography" of demographics.[3] Another implication is that urban sustainability is inherently a spatial issue. Because of this, agent-based models (ABMs) designed to study EJ issues can benefit greatly by taking local spatial data into account.

Fortunately, as the previous chapters have noted, new approaches to simulation are now allowing the integration of real-world data with the rule-based logic of the computational environment. Integrating geospatial data generated by geographic information systems (GIS) with agent-based modeling techniques opens up new vistas for theoretical research and especially for applied analysis of use to practitioners. This is particularly the case when the interactions of agents in an ABM, and subsequent emergent behaviors, are conditioned by properties that vary by location. For the policy analyst or researcher, GIS-ABM models can improve the empirical validity of explanations and provide decision support to policymakers.

In this chapter, our first goal is to introduce basic theoretical considerations for fusing GIS data and ABMs. Next, we highlight the advantages of coupling the approaches and examine some relevant software packages. We then present a spatially explicit multi-agent simulation, which we use to simulate two scenarios and make some inferences regarding EJ concerns over the siting of locally unwanted land use (LULU) facilities. We conclude with policy and research implications of our findings for urban sustainability.

## Integrating agent-based modeling with GIS

To begin, we discuss key definitions and theoretical considerations for integrating spatial data and agent-based models. Spatial data models represent geographical phenomena either as discrete objects on a layer of data, or as continuous fields that form surfaces. In the discrete objects approach, houses may be represented as points, highways as lines, and Census tracts as polygons. These real-world features are defined by attributes, such as population density or landscape cover, and by location in a fashion that allows placement on a computer-generated map.[4]

In contrast, agents within an ABM may contain location information and various data attributes, but agent interactions, according to various rules, are the focus. ABMs are process oriented and dynamic in that they simulate the interactions of agents over time and have detailed scheduling mechanisms that guide agent behavior.[5] The focus of an ABM is often on emergent patterns that arise out of micro-level interactions (as is described in the earlier chapters). On the other hand, GIS models are data oriented and express the structure of entities in the real world in relation to each other.[6] GIS models usually employ a static temporal representation consisting of a spatial "snapshot" of the arrangement of objects at a given time. In summary, ABMs are *process oriented* and GIS models are *spatially oriented*.

Integrated ABM-GIS models can be categorized as "loose," "moderate," or "tight" according to how data and processing are shared across the models.[7] Loosely coupled models share files, often across separate software packages, asynchronously. In a loosely coupled model, it is often the case that GIS is used to prepare data for the ABM simulation, and then results are returned for visualization to the GIS. Moderately coupled models have the ability to remotely access and share database information across the modules. Tightly coupled models allow the GIS and ABM components to communicate with each other during the simulation run. Although tightly coupled models may run faster, they are usually more difficult to program.[8] Regardless of the degree of coupling, an integrated model requires careful consideration of its advantages and challenges, and of the relationships between model components.

### Advantages and challenges

There are several theoretical and policy-relevant advantages—and also distinct challenges—that flow from integrating ABMs and GISs. The first advantage of integrated models is their ability to simulate distinct individuals and to model emergence. Emergence has been characterized as patterns arising from the *local* interactions of individual entities.[9] Being local, agent interactions are, at least partially, dependent on the spatial terrain.[10] Thus, in simulating emergent behavior, the built environment and natural features are often important factors—particularly in land-use planning and analysis of EJ issues. For instance, canyons and highways can inhibit or expedite the movement and interaction of agents and pollutants. Or, discontinuities in terrain and the built environment can lead to non-linear interactions that result in emergence. Since space in a GIS model is based on a geo-referenced coordinate system, an integrated model can model local interactions and "the effects of stochastic temporal and spatial variability," which in turn can be used to generate "phenomenologically realistic and complex behavior."[11]

The second advantage of integrating the two types of analytics is that real-world data allow rigorous validation of ABM results. Model verification and validation (as discussed earlier) is the process of evaluating whether the various components of the model behave as expected, and also whether the results of the model correspond to observed phenomena. In an ABM-GIS model, since simulation outputs are often presented in a geographic context, they can be compared to real-world outcomes and tested against real-world data.[12] Integrated ABM-GIS models can be validated against historical outcomes, demographic information, and other empirical data.

The final advantage of integrating GIS data with agent-based models is that ABM-GIS models can help decision makers optimize operational and resource allocation decisions.[13] ABM-GIS models can be constructed to create rigorous decision support systems (DSSs) which, in turn, can be used to analyze and plan projects and policies. DSSs allow users to simulate a range of possible policy inputs and outcomes, and can simulate the effects of a change in policy as compared to a business-as-usual path. A DSS can also be used for theoretical inquiry, as we demonstrate later in this chapter.

Our own experience with integrating agent-based modeling and GIS models has shown that it is not a trivial task—even though it may be crucial to working toward urban sustainability. Even with software that integrates the process and data models (as described below), considerable experience is needed in both agent-based modeling and GIS programming in order to get the integrated model to function properly. For example, modelers must clean and recode Census data so that the ABM software can process them. The map projection system used by the GIS model to translate location information needs to be recognized by the ABM software. Most importantly, procedures in the ABM code need to be carefully developed to account for the four relationships discussed below.

### What to consider

In order to achieve the advantages discussed above, which can help practitioners improve local sustainability, agent-based and geographic models must be carefully integrated. Brown et al. identify four key relationships to consider:[14]

1    It is crucial to establish valid identity relationships between agents and GIS data. Agents representing citizens, for instance, can be instantiated in the ABM on a 1:1 or a 1:many basis. Representing the citizens in a Census tract with fewer agents in the ABM can help the model run faster, but may harm model validity, especially if agent behavior is conditioned on the frequency of agent interactions or their movements across tracts.

2    Model integration requires careful attention to causal relationships and feedback loops. Agent behaviors can affect spatial features and their attributes, which in turn can influence agent behavior. One example is readily familiar to EJ researchers: an increasing number of polluting firms move into an area, which results in a change in the zoning of a parcel from commercial to industrial (cf. Chapter 8). In this case, the results of the ABM (e.g., decisions by firms to move) must update the GIS data model (e.g., the zoning attributes for each tract), which, in turn, may influence future decisions made by agents in the model.

3    Once causal relationships have been specified, temporal relationships must also be delineated. Changes to agents and to the features of the GIS model need to occur within a realistic timeframe and be updated as simulation time progresses.

4    In integrated models, careful attention must be paid to spatial relationships and interactions between ABM and GIS components. Spatial data include the location of agents upon model initialization, the topography of the model space, and the geographic rules that govern how agents move. Model builders must consider how agent interactions translate into movement, how far and how fast agents move, and whether they can cross boundaries such as rivers or roads. Similarly, spatial rules might also require that houses cannot be built on top of existing houses, or agents cannot occupy the same place at the same time.

Once analysts have considered these four types of relationships and made efforts to plan their model, programming can begin using a growing range of computer-based environments.

### Software platforms

The good news for the analyst who wishes to combine geographic information with agent-based simulation is that most ABM platforms have added at least basic spatial data capabilities. Given this, the most straightforward approach to model fusion is to include spatial data in one of the agent-based modeling platforms listed in Table 10.1, all of which are either open source or free.

*Table 10.1* Select software applications and platforms for GIS-ABM analysis

| ABM toolkit | Description and URL |
|---|---|
| NetLogo | NetLogo includes basic raster and vector GIS capabilities via a built-in extension; ccl.northwestern.edu/netlogo/docs/gis.html |
| MASON | The GeoMason extension adds advanced vector and raster capabilities to MASON; www.cs.gmu.edu/~eclab/projects/mason/extensions/geomason/ |
| Repast | Some GIS is provided within Repast by the GeoTools extension and Java Topology Suite, and Repast can be linked with Esri ArcGIS via Agent Analyst; repast.sourceforge.net |
| Agent Analyst | Agent Analyst provides a powerful integration of Esri ArcGIS with Repast; resources.arcgis.com/en/help/agent-analyst/ |
| R | The R statistical environment has basic spatial features, packages such as "sp" add power, and ABM capability can be added through the "RNetLogo" package; cran.r-project.org/web/views/Spatial.html |
| GAMA | A new, dedicated ABM-GIS platform; code.google.com/p/gama-plat form/wiki/GAMA |

Note: URLs provide links to additional information.

The software list in Table 10.1 is by no means comprehensive. Nikolai and Madey find over 50 different multi-agent modeling toolkits which range from open-source progenitors of agent-based modeling (such as Swarm), to commercial software (such as AnyLogic) that includes agent-based tools.[15] However, according to an analysis of research papers, the programs most frequently used by scholars in the past few years are NetLogo (used in previous chapters), Repast, Swarm, and MASON.[16] Given that Swarm is increasingly being supplanted by easier-to-use platforms such as Repast (which borrows many concepts from Swarm), we chose to highlight the applications presented in Table 10.1.

NetLogo is the first application we list because of its popularity and ease of use, and because it is used in previous chapters in this book. Given that the model we describe later in this chapter (the SEMPro DSS) was also authored in NetLogo, we discuss the capabilities of this platform in more detail below. Other ABM simulation platforms also include GIS capabilities, but require more complex programming. The MASON multi-agent simulation platform, for instance, provides very powerful capabilities, but must be programmed in Java. The MASON environment is broken into model-construction and visualization modules, and spatial data can be integrated using the GeoMason extension.[17] The Repast (aka the Recursive Porous Agent Simulation Toolkit) platform is another powerful multi-agent tool that can integrate spatial data. Although GIS data can be handled natively in Repast, more sophisticated capabilities are made available by using Agent

Analyst to integrate with Esri's ArcGIS suite of software.[18] R, an open-source statistical analysis platform, has the benefit of being able to run hundreds of different software modules. Available packages allow the addition of GIS capabilities within the R environment. Still other packages allow the integration of NetLogo within R or the use of R within NetLogo.[19]

*NetLogo and spatial data*

As described in Chapter 3, NetLogo has several advantages over other approaches: it is relatively simple to program and includes an intuitive, built-in user interface, giving it both ease of use and transparency in design. In addition, NetLogo imports GIS data using the now standard Esri "shapefile" format, or the Esri ASCII Grid file for raster data. The program can generate elements (such as agents representing people or firms) based on GIS data and can also generate variables based on the attributes of the spatial data.[20] To use these capabilities, spatial data must be created with a stand-alone GIS application or imported via an existing shapefile. After agents or patches are instantiated using the spatial data, agents within NetLogo can become spatially aware and thus interact with GIS data.

Although various attributes within the GIS data (e.g., population density) can be translated into elements within the NetLogo environment, more sophisticated kinds of geographic analysis are not yet supported. NetLogo is also limited in its ability to communicate with external datasets and cannot write back to shapefiles directly. However, it can update geographic information stored in the NetLogo program. Another drawback to using GIS data within NetLogo is that the GIS extension slows NetLogo's computational performance. Also potentially problematic is the small size of the graphical user interface (GUI) "window" available in NetLogo to view geographic data. These limits aside, NetLogo's ease of use makes it the go-to tool for many analysts, and programs such as ReLogo allow NetLogo code to be imported into more powerful environments such as Repast.

The fusion of agent-based simulation with spatial data is a rapidly evolving field. As this short introduction indicates, there are many different software applications and approaches to integration of ABMs and GISs. In the next section, we discuss the construction of the Sustainable Energy Modeling Program (SEMPro) and delve into the results of some simulation scenarios that analyze questions relevant to environmental justice and sustainability.

# A case of a GIS-enhanced ABM for decision support

*Power and environmental justice*

As any student of politics will tell you, power matters. The SEMPro model allows us to simulate decision outcomes under different levels of citizen power. The model can represent a project in a *physical* geography (including physical constraints) while accounting for the *social* geography of power, and then simulate the impact of interest-group bargaining on regulatory decision making. Our results indicate that despite all the money spent on assessing the engineering aspects of major infrastructure projects, citizen participation and political power are more important to stakeholder bargaining outcomes than the level of local (physical) disruption that a project causes.

The SEMPro decision-support model presented here simulates the complexity of infrastructure siting by fusing: GIS data for a specific locale, with an agent-based model of citizen attitude and behavior diffusion, and spatial bargaining models of stakeholder and regulatory decision making. Users can simulate the geospatial, engineering, social, and political attributes of each project (as explained in more detail in Abdollahian et al.[21]). SEMPro can be characterized as a loosely coupled ABM-GIS integrated with game-theoretic stakeholder bargaining modules. Although the results are not returned to a GIS application, they are presented within a real-world spatial context using the ABM graphical interface.

Below, we briefly summarize the basic architecture of the current iteration of the SEMPro model, and then simulate two different scenarios with the goal of examining EJ issues. By gaining insight into the dynamics of siting decisions, including how citizens interact and stakeholders bargain, users of the SEMPro DSS can reduce sociopolitical conflict and integrate a wider range of stakeholder concerns into a LULU project's design. DSSs like SEMPro allow users to improve planning outcomes by simulating tradeoffs and alternatives.[22] These capacities are key to sustainability, for the sustainable future will still require LULUs within or near urban environments.

### The SEMPro model

#### Agents and their decision-making modules

The Sustainable Energy Modeling Program is a decision-support software program specifically designed for energy facilities siting, but which can be used for almost any large-scale project useful for sustainable cities. The software simulates how competing interests, and community and project attributes, shape siting outcomes. The citizen agents, stakeholders, and regulators in the model are all trying to maximize their own utilities, given the assumption of bounded rationality. SEMPro has three sequential sub-modules that run for up to 25 time steps, with each time step representing 2 months of calendar time. Figure 10.1 depicts the overall model architecture and details key module processes.

Citizens react to infrastructure siting projects by forming opinions, interacting with their neighbors, multiplying their power by forming community-based organizations (CBOs), and engaging in extra-process legal or political

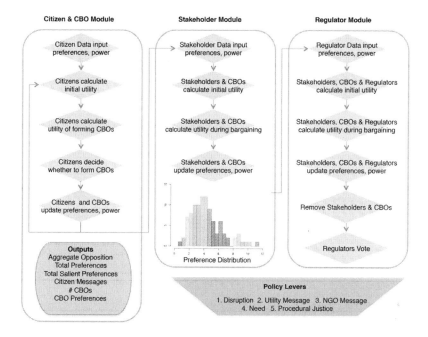

*Figure 10.1* SEMPro model architecture
(Abdollahian et al. 2013, used by permission)

activities.[23] In the first module of SEMPro (the Citizen & CBO Module), GIS-based data on the project size and route, on land use, and on the location of residents informs agent-based simulations of individual interactions. Figure 10.1 shows how these behaviors can result in the formation of CBOs that either support or oppose such projects. (CBOs are shown in the bottom part of Figure 10.2 as red (opposed) or blue (supportive) "faces.") Because citizens are typically opposed to the project, pro-development CBOs are uncommon and, if they do appear, not very influential because they have few members. As citizens interact to support or oppose the project, new agents representing citizen-based organizations may appear in the neighborhood.

The second module of SEMPro, shown in the center column of Figure 10.1, focuses on bargaining between CBOs and other organized stakeholders. In this context, "stakeholders" are non-CBO interest groups and government agencies that have the potential to influence the siting process. In the siting of energy projects, there are usually at least a dozen stakeholders that can include local, state and federal agencies, environmental organizations and other user groups, and utilities and power producers.[24]

Stakeholders seek to influence citizen opinions and emergent CBOs, and also other stakeholders, in order to maximize their organizational interests. (These stakeholders are shown in the circle in the top-right section of the

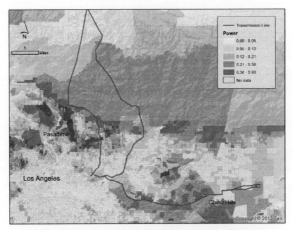

## (a) Census and Engineering Data

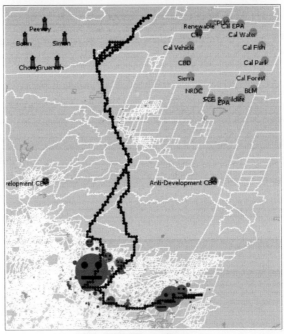

## (b) SEMPro Output

*Figure 10.2* Study area and SEMPro output

Note: Top panel shows the route of the Tehachapi Renewable Transmission Project (TRTP) transmission line, superimposed on the relative power of Census block groups, as it runs through Los Angeles and San Bernardino counties. Citizen power is the product of average household income and average household education. The bottom panel shows a similar area as seen through the "windshield" of the SEMPro ABM-GIS model, with CBOs depicted as either red (opposed) or blue faces. One portion of this figure, from Abdollahian, Yang and Nelson (2013), is used by permission.

bottom panel of Figure 10.2.) Preference data for stakeholders come from a web-based survey administered between July 2011 and March 2013.[25] The use of such stakeholder information is not standard in GIS or ABM, but shows another way in which an ABM can be enriched by real-world information. In the model, stakeholder bargaining incorporates non-cooperative game theory to reflect competing interests during the process.

The final module of SEMPro, shown in the far-right column of Figure 10.1, simulates the regulatory decision-making process, which is based on the interplay between CBOs (representing the public), stakeholders, and regulators. This module makes use of the same non-cooperative bargaining theory as the previous module. Regulators participate in the stakeholder bargaining process during time-steps 16–20. After time-step 20, regulators bargain among themselves and decide the project's fate using a majority-voting rule. (Regulators and their preferences are represented as chess pieces in Figure 10.2 in the upper left-hand side of the bottom panel.)

### GIS data in SEMPro

As discussed above, GIS data are critical for representing the real-world attributes of the project in the decision support system. As described in the next paragraphs, spatial data used in the SEMPro model include project route and size, topographical data, and US Census data.

Data on project route and size can take the form of lines or polygons (representing power lines) or points (representing power plants or waste incinerators). By overlaying GIS project data onto US Census data, the project then follows, or is placed into, the real-life attributes of the community. The top panel in Figure 10.2 shows the transmission line route for the SEMPro case study, as well as the varying levels of citizen power in the area. With greater resolution, Figure 10.2 would reveal that the transmission line mostly follows existing rights of way through the region. These rights of way constitute the setback between the project and the houses along the route. The proximity of the citizen agents to the project is a key driver of attitudes to the project. We assume that the importance (salience) of the project to citizens is relative to the inverse of its distance. Less proximate citizens are less likely to get involved in the siting process because it is not as important to them.

We have also included gridded, topographical data into the model that represents the "viewshed," or the region where an agent could view the 200 foot-tall transmission towers analyzed in this particular instance. The current version of the model takes a simple approach based only on proximity, but future versions could integrate a more sophisticated use of topographic data.

US Census block-group-level data on population density are used to locate citizen agents in the ABM. Citizen agents are instantiated in the model at a rate consistent with US Census data and with one agent representing 1,000 people. GIS-based Census data on education and income, by block group, are also included as attributes of the citizen agents. Higher levels of income and education imbue citizens with greater political power, and more powerful citizens, because they have a stronger sense of self-efficacy as well as more resources and access, are more influential in affecting project outcomes.[26]

After the geographic information summarized above is input into the model, different parameters and policy "levers" can be adjusted. One of the primary policy levers simulated in the model is the level of *disruption* that the project imposes on the community. Disruption is the cumulative effect of negative externalities such as aesthetic impact, risk of exposure to electric and magnetic fields, and reduction in residential property values. For transmission lines, disruption is measured as the height of the transmission tower, with 0 indicating no change to the existing landscape, and 1 indicating the maximum above-ground disruption of a 200-foot pylon. Smaller transmission towers are measured as values between 0 and 1 (e.g., 0.6).

*Need* is the perceived project need. The highest value for need is when the project has been approved by the state transmission operator and it improves reliability for the communities affected by the power line. Need is lowest when the power line carries power to other regions without significant local benefits. Need is assessed by subject-matter experts based on public statements from the project proponent and the independent system operator.

*Procedure* is an indicator of procedural justice, or to what extent the citizens think their preferences will be included in regulatory decision making. Gross has shown that the level of trust residents have in the decision-making procedure is critical to sentiment regarding a project—a reason why sustainability is assisted by trust between citizens, including minority citizens, and government.[27] Although this can be difficult to control in practice, work by Beierle and Cayford has shown that how policymakers shape public participation and integrate public comment can have a substantial effect on citizen sentiment.[28]

*Utility message* represents the number of pro-development messages the project sponsor sends to citizens to shape public attitudes. *NGO message* represents the number of anti-development outreach messages that nongovernmental organizations (NGOs) send.

One important parameter that is a constant rather than a policy lever is *talk-span*, which is the distance or neighborhood within which agents talk to each other and make decisions on whether to form CBOs.

### Simulation study area

SEMPro was initially designed to simulate the siting of high-voltage transmission lines (HVTL). The Tehachapi Renewable Transmission Project (TRTP), located in southern California, was the case used for model construction. TRTP is a 173 mile-long HVTL project being constructed to connect wind generators in the Tehachapi-Mojave Wind Resource Area with customers located in the Los Angeles metropolitan area. By using extra-urban area wind sources to provide power in Los Angeles, it should enhance urban sustainability, but the project has not been popular. Our model correctly highlights the opposition to Segment 8A of the project, which runs through the City of Chino Hills, located in the southwest corner of San Bernardino County.

The top of Figure 10.2 shows "political power" data for the study region. We calculate citizen political power by multiplying average household income by average education level and normalizing the data. As shown in Figure 10.2, darker colors represent higher levels of education and income. The bottom panel of Figure 10.2 shows the model's predictions for the spatial location of citizen messages in high-population-density Census block groups.

As one element of its validation, the model's predictions were compared with actual public comments. The SEMPro model's predictions match the comments submitted by residents of Chino Hills, and slightly over-predict comments from the Pasadena area (another city in the region).[29] Other model validation efforts included comparing the modeling outcomes with *a priori* theoretical expectations.[30]

### *Adding an EJ component*

Given this model design and the validity tests performed, we now describe scenarios of interest to environmental justice researchers and sustainability practitioners. Although the SEMPro model was not explicitly designed for EJ analysis, we can use it for this purpose by simulating outcomes under two different scenarios. In the reference-case scenario, the power of agents varies according to Census-derived data as shown in the top panel of Figure 10.2 and described above. We contrast this with an egalitarian case scenario, where all agents have the same (maximum) level of power. In this case (not shown), a power map of the region would be entirely dark blue.

Since the model's algorithms dictate that more powerful citizens are more influential (because they are more likely to send messages to regulators and more likely to form CBOs), in the reference case we expect fewer citizen comments and less advocacy, as many citizens have less than full power. In contrast, in the egalitarian world scenario, we expect that more messages will be sent and more CBOs will form as all citizens have a high level of power. Thus, comparing the reference (GIS-based) scenario to an egalitarian scenario allows us to consider what outcomes would look like in the *absence* of environmental *in*justice.

### *Model outcomes*

We conducted a quasi-global sensitivity analysis by varying all input parameters across their entire range in three steps (minimum, mean, maximum), which resulted in 729 runs for each of the two scenarios, or a total of 1,458 runs. Each run contained up to 25 time steps for a total of 29,154 observations. The simulation results were pooled together and ordinary least squares (OLS) estimation was used to create standardized β (beta) coefficients for input parameter comparability and model performance.[31]

In Table 10.2, Model 1 shows the impact of input parameters on citizen opposition to the project, which in turn drives formation of CBOs and thus influences regulators in the subsequent modules, as shown in Figure 10.1. The dependent variable is the result of the interaction of the total number of citizen messages and the median preferences of citizen agents. This captures *both* the direction and intensity of public sentiment at the level of the study

*Table 10.2* Pooled OLS estimations of citizen, CBO, and stakeholder preferences

| | Model 1 | Model 2 | Model 3 | Model 4 |
|---|---|---|---|---|
| | *Citizen preferences (opposition)* | *CBO preferences* | *Stakeholder preferences* | *Citizen preferences* |
| Disruption | 0.113*** | 0.001 | -0.002 | 0.146*** |
| | (0.000) | (0.506) | (0.333) | (0.000) |
| Talk-span | 0.609*** | 0.904*** | 0.898*** | 0.609*** |
| | (0.000) | (0.000) | (0.000) | (0.000) |
| NGO message | 0.024*** | 0.008*** | 0.004* | 0.024*** |
| | (0.000) | (0.000) | (0.028) | (0.000) |
| Utility message | 0.013*** | 0.003 | 0.002 | 0.013*** |
| | (0.000) | (0.211) | (0.313) | (0.000) |
| Need | -0.015*** | -0.007*** | -0.008*** | -0.015*** |
| | (0.000) | (0.001) | (0.000) | (0.000) |
| Procedure | 0.015*** | 0.002 | -0.001 | 0.015*** |
| | (0.000) | (0.428) | (0.689) | (0.000) |
| Power diff. | -0.125*** | 0.001 | -0.004* | -0.077*** |
| | (0.000) | (0.509) | (0.039) | (0.000) |
| Time step | 0.632*** | 0.251*** | 0.296*** | 0.632*** |
| | (0.000) | (0.000) | (0.000) | (0.000) |
| Power diff. * disruption | | | | -0.067*** |
| | | | | (0.000) |
| N | 29,154 | 29,154 | 29,154 | 29,154 |
| Prob > F | 0.000 | 0.000 | 0.000 | 0.000 |
| Adj. $R^2$ | 0.800 | 0.880 | 0.895 | 0.801 |

Note: Standardized beta coefficients; p-values in parentheses. * $p<0.05$, ** $p<0.01$, *** $p<0.001$. The dependent variable for Model 1 is a measure of citizen opposition.

area. Models 2 and 3 measure the impact of the drivers on dependent variables that are created within each module of SEMPro. The dependent variable of Model 2 measures CBO preferences and the dependent variable of Model 3 measures stakeholder preferences in a similar fashion.

As shown in the first column of Table 10.2, all Model 1 drivers are statistically significant and all of the signs are in the expected direction (with the exception of procedural justice). Community attributes and other control variables have a large impact on citizen advocacy and activism. First, the value of *talk-span* ($\beta$ = 0.61) in Model 1 suggests that citizens communicate their opinions to regulators more frequently in well-connected communities. The implications of this finding are discussed in more detail below. As expected, each model time step, which represents 2 months of calendar time ($\beta$ = 0.63), has a positive and significant impact on the number of citizen messages. Given the structure of the SEMPro model, we expect a high Adjusted-$R^2$, which we can see with Model 1 at 80%.

The level of disruption has the most substantial effects among the policy levers in the SEMPro model. Given the value ($\beta$ = 0.113), we can say that an increase of one standard deviation in the level of project disruption results in a 0.11 standard deviation increase in negative citizen response. Looking at the other policy levers, although effect sizes are small, both NGO messages and utility messages increase citizen opposition. The relationship of utility messages to citizen opposition is counterintuitive but logical. The harder utilities "push" citizens, the more citizens push back.[32] The impact of project *need* in Model 1 is negative ($\beta$ = -0.015), which is consistent with existing theory that when a project is perceived as necessary, it will generate less opposition. Perceptions of procedural justice have a positive effect ($\beta$ = 0.015), which suggests that citizens who view the process as fair are more likely to participate by expressing opposition. This finding is counter to theoretical expectations and previous research, and requires further investigation.[33]

Looking at the results for *power diff.*, we can gain some insight into the differences between the EJ scenarios. Recall that we have 729 simulations for the reference case with power levels calculated from US Census data, and the same number of simulations with all citizens having maximum power. In the regression models, *power diff.* is a dummy variable, with 0 for the EJ simulations and 1 for the reference-case simulations. The negative coefficient for *power diff.* indicates that in the reference-case scenario where power levels vary based on Census data, fewer messages are sent to regulators. This implies that in an egalitarian siting process more citizens would participate. The effect of power is strong: the standardized coefficient for power differential is larger than the coefficient for disruption, one of the primary drivers of opposition.

In Model 2, the coefficient for *power diff.* indicates that varying levels of citizen power have no significant effects on CBO preferences. Variation in citizen power impacts CBO influence in the siting process (as more powerful citizens are more likely to create CBOs and more CBOs are more effective), but in our simulations has no significant impact on CBO preferences. Turning to Model 3, the *power diff.* coefficient indicates a very small (β = -0.004) and significant (p<0.05) effect on stakeholder preferences. In other words, we can expect slightly more opposition in a more egalitarian world. Since power differentials do not directly affect CBO preferences in the model, the unequal distribution of citizen power affects stakeholders through other channels.

Finally, in Model 4, we interact two of the most important variables from an EJ perspective, disruption and power differential, and then assess their effects on citizen messages. The negative interaction coefficient indicates that variation in citizen power in the reference case reduces the effect of disruption on the number of citizen opposition messages sent to regulators. The interaction term predicts that, holding all other variables constant, reduced equality of citizens reduces the effect of disruption on messages sent to regulators. *Ceteris paribus*, we can predict that proponents of very disruptive projects are more likely to get their projects approved in areas where citizens have lower levels of income and education.

## Discussion

Our simulation analysis in this chapter finds that low levels of individual income and education reduce public participation in energy facility siting. Less powerful individuals are less influential in influencing project outcomes. The findings of the effects of power differentials are not surprising as they are coded into the SEMPro model structure. What is surprising is the relatively large effect size of power inequality. The standardized coefficient for power inequality is larger than that of project disruption, holding other variables constant.

Our findings may be of use to several debates in EJ research and practice, and thus have relevance to our pursuit of sustainable cities. First, we find support for sociopolitical explanations that argue that poor and/or uneducated communities have more difficulty developing effective opposition to disruptive projects.[34] A second implication relates to the temporal debate about which came first: locally unwanted land uses, or poor and minority communities. While not explicitly a panel analysis, our ABM results are consistent with research that finds that unwanted facilities are imposed on existing communities with a low ability to oppose them.[35] This is consistent with the infamous Cerrell Associates report of 1984, which recommended that new waste incineration facilities be sited in poor communities.[36]

The results from the interaction between disruption and power also show that the inability of less powerful communities to participate in siting decisions attenuates the negative effects of a project's disruption on planning processes. This supports research showing that project sponsors are aware of the relative ease of siting projects in less powerful communities and that this has guided siting decisions.[37] The implication is that while low-disruption projects may be sited through high-education and high-income communities, high-disruption projects are more likely to go through less powerful communities. More egalitarian residential power relationships, or siting processes that treat groups in a more egalitarian manner, would mean that very disruptive projects would face higher levels of opposition. This is troubling for practitioners who seek to develop more sustainable cities since, in this case, there is a tradeoff between siting an environmentally beneficial project and imposing its costs on the poorer and less well educated.

We also find some methodological implications from our simulation and analysis. Some EJ research has treated hazardous waste facilities and other environmentally harmful projects as dichotomous units where the facilities either exist or do not exist.[38] However, this coding could actually be understating the effects of race- and class-based biases on facility siting. For example, if small facilities with few toxic emissions sited in wealthy communities are coded the same as larger, high-emissions facilities sited in poorer, more diverse neighborhoods, then multivariate regression will underestimate the impact of race and income on pollution exposure. Our model represents the size of the project (measured as a variable taking on values between 0 and 1), as well as agent proximity to the project, as continuous variables within a specific physical context. As we detail above, this provides greater precision in measuring disruption and understanding the impact of geography on agent decisions—key issues for decision makers. We suggest improving measurement of disruption whenever possible. This research recommendation is consistent with social epidemiology methodologies that use GIS and facility-level emissions data to estimate individual health impacts across spatial scales.[39]

There are also several policy implications from the findings of our ABM-GIS model. The first policy implication is that a more egalitarian process for siting infrastructure would result in more citizen opposition, fewer highly disruptive projects near citizens and, possibly, greater social justice in the long run. Our findings support the importance of institutionalized public participation, which tends to increase communication and ensure stakeholders are representing community sentiment.[40] A more egalitarian planning process could proactively survey all the citizens impacted by a project, rather than employing the passive notification and comment period approach, which tends to favor wealthier and more educated individuals. Such an approach could enhance sustainability in more than one way, by increasing the justice of LULU placements, and also enhancing government-citizen trust.

The second policy implication is that ABM-GIS models can be an effective way to integrate social justice issues into planning for specific projects. Siting issues are quite complex, and decision makers must balance competing concerns while following a highly institutionalized process. The California Environmental Protection Agency has created a web-based GIS tool showing the communities in California with the highest burden of pollution from a variety of sources.[41] Adding the ability to simulate the manipulation of policy levers, such as disruption or project location, could result in better understanding of the costs and benefits of different project scenarios, which in turn can reduce conflict and delays, lower project costs, and allow more successful implementation of sustainability-supporting projects such as TRTP.

Using the SEMPro DSS to simulate EJ issues as is done herein is not without limitations. The current version of the SEMPro DSS only includes parameters for the simulation of class-based EJ outcomes, and does not include Census data on race and ethnicity. Since it has been shown that minorities often also have less education and income, our findings could be generalizable to these demographics—but earlier chapters indicate there is something particular about being in the minority.[42] Given the findings of Chapter 6, which show that minorities may cluster near amenities as well as disamenities, there is room for further study of how race, education, and income influence infrastructure siting. Nonetheless, the case illustrates the use of an ABM-GIS, and these considerations suggest how policy analysts and planners, researchers, and practitioners can develop models that are appropriate to their own locales and issues.

This chapter has presented some core concepts, issues, and platforms for integrating agent-based models with spatially explicit GIS data. After discussing some of the advantages and challenges associated with ABM-GIS, we have described the design of the SEMPro DSS and shown how it can provide insight into questions of relevance to the EJ community—and, in turn, to sustainable cities.

The integration of these two technologies can yield substantial benefits to researchers, and to policymakers and practitioners. For the research community and concerned practitioners, use of the ABM-GIS SEMPro provides support for the theory that hazardous facilities are imposed on communities that lack as much power to resist them. Methodologically, our simulations also provide support for the importance of analyzing externalities using continuous (rather than discrete) variables in a geographic context.

Future research could also analyze siting cases for which the scale of the disruption of harmful projects was reduced at the design phase and compare these to projects that were approved without modifications. The predictors of this outcome variable could then be investigated for biases in race and class, which could provide evidence regarding the proposition that more powerful communities are able to reduce project impacts more successfully than less powerful communities.

For practitioners who want to integrate EJ concerns into existing frameworks, spatial DSS and ABM-GIS platforms show considerable promise. At the beginning of this chapter we posited that "all politics is spatial." While this may be a slight exaggeration, the theory and empirics presented here show strong support for the conclusion that spatial heterogeneity is an important factor in siting outcomes. In other words, what matters to individuals varies by physical location, as well as by other factors such as income. Therefore, integrating GIS data into environmental justice and sustainability research and simulation is critical to modeling, analyzing, and addressing these issues in specific locales.

In our simulations, individual-level attributes, such as income and education, have effects of a magnitude similar to that of the level of disruption caused by a project. We also find that the effect of the project's disruption on the number of citizen messages is dependent on citizen attributes that vary geographically. All of these factors stress the value of coupling agent-based modeling with GIS data for local policy and planning. As any student of politics will tell you, power matters. Despite all the money spent on assessing the engineering aspects of siting projects, citizen power and participation are more important to stakeholder bargaining outcomes than project disruption—the physical nature of the project—in our modeling. Our research highlights how the spatial attributes of power can be integrated with agent-based simulation to provide actionable insights for policymakers, researchers, and citizens.

## Notes

1  Tip O'Neill and Gary Hymel, *All Politics is Local* (London: Crown, 1994).
2  Ibid.
3  Susan L. Cutter, "Race, Class and Environmental Justice," *Progress in Human Geography* 19, no. 1 (1995): 111–22.
4  Michael J. de Smith, Michael F. Goodchild and Paul A. Longley, *Geospatial Analysis: A Comprehensive Guide to Principles, Techniques and Software Tools*, fourth edn (Winchelsea: The Winchelsea Press, 2007), 40.
5  Daniel G. Brown, Rick Riolo, Derek T. Robinson, Michael North and William Rand, "Spatial Process and Data Models: Toward Integration of Agent-Based Models and GIS," *Journal of Geographical Systems* 7, no. 1 (2005): 25–47.
6  Jonathan Raper and David Livingstone, "Development of a Geomorphological Spatial Model Using Object-Oriented Design," *International Journal of Geographical Information Systems* 9, no. 4 (1995): 359–83.
7  Andrew T. Crooks and Christian J.E. Castle, "The Integration of Agent-Based Modelling and Geographical Information for Geospatial Simulation," in *Agent-based Models of Geographical Systems*, eds Alison J. Heppenstall, Andrew T. Crooks, Linda M. See and Michael Batty (Dordrecht, Netherlands: Springer, 2012), 224.
8  Ibid., 225.
9  Joshua M. Epstein and Robert L. Axtell, *Growing Artificial Societies: Social Science from the Bottom Up* (Washington, DC: The Brookings Institute, 1996).
10 H. Randy Gimblett, "Integrating Geographic Information Systems and Agent-Based Modeling Techniques for Simulating Social and Ecological Processes," in *Integrating Geographic Information Systems and Agent-Based Modeling Techniques for Simulating Social and Ecological Processes*, ed. H. Randy Gimblett (New York: Oxford University Press Inc., 2002), 6.
11 Ibid., 5.
12 Peter J. Deadman and Edella Schlager, "Models of Individual Decision Making in Agent-Based Simulation of Common-Pool Resource Management Institutions," in *Integrating Geographic Information Systems and Agent-Based Modeling Techniques for Simulating Social and Ecological Processes*, ed. H. Randy Gimblett (New York: Oxford University Press Inc., 2002), 139.

13  Gregory E. Kersten, "Decision Making and Decision Support," in *Decision Support Systems for Sustainable Development: A Resource Book of Methods and Application*, ed. Gregory E. Kersten, Zbigniew Mikolajuk. and Anthony Gar-On Yeh (Dordrecht, Netherlands: Springer, 2000), 29–51.

14  Brown et al., "Spatial Process and Data Models."

15  Cynthia Nikolai and Gregory Madey, "Tools of the Trade: A Survey of Various Agent-Based Modeling Platforms," *Journal of Artificial Societies and Social Simulation* 12, no. 2 (2009).

16  Christophe Le Page, Nicolas Becu, Pierre Bommel and François Bousquet, "Participatory Agent-Based Simulation for Renewable Resource Management: The Role of the Cormas Simulation Platform to Nurture a Community of Practice," *Journal of Artificial Societies and Social Simulation* 15, no. 1 (2012): 10.

17  Sean Luke, "Multiagent Simulation and the MASON Library," Manual, George Mason University (2013), 11.

18  Kevin Johnston, *Agent Analyst: Agent-Based Modeling in ArcGIS* (Redlands, CA: Esri Press, 2013).

19  Jan C. Thiele, Winfried Kurth and Volker Grimm, "Agent-Based Modelling: Tools for Linking NetLogo and R," *Journal of Artificial Societies and Social Simulation* 15, no. 3 (2012): 8.

20  Uri Wilensky, *NetLogo User Manual, version 5.0.5* (Center for Connected Learning and Computer-Based Modeling, Northwestern University Evanston, IL: 2013), 12.

21  Mark Abdollahian, Zining Yang and Hal Nelson, "Techno-Social Energy Infrastructure Siting: Sustainable Energy Modeling Programming (SEMPro)," *Journal of Artificial Societies and Social Simulation* 16, no. 3 (2013): 6.

22  S.D. Pohekar and M. Ramachandran, "Application of Multi-Criteria Decision Making to Sustainable Energy Planning—A Review," *Renewable and Sustainable Energy Reviews* 8, no. 4 (2004): 365–81.

23  Nicholas L. Cain and Hal T. Nelson, "What Drives Opposition to High-Voltage Transmission Lines?" *Land Use Policy* 33 (2013): 204–13.

24  Ibid.

25  Those surveyed were stakeholders that had been involved in previous transmission siting decisions. Approximately 38 of 122 stakeholders (31%) responded to the survey invitations, which included a US$20 Starbucks gift card for completing the survey.

26  Masami Nishishiba, Hal Nelson and Craig Shinn, "Explicating the Factors that Foster Civic Engagement Among Students,"*Journal of Public Affairs Education* 11, no. 4 (2005): 269–86.

27  Catherine Gross, "Community Perspectives of Wind Energy in Australia: The Application of a Justice and Community Fairness Framework to Increase Social Acceptance," *Energy Policy* 35, no. 5 (2007): 2727–36.

28  Thomas C. Beierle and Jerry Cayford, *Democracy in Practice: Public Participation in Environmental Decisions* (Washington, DC: Resources for the Future, 2002).

29  California Public Utilities Commission (CPUC), SCE Tehachapi Renewable Transmission Project (2009), ftp.cpuc.ca.gov/gopher-data/environ/tehachapire newables/TRTP.htm.

30  Abdollahian et al., "Techno-Social Energy Infrastructure Siting."

31  Although King cautions against the use of standardized coefficients, we present them here since many of the variables are measured on a comparable scale, and have similar levels of variance, which allows for more straightforward interpretation. Gary King, "How Not to Lie with Statistics: Avoiding Common Mistakes in Quantitative Political Science," *American Journal of Political Science* 30 (1986): 666–87.

32 Abdollahian et al., "Techno-Social Energy Infrastructure Siting."
33 Ibid.
34 Paul Mohai, David Pellow and J. Timmons Roberts, "Environmental Justice," *Annual Review of Environment and Resources* 34 (2009): 405–30.
35 See James T. Hamilton, "Testing for Environmental Racism: Prejudice, Profits, Political Power?" *Journal of Policy Analysis and Management* 14, no. 1 (1995): 107–32.
36 Mike Ward, "State Board Denies Using Siting Report: Study Identifies Least Likely Incinerator Foes," *Los Angeles Times* (1987), articles.latimes.com/1987-07-16/news/cb-4317_1_waste-incineration-plant.
37 Robin Saha and Paul Mohai, "Historical Context and Hazardous Waste Facility Siting: Understanding Temporal Patterns in Michigan," *Social Problems* 52, no. 4 (2005): 618–48.
38 For example, Rachel Morello-Frosch, Manuel Pastor Jr, Carlos Porras and James Sadd, "Environmental Justice and Regional Inequality in Southern California: Implications for Future Research," *Environmental Health Perspectives* 110, no. Suppl 2 (2002): 149.
39 Marie S. O'Neill, Michael Jerrett, Ichiro Kawachi, Jonathan I. Levy, Aaron J. Cohen, Nelson Gouveia, Paul Wilkinson, Tony Fletcher, Luis Cifuentes and Joel Schwartz, "Health, Wealth, and Air Pollution: Advancing Theory and Methods," *Environmental Health Perspectives* 111, no. 16 (2003): 1861.
40 Beierle and Cayford, *Democracy in Practice*.
41 California Environmental Protection Agency. California Communities Environmental Health Screening Tool (Calenviroscreen 1.0), oehha.ca.gov/ej/ces042313.html#sensitivity (accessed August 15, 2013).
42 Mohai et al., "Environmental Justice."

## References

Abdollahian, Mark, Zining Yang and Hal Nelson. "Techno-Social Energy Infrastructure Siting: Sustainable Energy Modeling Programming (SEMPro)." *Journal of Artificial Societies and Social Simulation* 16, no. 3 (2013): 6.
Beierle, Thomas C. and Jerry Cayford. *Democracy in Practice: Public Participation in Environmental Decisions*. Washington, DC: Resources for the Future, 2002.
Brown, Daniel G., Rick Riolo, Derek T. Robinson, Michael North and William Rand. "Spatial Process and Data Models: Toward Integration of Agent-Based Models and GIS." *Journal of Geographical Systems* 7, no. 1 (2005): 25–47.
Cain, Nicholas L. and Hal T. Nelson. "What Drives Opposition to High-voltage Transmission Lines?" *Land Use Policy* 33 (2013): 204–213.
California Environmental Protection Agency. *California Communities Environmental Health Screening Tool (Calenviroscreen 1.0)*. oehha.ca.gov/ej/ces042313.html#sensitivity (accessed August 15, 2013).
California Office of Planning and Research. *Environmental Justice in California State Government*. October 2003. www.opr.ca.gov/docs/OPR_EJ_Report_Oct2003.pdf.
CPUC (California Public Utilities Commission). *SCE Tehachapi Renewable Transmission Project*. 2009. ftp.cpuc.ca.gov/gopher-data/environ/tehachapi renewables/TRTP.htm.
Crooks, Andrew T. and Christian J.E. Castle. "The Integration of Agent-Based Modelling and Geographical Information for Geospatial Simulation." In *Agent-based Models of Geographical Systems*, edited by Alison J. Heppenstall, Andrew T. Crooks, Linda M. See and Michael Batty. Springer Netherlands, 2012, 219–251.

Cutter, Susan L. "Race, Class and Environmental Justice." *Progress in Human Geography* 19, no. 1 (1995): 111–122.

Deadman, Peter J. and Edella Schlager. "Models of Individual Decision Making in Agent-based Simulation of Common-pool Resource Management Institutions." In *Integrating Geographic Information Systems and Agent-Based Modeling Techniques for Simulating Social and Ecological Processes*, edited by H. Randy Gimblett. New York: Oxford University Press Inc., 2002, 137–169.

De Smith, Michael J., Michael F. Goodchild and Paul A. Longley. *Geospatial Analysis: A Comprehensive Guide to Principles, Techniques and Software Tools.* Fourth edn. Winchelsea: The Winchelsea Press, 2007.

Epstein, Joshua M. and Robert L. Axtell. *Growing Artificial Societies: Social Science from the Bottom Up.* Washington, DC: The Brookings Institute, 1996.

Gimblett, H. Randy. "Integrating Geographic Information Systems and Agent-based Modeling Techniques for Simulating Social and Ecological Processes." In *Integrating Geographic Information Systems and Agent-Based Modeling Techniques for Simulating Social and Ecological Processes*, edited by H. Randy Gimblett. New York: Oxford University Press Inc., 2002, 1–20.

Gross, Catherine. "Community Perspectives of Wind Energy in Australia: The Application of a Justice and Community Fairness Framework to Increase Social Acceptance." *Energy Policy* 35, no. 5 (2007): 2727–2736.

Hamilton, James T. "Testing for Environmental Racism: Prejudice, Profits, Political Power?" *Journal of Policy Analysis and Management* 14, no. 1 (1995): 107–132.

Johnston, Kevin. *Agent Analyst: Agent-Based Modeling in ArcGIS.* Redlands, CA: Esri Press, 2013.

Kersten, Gregory E. "Decision Making and Decision Support." In *Decision Support Systems for Sustainable Development: A Resource Book of Methods and Applications*, edited by Gregory E. Kersten, Zbigniew Mikolajuk and Anthony Gar-On Yeh. Dordrecht, Netherlands: Springer, 2000, 29–51.

King, Gary. "How Not to Lie with Statistics: Avoiding Common Mistakes in Quantitative Political Science." *American Journal of Political Science* 30 (1986): 666–687.

Le Page, Christophe, Nicolas Becu, Pierre Bommel and François Bousquet. "Participatory Agent-based Simulation for Renewable Resource Management: The Role of the Cormas Simulation Platform to Nurture a Community of Practice." *Journal of Artificial Societies and Social Simulation* 15, no. 1 (2012): 10.

Luke, Sean. "Multiagent Simulation and the MASON Library." Manual, George Mason University (2011).

Mohai, Paul, David Pellow and J. Timmons Roberts. "Environmental Justice." *Annual Review of Environment and Resources* 34 (2009): 405–430.

Morello-Frosch, Rachel, Manuel Pastor Jr, Carlos Porras and James Sadd. "Environmental Justice and Regional Inequality in Southern California: Implications for Future Research." *Environmental Health Perspectives* 110, no. Suppl 2 (2002): 149.

Nikolai, Cynthia and Gregory Madey. "Tools of the Trade: A Survey of Various Agent-based Modeling Platforms." *Journal of Artificial Societies and Social Simulation* 12, no. 2 (2009).

Nishishiba, Masami, Hal Nelson and Craig Shinn. "Explicating the Factors that Foster Civic Engagement Among Students." *Journal of Public Affairs Education* 11, no. 4 (2005): 269–286.

O'Neill, Marie S., Michael Jerrett, Ichiro Kawachi, Jonathan I. Levy, Aaron J. Cohen, Nelson Gouveia, Paul Wilkinson, Tony Fletcher, Luis Cifuentes and Joel Schwartz. "Health, Wealth, and Air Pollution: Advancing Theory and Methods." *Environmental Health Perspectives* 111, no. 16 (2003): 1861.

O'Neill, Tip and Gary Hymel. *All Politics is Local*. London: Crown, 1994.

Pohekar, S.D. and M. Ramachandran. "Application of Multi-criteria Decision Making to Sustainable Energy Planning—A Review." *Renewable and Sustainable Energy Reviews* 8, no. 4 (2004): 365–381.

Raper, Jonathan and David Livingstone. "Development of a Geomorphological Spatial Model Using Object-oriented Design." *International Journal of Geographical Information Systems* 9, no. 4 (1995): 359–383.

Saha, Robin and Paul Mohai. "Historical Context and Hazardous Waste Facility Siting: Understanding Temporal Patterns in Michigan." *Social Problems* 52, no. 4 (2005): 618–648.

Thiele, Jan C., Winfried Kurth and Volker Grimm. "Agent-Based Modelling: Tools for Linking NetLogo and R." *Journal of Artificial Societies and Social Simulation* 15, no. 3 (2012): 8.

Ward, Mike. "State Board Denies Using Siting Report: Study Identifies Least Likely Incinerator Foes." *Los Angeles Times*, 1987. articles.latimes.com/1987-07-16/news/cb-4317_1_waste-incineration-plant.

Wilensky, Uri. *NetLogo User Manual, version 5.0.5* Evanston, IL: Center for Connected Learning and Computer-based Modeling, Northwestern University, 2013.

# 11 Conclusions

This book aimed to analyze and understand observed environmental injustice as an emergent outcome of dynamic cities, to examine and demonstrate the use of agent-based modeling in urban policy and planning settings, and, perhaps most importantly, to offer useful insights for environmental justice research and urban sustainability policies. We came to this project with a concern about EJ, its relationship to sustainable cities, and our dissatisfaction with the state of environmental justice research in offering policy guidance.

We do not suggest that previous environmental justice research is not useful, but we do believe it is limited and beset by a static frame of mind—in terms of how we model cities—and methodological challenges, not the least of which is the use of linear statistical analysis, often using cross-sectional data. Cities are neither static nor linear. Cities consist of inherently interdependent, dynamic, and interactive subsystems. Indeed, this is the basis of three pillars of sustainability itself.

In cities, social systems interact with economic systems, environmental systems, and policy systems, all within a specific physical space. Therefore, cities can exhibit unintended or unexpected problems, issues, and benefits. Any time a new problem arises, the nature, character, and degree of the problem can change quickly. Given the magnitude of urbanization in our era, successful sustainability relies on our ability to understand emergent outcomes within cities. To do this, we must use nonlinear analytic methods, such as agent-based modeling.

Environmental injustice has been widely visible since the 1980s, and hence a concern of researchers and policymakers at all levels of government. Originally it was conceptualized as an issue of the disproportionate collocation of toxic wastes and race. Now it includes extended or emerging themes—such as sustainability, climate change, open space, e-waste, etc.—and the perceived scope has also changed, incorporating not only substantive but also procedural rights.[1]

Scholars' understanding of the source of the EJ problem has also been changed, from a simple expectation of pure discriminatory actions, to a more nuanced perspective incorporating social institutions. While this expanded understanding has been possible due to many EJ studies since the 1980s, the question still remains: Is the current environmental justice research responsive to such an evolving problem in a dynamic but location-specific setting? If it is not, are we diminishing our chances to advance both theory and practice on this important topic? In our view, with an emphasis on research methods that implicitly assume static worlds, proposed explanations for the observation that minority neighborhoods tend to have worse environmental quality than majority neighborhoods have been oversimplified.

Our starting point for this research was a shared agreement that the working explanations for the environmental justice problem were, at best, insufficient, owing largely to the research approaches commonly taken— approaches that we ourselves have used to study the problem. Even when we knew what, we did not know *why*. Further, policies based on the commonly taken approach have not been effective at solving the EJ problem. We think that the intentional/discrimination argument, the institutional/political argument, and the market/residential-sorting argument are all viable but incomplete explanations of the EJ problem, and that any policy assuming the veracity of one argument while ignoring the unintended interactive complexity of social behavior is unlikely to be effective. In general, this concern will only be magnified for broader sustainability outcomes.

Given the complexity of urbanized regions, we believe—and hope that we have demonstrated in this book—that agent-based modeling is well suited to the study of urban environmental injustice in particular, and more widely to other issues of urban sustainability. Agent-based modeling instantiates a complex adaptive system that consists of the actions of individuated entities (e.g., residents, firms, and government) who are disaggregated and hetero-geneous across both time and space while also constrained by the environment and by previous actions. We argue that these are crucial factors for understanding cities, environmental injustice, and urban sustainability. Therefore, we developed the EJ ABM to reflect this complexity and to provide insight into the EJ problem—and other urban environmental and sustainability issues. Through this effort, we have learned much about the challenges of trying to model the complexity of the world, about the dynamism of the urban system, and about the unintended intractability of the environmental justice problem.

## What we learned

In the past, there have been many cases in which urban planners and policymakers, with nothing but the best intentions, have instituted policies that led to severe, damaging, unintended consequences. Consider, for example, urban renewal. While some policymakers may not have had good intentions, the fundamental idea of providing public housing to people who could not afford housing, and clustering that housing together to deliver services more efficiently, was often well intentioned. However, the unforeseen consequences of concentrating poverty were drastic, defined components of the urban structure for 50 years, and, by concentrating poor minorities, likely contributed to the environmental injustice problem.

Thus, the issue may be less one of intentionality, and more an outgrowth of lack of understanding of the hidden structure of the system that policy-makers deal with, the intertwining of social problems, and the evolving nature of the system and the problem. Although the full value of agent-based model-ing is, as yet, unknown, its ability to simulate complex adaptive systems and provide insight into the unexpected consequences of interdependencies and interactions of systems could help prevent such unfortunate outcomes, or at least help make sense of and heighten awareness of them.

It is on this point that we find what we consider to be the most important, and generally unexpected, result of our EJ ABM experiments. We found some limited evidence to suggest that the intentional model of environmental injustice—the idea that polluting facilities target minority communities—could explain the EJ problem. However, this evidence was mostly marginal. In the EJ ABM, when *all* firms act in a discriminatory manner and purposely site near minority populations, it does make environmental disparities larger; however, the change is barely significant in and of itself.

Assuming that all firms behave in this way is a problematic assumption in terms of current reality in most industrialized nations; if all do not behave this way, we expect the small results to be reduced even further. Thus, our skepticism about the veracity of discrimination being the only cause of environmental injustice appears well founded. Further, the simulated mag-nitude of the EJ problem in these conditions seems too small compared to observed levels of environmental injustice.

However, our most consistent finding in this research is that most of the common explanations for environmental injustice, like discrimination and mobility, have marginal effects that interact with one key facet of the story that had heretofore not been considered—our own preferences to live near others like ourselves.

The analysis in Chapter 4 shows that the largest environmental quality gaps emerge when residents hold the highest similarity preferences. Dis-crimination by polluting firms and, as shown in Chapter 7, mobility do have effects on the size of the gap, but this is mostly when combined with high residential similarity preferences. Indeed, in Chapter 9, when we sought to engineer regions with a significant environmental justice problem and regions with a more modest environmental justice problem, we simply altered similarity preferences.

This insight illustrates a value of the agent-based modeling approach to understanding urban problems. At its root, as we show in Chapter 5, the similarity preference effect led us to recognize that environmental injustice is, in some sense, a problem of being in the numerical minority. For it is worth noting that the EJ problems that emerge in the EJ ABM are rarely caused by some sort of explicit discrimination.

The polluting firm may discriminate by preferring to locate in minority communities, but the majority is quiescent and does not taunt, stereotype, or problematize the minority, does not refuse to sell it houses in its neighborhoods, does not limit its access to jobs. The worst thing the majority does in these scenarios is prefer to live in communities with proportions of majorities somewhat above their own representation in the population.[2] The agent-based minority does not live with a history of slavery or other legal inferiority.

Yet, even in this bloodless world, if residents have similarity preferences, and space is constrained, then minority residents, *because* they are in the numerical minority, will have far fewer choices for settlement than majority residents.[3] With fewer choices—but the same preferences—balancing multiple goals is more difficult, and one element that may suffer is environmental quality.

When modeled similarity preferences were informed by empirical observations about empirically found similarity preferences, we saw a persistent and significant environmental quality gap between majority residents and minority residents, controlling for as well as varying income, mobility, firm behavior, and/or regional characteristics such as growth rate. Further, when both groups held lower (or no) similarity preferences, outcomes for both groups were better.

This suggests an important hypothesis: If people are more willing to live among people unlike themselves, then not only might environmental injustice be mitigated, but environmental quality outcomes could be better for everyone. This would enhance urban sustainability. On the one hand, this is encouraging because the Millennial generation seems not only to show a tolerance for, but to see value in, living in diverse communities;[4] this may bode well for the future. On the other hand, however, there is evidence that people are increasingly sorting themselves into communities with like-minded people (the so-called Big Sort),[5] which could mean that the form of the environmental justice problem will change, but that it will remain a problem.

However, we are careful to note that this is only a hypothesis. As described in Chapter 1, to this point agent-based modeling in the social sciences has mostly been used as a generator of hypotheses rather than as a predictor of outcomes. It is with this caveat in mind that we consider our results.

The EJ ABM developed for this series of studies and experiments has helped us develop new, empirically testable hypotheses, and make cautious policy recommendations. Of course, both hypotheses and policy recommendations are based on the model we use in our simulations. As with all models, the EJ ABM is formed of a set of simplifying assumptions. Therefore, model implications need to be tested in real cities using observational data, along the lines of the project illustrated in Chapter 10. Only then may we improve our confidence that the policy insights of the model are worth pursuing.

Nevertheless, based on the EJ ABM, which mimics the real world in useful respects, we have identified a number of different hypotheses that have implications for both research and policy regarding environmental justice, and, hence, the development of fully viable sustainable cities. We hypothesize the following:

- Environmental injustice is less severe in cities where communities are more diverse.
- Environmental injustice is less severe where the minority group is larger.
- Environmental injustice is less severe in cities where residents are moderately mobile, provided that communities are diverse (i.e., that there is reasonable balance between the number of the majority and the minority).
- Environmental injustice is more severe in cities with years of no zoning.
- Closing the environmental justice gap and improving the level of environmental quality for a group may not be the same.

Beyond these implications for environmental justice study, we also see some broader implications for urban research more generally.

- An important implication of the EJ ABM research is about "revealed preference," a mainstay of certain types of economic analysis. The results imply that in a complex, dynamic, interactive system, observed behavior does not necessarily reveal true preferences. Early on this was implied by Schelling's work, for in his first (checker-based) ABM, "people" routinely lived in communities that were more segregated than their preference.[6] In making locational choices, people have to balance a large number of different considerations. People may not reveal preferences so much as they compromise amongst those various considerations and select locations that are satisfactory, but not necessarily optimal along any one dimension. Further, recall that interaction in a dynamic, nonlinear system may result in outcomes unintended by any.
- Similarly, the complexity and interactivity of some results imply that estimating a useful hedonic-pricing model is more difficult than typically thought. Emergence of location choices may be too complex to allow independent valuation of any particular locational aspect.
- Our research suggests paying close attention to changes in the overall context of cities such as racial composition changes, rates of population growth, and industrial growth or decline, and how urban studies reflect such changes, in order to provide a proper understanding of problems like environmental injustice and other sustainability factors.
- In cities, both amenities *and* disamenities are present. Studies that focus on either disamenities *or* amenities may ignore the overall environmental reality of neighborhoods. This finding may be relevant for other urban issues, like access to healthful food or other residential services.
- Social outcomes may be asymmetric. The collocation of environmental harms with the poor does not necessarily imply that the rich are the

winners of the environmental quality stakes. In our study, the middle class often enjoyed higher quality than the rich. This result may be surprising, but is not necessarily implausible, especially if numerical size matters. A review of the literature finds much evidence of the poor living with worse environmental quality than the middle class and the wealthy, but we found no studies comparing environmental quality between the wealthy and the middle class. While a simple version of microeconomic theory would certainly predict the wealthy to have the highest quality, our model result, which incorporates wealth clustering, suggests that considering quality variability between the middle and upper classes may be a worthwhile empirical question. Assuming symmetry of a concept can hide an important facet of the problem and hinder our understanding.

We are policy analysts, and so we are particularly keen to derive policy implications from the EJ ABM. Though requiring empirical investigation, the EJ ABM implies the following:

- Zoning, a common tool of urban policy, appears tricksome in the complex, interactive context of a city. We found that proactive zoning can be used as a tool to mitigate the emergence of an environmental injustice problem, and to enhance urban sustainability, but this finding is only clear in new development. For a variety of reasons such as politics, tradition, or geographic constraints, existing communities may not have the ability to alter historic zoning schemes dramatically, but if they can, zoning can be a tool to address environmental inequities and sustainability— but with caution since reactive zoning may also degrade overall environmental quality.
- More encouraging are the results showing that hazardous-site remediation can be a tool to address environmental disparities. In regions with significant environmental justice problems, the policy could even be particularly easy—cleaning up sites based on EJ concerns, property values, or levels of pollution will all improve matters. In regions with less severe problems, for EJ concerns it may be better specifically to target cleanup near the largest clusters of minority populations, but ultimately the message from Chapter 9 is almost astonishingly simple: clean up brownfields and cities can improve environmental quality for minority groups without worsening conditions for majority groups; clean up brownfields to improve both narrow and broad urban sustainability. For policymakers in search of the rare potential for Pareto improvement, brownfield cleanup may offer that opportunity.

While the use of agent-based modeling in Chapters 4–9 primarily shows how agent-based simulation can serve as a hypothesis generator for urban systems, Chapter 10 highlights agent-based modeling as a decision-support tool tailored with more localized, context-specific information. This chapter hints at two important potential uses of an agent-based modeling approach. First, agent-based modeling as a tool is flexible in working with other technical developments such as GIS, and agent-based modeling can be linked to statistical packages such as R, providing real-time statistical analysis of the system modeled. Second, while general abstract knowledge of EJ is useful, policymakers in cities need city-specific analysis to inform their local decisions. Agent-based modeling can be tailored and calibrated for decision support in individual cities, regions, and states.

However, these claims raise the question of whether policy decision makers will be willing to use such a synthetic, artificial approach to understanding the world. The first question under this category might be why would they use agent-based modeling in the first place? One answer is that environmental injustice, other sustainability issues, and many other urban issues have proven resistant to policy efforts to address them, and also cause political discord in communities. Given that traditional analytical methods have not yielded effective policies, decision makers are often willing to try new methods such as agent-based modeling.

In fact, Southern California Edison funded the development of the ABM underlying the work in Chapter 10 in order to help with the increasingly difficult work of dealing with political opposition to the siting of transmission lines—even transmission lines for green energy, which we think of as pro-sustainability.[7] Further, agent-based modeling is successfully used in many commercial applications, including for international insurance claims and optimization of large-scale transport.[8] If a method is seen to be successful in commerce, many governmental decision makers will be open to at least considering it. Indeed, agent-based modeling is already being used in government settings, such as by the Chicago Housing Authority and the UK Ministry of Defence.[9]

Many urban studies and policies can benefit from this versatility of ABMs. In the future, we would like to see more environmental justice and policy research that leverages this capacity of agent-based modeling as a way of moving toward urban sustainability.

## Limitations of the agent-based modeling approach

While we believe the results presented in this book are valuable, we would be remiss if we did not discuss some limitations and critiques of agent-based modeling as a research method. In so doing we also provide some counter-arguments.[10]

When confronting research using social simulation models like our EJ ABM, critiques often relate to the underlying *assumptions* that drive model behavior. Some argue that ABMs are black boxes, implying that they are not sure what assumptions have been made, why, and how the assumptions play out. If readers fail to understand how an ABM is structured, it is unlikely that they will accept the model and its results. Therefore, it is imperative for model developers to articulate clearly an ABM's assumptions and structures, as we have tried to do throughout this book.

On the other hand, it is worth noting that an ABM is constructed to represent a system. The system is often depicted in a conceptual framework (as seen in Figure 3.1), and modeled using a computer programming language that explicitly encodes underlying assumptions (e.g., as shown in the Appendix). Our EJ ABM represents our understanding of both environmental injustice and sustainability as social outcomes that emerge from the urban system. If some social outcomes truly are emergent, then in order to understand them correctly we must use a modeling method that can model emergence. Right now, agent-based modeling is one of our best tools that meets this requirement.

Others argue that the assumptions and parameters in some models are too many or too arbitrary. "Too many" is related to the complexity of an ABM. One must be more cautious of understanding, analyzing, and interpreting simulation results as the complexity of an ABM increases. However, this does not imply that we should only represent the world in a simple and linear way. Models need to be complex enough to capture the key features of the problem at hand. Jane Jacobs asked what kind of problem a city is, and answered that a city is a problem in organized complexity.[11] If so, to capture key causal structures, analytic tools must reflect that. When a researcher carefully adds details to a simple model, ABMs can enhance our understanding and bring new insights to a complex problem. In other words, though the EJ ABM ended up with a significant number of variables, parameters, and behaviors in order to represent and test key assumptions in each chapter, this was the result of step-by-step additions of complexity in order to address specific questions—not the result of complexity for complexity's sake.

The charge that an ABM is "too arbitrary" often concerns the choice to use non-empirical numerical scales for concepts that are necessary and crucial but lack empirical measurement. For example, in the EJ ABM we used an expected value of 50 (ranging from 0–100) to initialize and update an environmental quality level for each plot, and a pollution value for firms that arbitrarily ranges from zero to nine. The values are arbitrary, yet they meet certain needs for the model. We·know that firms produce different levels of pollution and that pollution diffuses over space, influencing environmental quality. However, though it is extremely difficult to measure or get data about these levels, they are vital to understanding environmental justice. Lack of or incomplete empirical data should not stymie our efforts to understand important social problems.

In addition, although the values used are arbitrary, the development of these two key variables was not arbitrary; they were developed through an iterative process of testing, exploring, and revising until pollution and environmental quality in the model provided sufficient and appropriate variability to represent important elements of what we observe in the real world.

Another common critique of agent-based modeling is that results are built into the model. This is true in the sense that what we find from simulations are the logical consequences of assumptions made in the model (as is also true in other types of formal modeling, including formal logic), but this critique overlooks the real value of agent-based modeling. In agent-based modeling, though assumptions may be simple, interactions are often structured in a complex manner such that one cannot envision the result without running the model.

As an example, NetLogo's Fire ABM[12] simulates the spread of a fire through a forest. What is the chance that a fire on the left edge can reach the right edge given the density of trees? In the Fire model, assumptions are made that: 1 the fire starts on the left edge of the forest; and 2 it spreads to neighboring trees in four directions. Obviously, neither of these assumptions necessarily represents the way a forest fire actually spreads, as fires can start anywhere and move in more (or fewer) than four directions. However, using the model, researchers find that the density of trees in the forest is a critical and nonlinear parameter: at a certain density (i.e., 59% in the example model), the fire has a 50/50 chance of reaching the right edge. Though the model makes artificial assumptions, results are still of value in the real world.

Similarly, Chapter 7 provides the nonlinear assessment that at some levels mobility increases can improve EJ outcomes, but perfect mobility cannot solve the EJ problem—and may exacerbate it—in a world with income differentials and race/ethnicity-based residential preferences. The finding is revealed as a result of the dynamic system rather than because we built this result into the model.

While the complexity of ABMs has been a primary focus of many critiques, conversely, agent-based modeling is also sometimes criticized for excess simplicity: excluding crucial components of the system. For those critics, ABMs are wrong because they do not mirror the richness of the real world (or at least do not include some important aspects that it is argued must be included). This critique is especially valid when there are compelling theoretical and empirical reasons to include a particular aspect of the system under scrutiny, but a model is missing that component.

However, there are a couple of things to keep in mind. First, it is impossible (and would not be useful) to make one-to-one correspondence between the real system and an ABM. No model can mirror the complexity of the real world, and the more complexity built into a model, the less ability researchers have to understand and pinpoint causes and effects.[13] Second, the assessment of whether an agent-based model is "right" or "wrong" is not straightforward, especially when the ABM aims to model social realities. The model as a duplication of reality will (always) be wrong, but it still can be right in helping researchers understand and/or explain reality.[14]

Perhaps the most important point to make regarding assumptions in agent-based modeling is that, as for every model, the quality of assumptions matters in understanding and evaluating the results. In an ABM, good assumptions are driven by appropriate theoretical rationales, empirical observations, thoughtful reasoning, and careful testing. This is not different from other research methods. Agent-based modeling as a technique can easily offer multiple representations of the system under analysis.

Though we provide sensitivity assessments of the EJ ABM in Chapter 3,[15] there are still literally hundreds or maybe even thousands of other experiments we could have done: we did not alter preferences in the utility function, analyze changes to population density (e.g., allow more than one resident per plot), use additional "races," change diffusion rates, consider differences in "poor" and "rich" cities, etc. Which assumptions are ancillary and which assumptions are central depends upon what questions ABM researchers and policymakers are interested in and for what purpose.

## Summary

The research presented in this book identifies strengths of using agent-based modeling to explore policy problems, with a particular focus on environmental injustice and extensions to other elements of urban sustainability. While the model presented here is not fully representative of the richness and detail of the real world (and it will never be!), the model and our results provide us with a new way to think about EJ outcomes and the social pillar of urban sustainability. Rather than investigating whether or not an unequal distribution of environmental quality exists, we have explored the conditions under which an unequal distribution could emerge *even when unintended*, and how some common tools of government policy could be used to address the problem.

Further, this model allows us to consider *overall* levels of environmental quality, rather than only the *relative* levels, finding that some conditions lead to better quality for both groups, and some to worse—key issues in sustainability. Although our model presents very simplified and pure versions of two tools of government policy, using an ABM allows us to explore implications of utilizing zoning or remediating hazardous sites in a consequence-free environment that holds the potential to inform both theory—through the modeling of complex interactivity and the derivation of hypotheses—and practice.

While we have noted several times that the academic literature is undecided about the causes of the EJ problem, we do not expect that we have solved that conundrum here. However, our goal was to try to move the EJ discussion forward from its current impasse, by acknowledging the likely veracity of the multiple causal claims, and testing them in a way that acknowledges interaction and emergence and does not assume that any particular explanation is "right" or "wrong," but that each explanation is limited. By taking into account a system in which there are multiple causes interdependently acting together, we have not only identified combined effects of spatial constraints, race, income, mobility, and land-use policy, but we have also added new potential explanations and solutions for the seemingly intractable EJ problem.

It is our hope that this book moves urban environmental policy conversations away from arguing about one cause versus another, and toward considering the nature of social emergence in urban environments and how taking into account dynamic causal interactions may allow us to create more effective policies. Such an effort can more fully assist the aims of sustainable city advocates and practitioners.

## Notes

1 Steven Bonorris, *Environmental Justice for All: A Fifty State Survey of Legislation, Policies and Cases*, fourth edn (San Francisco, CA: American Bar Association and Hastings College of the Law, 2010), www.abanet.org/environ/resources. html.

2 In the 2010 US Census, people identifying themselves as "white alone" were 72.4% of the population, and white alone, not Hispanic or Latino were 63.7%. Thus, an 80% similarity preference is between 7.6 and 16.3 percentage points above base representation. *The White Population: 2010*, www.census.gov/prod/ccn2010/briefs/c2010br-05.pdf.

3 In the version of the EJ ABM used in this book, the minority also usually has lower income than the majority. However, in our earlier work (published in journals and presented at APPAM), we still find these results even when incomes are identical.

4 For evidence that Millennials are more accepting of difference, see e.g., Scott Keeter and Paul Taylor, "The Millennials," Pew Research Center, December 10, 2009, www.pewresearch.org/2009/12/10/the-millennials/. For evidence that they prefer diverse communities, see Nielsen, "Millennials Prefer Cities to Suburbs, Subways to Driveways," March 4, 2014, www.nielsen.com/content/corporate/us/cn/insights/news/2014/millennials-prefer-cities-to-suburbs-subways-to-driveways.html.

5 Bill Bishop, *The Big Sort: Why the Clustering of Like-Minded America is Tearing Us Apart* (New York: Mariner Books, 2009).

6 See also NetLogo's Segregation applet, ccl.northwestern.edu/netlogo/models/Segregation.

7 For additional information, see Mark Abdollahian, Zining Yang and Hal Nelson, "Techno-Social Energy Infrastructure Siting: Sustainable Energy Modeling Programming (SEMPro)," *Journal of Artificial Societies and Social Simulation*, 16, no. 3 (2013): 6, and this website on the Sustainable Energy Modeling Project: www.cgu.edu/pages/10771.asp (available August 2014).

8 Michael Luck, *AgentLink*, "50 Facts about Agent-Based Computing," Published by the University of Southampton on behalf of AgentLinkIII (2005), www2.econ. iastate.edu/tesfatsi/AgentLink.50CommercialApplic.MLuck.pdf.

9 Ibid.

10 See Annie Waldherr and Nanda Wijermans, "Communicating Social Simulation Models to Sceptical Minds," *Journal of Artificial Societies and Social Simulation* 16, no. 4 (2003), for a discussion of common criticisms of social simulation models, jasss.soc.surrey.ac.uk/16/4/13.html.

11 Jane Jacobs, *The Death and Life of Great American Cities* (New York: Random House, 1961); Luis M.A. Bettencourt, "The Kind of Problem a City Is," SFI Working Paper 2013-03-008, www.santafe.edu/media/workingpapers/13-03-008. pdf.

12 NetLogo Models Library, Sample Models/Earth Science, Fire, ccl.northwestern. edu/netlogo/models/Fire.

13 This result is known as Bonini's Paradox: see William H. Starbuck, "Why I Stopped Trying to Understand the Real World," *Organization Studies* 57, no. 7 (2004): 1233–54.

14 George E.P. Box and Norman Richard Draper, *Empirical Model Building and Response Surfaces* (New York: John Wiley & Sons, 1987).

15 For most parameters, we calculated the local sensitivity as recommended by Steven Railsback and Volker Grimm, *Agent-Based and Individual-Based Modeling* (Princeton, NJ: Princeton University Press, 2011), 293–95. See Table 3.5 in Chapter 3 of this volume.

## References

Abdollahian, Mark, Zining Yang and Hal Nelson. "Techno-Social Energy Infrastructure Siting: Sustainable Energy Modeling Programming (SEMPro)." *Journal of Artificial Societies and Social Simulation* 16, no. 3 (2013): 6.

Bettencourt, Luis M.A. "The Kind of Problem a City Is." SFI Working Paper 2013-03-008. www.santafe.edu/media/workingpapers/13-03-008.pdf.

Bishop, Bill. *The Big Sort: Why the Clustering of Like-minded America is Tearing Us Apart*. New York: Mariner Books, 2009.

Bonorris, Steven. *Environmental Justice for All: A Fifty State Survey of Legislation, Policies and Cases*. Fourth edn. San Francisco, CA: American Bar Association and Hastings College of the Law, 2010. www.abanet.org/environ/resources.html.

Box, George. E.P. and Norman Richard Draper. *Empirical Model Building and Response Surfaces*. New York: John Wiley & Sons, 1987.

Jacobs, Jane. *The Death and Life of Great American Cities*. New York: Random House, 1961.

Keeter, Scott and Paul Taylor. "The Millennials." Pew Research Center. December 10, 2009. www.pewresearch.org/2009/12/10/the-millennials/.

Luck, Michael. "50 Facts about Agent-Based Computing." Published by the University of Southampton on behalf of *AgentLinkIII*, 2005. www2.econ.iastate.edu/tesfatsi/AgentLink.50CommercialApplic.MLuck.pdf.

NetLogo. *NetLogo Models Library, Sample Models, Earth Science, Fire*. ccl.north western.edu/netlogo/models/Fire.

NetLogo. *NetLogo Models Library, Sample Models, Social Science, Segregation*.

Nielsen. "Millennials Prefer Cities to Suburbs, Subways to Driveways." March 4, 2014. www.nielsen.com/content/corporate/us/en/insights/news/2014/millennials-prefer-cities-to-suburbs-subways-to-driveways.html (accessed August 18, 2014).

Railsback, Steven F. and Volker Grimm. *Agent-Based and Individual-Based Modeling*. Princeton, NJ: Princeton University Press, 2011.

Starbuck, William H. "Why I Stopped Trying To Understand the Real World." *Organization Studies* 57, no. 7 (2004): 1233–1254.

US Census. *The White Population: 2010*. Table 1: White Population, 2000 and 2010. 2010. www.census.gov/prod/cen2010/briefs/c2010br-05.pdf (accessed July 1, 2010).

Waldherr, Annie and Nanda Wijermans. "Communicating Social Simulation Models to Sceptical Minds." *Journal of Artificial Societies and Social Simulation* 16, no. 4 (2003). jasss.soc.surrey.ac.uk/16/4/13.html.

# Appendix
## NetLogo code for EJ ABM 1.0

This appendix reproduces version 1.0 of our EJ ABM, which was used for Eckerd, Campbell and Kim (2012). While we cleaned up some unnecessary parts of the original model for this reproduction, the basic function and procedure remain the same. Readers can reproduce the original EJ ABM using the code herein. To make the model function in NetLogo, readers may also need to create buttons, sliders, switches and output panels. In NetLogo code, comments (which are not executed) are preceded by semicolons (;;;).

```
;;; DECLARATION OF VARIABLES AND COLLECTIVES
breed [ jobs job ]
breed [ residents a-resident ]
residents-own [ race ]
jobs-own [ pollution trif ]
patches-own [ quality price sddist prop-min prop-maj prop-
trif prop-non-trif utility local-vacancy ]
globals [ growth ]


;;; MODEL INITIALIZATION
to setup
  reset-ticks
  clear-turtles
  clear-patches
  clear-all-plots
  set growth 0
  setup-jobs
  setup-patches
  setup-residents
  ask patches [ update-patch-color ]
end
to setup-jobs
```

```
    create-jobs 1
    ask jobs [
      set shape "circle"
      set pollution 0
      set trif 0
      set color orange + 2
      set size 3 ]
end

to setup-patches
  ask patches [
    set quality 50
    set price 50 ]
  ask patches [
    set sddist min [distance myself] of jobs ]
end

to setup-residents
  create-residents 50
  ask n-of 35 residents [
    set color red
    set shape "box"
    set race 1→ ;;; majority
    let radius 20
    setxy ( ( radius / 2) - random-float ( radius * 1.0 ) )
          ( ( radius / 2 ) - random-float ( radius * 1.0 ) ) ]
  ask residents with [ race != 1 ] [
    set color yellow
    set shape "box"
    set race 2→ ;;; minority
    let radius 20
    setxy ( ( radius / 2 ) - random-float ( radius * 1.0 ) )
          ( ( radius / 2 ) - random-float ( radius * 1.0 ) ) ]
end


;;; SCHEDULE ACTIONS

to go
  locate-residents
  if count (residents) / count (jobs) > residents-per-job
     [ locate-service ]
  if count (residents) >= 500 [ kill-residents ]
  calc-utility
  trif-effect
  ask patches [ update-patch-color ]
  do-plots
```

```
    tick
  end


  ;;; SUB-MODELS

to calc-utility
  ask patches [
    if count residents in-radius 1 > 0 [
      set prop-min ( count residents with [ race = 2 ]
        in-radius 2 ) / ( count residents in-radius 2 )
      set prop-maj ( count residents with [ race = 1 ]
        in-radius 2 ) / ( count residents in-radius 2 )
      set prop-trif ( count jobs with [ trif = 1 ]
        in-radius 20 )
      set prop-non-trif ( count jobs with [ trif = 0 ]
        in-radius 20 ) ]
    set local-vacancy count residents-on neighbors / 8
    set utility ( quality ^ quality-preference ) *
      ( price ^ price-preference ) * ( ( 1 / ( sddist + .01 ) )
      ^ ( distance-preference ) )
    set price price + ( utility * local-vacancy ) ]
end

to locate-residents
  set growth count (residents) * growth-rate * 1.20
  set growth ceiling (growth)
  ask n-of growth residents [
    hatch 1 [
      evaluate ] ]
end

to evaluate
  let candidate-patches n-of random 100 patches with
    [ not any? turtles-here ]
  if (not any? candidate-patches) [ stop ]
  if race = 1 [
    let qualifying-patches candidate-patches with
      [ prop-min <= ( 1 - similarity-preference ) ]
    if (not any? qualifying-patches) [ set qualifying-
      patches candidate-patches ]
    let best-candidate max-one-of qualifying-patches
      [ utility ]
    move-to best-candidate ]
  if race = 2 [
    let qualifying-patches candidate-patches with
      [ prop-maj <= ( 1 - similarity-preference ) ]
```

```
      if (not any? qualifying-patches) [ set qualifying-
        patches candidate-patches ]
      let best-candidate max-one-of qualifying-patches
        [ utility ]
      move-to best-candidate ]
  end

  to kill-residents
    set growth count (residents) * growth-rate * .20
    repeat floor (growth) [ ask min-one-of residents [who]
      [ die ] ]
  end

  to locate-service
    let empty-patches patches with [ not any? turtles-here ]
    if any? empty-patches [
      ask one-of empty-patches [
        sprout-jobs 1
          set shape "circle"
          set pollution random 10
          if pollution > 5 [
            set trif 1
            set color orange - 2 ]
          if pollution <= 5 [
            set trif 0
            set color orange + 2 ]
          set size 3
          evaluate-trif ] ]
    ask patches [
      set sddist min [distance myself + .01] of jobs ] ]
  end

  to evaluate-trif
    let candidate-patches n-of random 100 patches with
      [ not any? turtles-here ]
    if (not any? candidate-patches) [ stop ]
    if trif = 0 [
      let qualifying-patches candidate-patches with
        [ prop-non-trif > 0 ]
      if (not any? qualifying-patches) [ set qualifying-
        patches candidate-patches ]
      let best-candidate min-one-of qualifying-patches
        [ price ]
      move-to best-candidate ]
    if trif = 1 [
```

```
      let qualifying-patches candidate-patches with
        [ prop-trif > 0 ]
      if (not any? qualifying-patches) [ set qualifying-
        patches candidate-patches ]
    if trifs-choose = "near minority" [
      let best-candidate max-one-of qualifying-patches
        [ count residents with [ race = 2 ] in-radius 4 ]
      move-to best-candidate ]
    if trifs-choose = "away from majority" [
      let best-candidate min-one-of qualifying-patches
        [ count residents with [ race = 1 ] in-radius 4 ]
      move-to best-candidate ]
    if trifs-choose = "low price" [
      let best-candidate min-one-of qualifying-patches
        [ price ]
      move-to best-candidate ] ]
    pollute
end

to pollute
  ask jobs [
    if pollution = 6 [ decrease-value ]
    if pollution = 7 [ repeat 2 [ decrease-value ] ]
    if pollution = 8 [ repeat 3 [ decrease-value ] ]
    if pollution = 9 [ repeat 4 [ decrease-value ] ]
    if pollution = 10 [ repeat 5 [ decrease-value ] ] ]
end

to trif-effect
  ask jobs [ if trif = 1 [ decrease-value ] ]
  ask jobs [ if trif = 0 [ raise-value ] ]
  diffuse quality random-normal .5 0.05
  diffuse price random-normal .5 0.05
end

to decrease-value
  ask patch-here [ set quality ( quality * 0.70 ) ]
  ask patches in-radius 1 [ set quality ( quality * 0.80 ) ]
  ask patches in-radius 2 [ set quality ( quality * 0.90 ) ]
end

to raise-value
  ask patch-here [ set quality ( quality * 1.06 ) ]
  ask patches in-radius 1 [ set quality ( quality * 1.04 ) ]
  ask patches in-radius 2 [ set quality ( quality * 1.02 ) ]
end
```

```
;;; VISUALIZATION

to update-patch-color
  if quality > 100 [ set quality 100 ]
  if price > 100 [ set price 100 ]
  if quality < 1 or quality = "NaN" [ set quality 1 ]
  if price < 1 or price = "NaN" [ set price 1 ]
  set pcolor scale-color green quality 0 100
end

to do-plots
  set-current-plot "environmental quality"
  set-current-plot-pen "majority"
  plot mean [ quality ] of patches with [ any? residents-
    here with [ race = 1 ] ]
  set-current-plot-pen "minority"
  plot mean [ quality ] of patches with [ any? residents-
    here with [ race = 2 ] ]
  set-current-plot-pen "mean"
  plot mean [ quality ] of patches with [ any? residents-
    here ]
end
```

## References

Eckerd, Adam, Heather E. Campbell and Yushim Kim. "Helping those Like Us or Harming those Unlike Us: Agent-based Modeling to Illuminate Social Processes Leading to Environmental Injustice." *Environment & Planning B* 39, no. 5 (2012): 945–964.

# References

Abdollahian, Mark, Zining Yang and Hal Nelson. "Techno-Social Energy Infrastructure Siting: Sustainable Energy Modeling Programming (SEMPro)." *Journal of Artificial Societies and Social Simulation* 16, no. 3 (2013): 6.

Alonso, William. *Location and Land Use: Toward a General Theory of Land Rent.* Cambridge, MA: Harvard University Press, 1964.

Alusi, Annıssa, Robert G. Eccles, Amy C. Edmondson and Tiona Zuzul. "Sustainable Cities: Oxymoron or The Shape of the Future?" *Harvard Business School Working Paper* 11–062 (2011).

Arora, Seema and Timothy N. Cason. "Do Community Characteristics Influence Environmental Outcomes? Evidence from the Toxics Release Inventory." *Journal of Applied Economics* 1, no. 2 (1998): 413–453.

Baden, Brett, Douglas Noonan and Rama Mohana Turaga. "Scales of Justice: Is there a Geographic Bias in Environmental Equity Analysis?" *Journal of Environmental Planning and Management* 50, no. 2 (2007): 163–185.

Banzhaf, H. Spencer and Eleanor McCormick. "Moving Beyond Cleanup: Identifying the Crucibles of Environmental Gentrification." Andrew Young School of Policy Studies Research Paper Series, Working Paper 07–29 (2007).

Banzhaf, H. Spencer and Randall P. Walsh. "Do People Vote with their Feet? An Empirical Test of Tiebout's Mechanism." *American Economic Review* 98, no. 3 (2008): 843–863.

Batty, Michael, Yichun Xie and Zhanli Sun. "Modeling Urban Dynamics Through GIS-Based Cellular Automata." *Computers, Environment and Urban Systems* 23, no. 3 (1999): 205–233.

Bedau, Mark A. and Paul Humphreys, eds. *Emergence: Contemporary Readings in Philosophy and Science.* Cambridge, MA: The MIT Press, 2008.

Been, Vicki and Francis Gupta. "Coming to the Nuisance or Going to the Barrios? A Longitudinal Analysis of Environmental Justice Claims." *Ecology Law Quarterly* 24, no. 1 (1997): 1–56.

Beierle, Thomas C. and Jerry Cayford. *Democracy in Practice: Public Participation in Environmental Decisions.* Resources for the Future, 2002.

Benfield, Kaid. "Miami 21 Leads the Way on Zoning Reform." *Switchboard: National Resources Defense Council Staff Blog.* January 7, 2010. Switchboard. nrdc.org/blogs/kbenfield/miami_21_leads_the_way_on_zoni.html.

Bettencourt, Luis M.A. "The Kind of Problem a City Is." SFI Working Paper 2013-03-008. www.santafe.edu/media/workingpapers/13-03-008.pdf.

Bishop, Bill. *The Big Sort: Why the Clustering of Like-minded America is Tearing Us Apart*. Mariner Books, 2009.

Blitz, David. *Emergent Evolution*. Dordrecht, The Netherlands: Kluwer Academic Publishers, 2010.

Bolin, Bob, Eric Matranga, Edward J. Hackett, Edward K. Sadalla, K. David Pijawka, Debbie Brewer and Diane Sicotte . "Environmental Equity in a Sunbelt City: the Spatial Distribution of Toxic Hazards in Phoenix, Arizona." *Environmental Hazards* 2, no. 1 (2000): 11–24.

Bolin, Bob, Amy Nelson, Edward J. Hackett, K. David Pijawka, C. Scott Smith, Diane Sicotte, Edward K. Sadalla, Eric Matranga and Maureen O'Donnell. "The Ecology of Technological Risk in a Sunbelt City." *Environment and Planning A* 34, no. 2 (2002): 317–339.

Bonorris, Steven. *Environmental Justice for All: A Fifty-state Survey of Legislation, Policies and Initiatives*. San Francisco, CA: American Bar Association and Hastings College of Law, 2004.

Bonorris, Steven. *Environmental Justice for All: A Fifty State Survey of Legislation, Policies and Cases*. Fourth edn. San Francisco, CA: American Bar Association and Hastings College of the Law, 2010. www.abanet.org/environ/resources.html.

Bowen, William M. "An Analytical Review of Environmental Justice Research: What Do We Really Know?" *Environmental Management* 29, no. 1 (2002): 3–15.

Bowen, William M., Mark Atlas and Sugie Lee. "Industrial Agglomeration and the Regional Scientific Explanation of Perceived Environmental Injustice." *The Annals of Regional Science* 43, no. 4 (2009): 1013–1031.

Bowen, William M. and Michael V. Wells. "The Politics and Reality of Environmental Justice: A History and Considerations for Administrators and Policy Makers." *Public Administration Review* 62, no. 6 (2002): 688–699.

Box, George E.P. and Norman Richard Draper. *Empirical Model Building and Response Surfaces*. New York: John Wiley & Sons, 1987.

Brown, Daniel G., Rick Riolo, Derek T. Robinson, Michael North and William Rand. "Spatial Process and Data Models: Toward Integration of Agent-Based Models and GIS." *Journal of Geographical Systems* 7, no. 1 (2005): 25–47.

Brown, Daniel G. and Derek T. Robinson. "Effects of Heterogeneity in Residential Preferences on an Agent-based Model of Urban Sprawl." *Ecology and Society* 11, no. 1 (2006): 46–66.

Brown, Daniel G., Scott E. Page, Rick Riolo, Moira Zellner and William Rand. "Path Dependence and the Validation of Agent-based Spatial Models of Land Use." *International Journal of Geographical Information Science* 19, no. 2 (2005): 153–174.

Brown, Phil. "Race, Class, and Environmental Health: A Review and Systematization of the Literature." *Environmental Research*, no. 69 (1995): 15–30.

Bullard, Robert D. "Environmental Justice: It's More than Waste Facility Siting." *Social Science Quarterly* 77, no. 30 (1996): 493–499.

Bullard, Robert D. "Environmental Justice in the 21st Century: Race Still Matters." *Phylon* 49, no. 3/4 (2001): 151–171.

Cain, Nicholas L. and Hal T. Nelson. "What Drives Opposition to High-voltage Transmission Lines?" *Land Use Policy* 33 (2013): 204–213.

California Environmental Protection Agency. California Communities Environmental Health Screening Tool (Calenviroscreen 1.0). oehha.ca.gov/ej/ces042313.html#sensitivity (accessed August 15, 2013).

California Office of Planning and Research. *Environmental Justice in California State Government.* October 2003. www.opr.ca.gov/docs/OPR_EJ_Report_Oct2003.pdf.

Campbell, Heather E. and Elizabeth A. Corley. *Urban Environmental Policy Analysis.* Armonk, NY: ME Sharpe, 2012.

Campbell, Heather E., Laura R. Peck and Michael K. Tschudi. "Justice for All? A Cross-Time Analysis of Toxics Release Inventory Facility Location." *Review of Policy Research* 27, no. 1 (2010): 1–25.

Campbell, Heather E., Yushim Kim and Adam Eckerd. "Local Zoning and Environmental Justice: An Agent-Based Model Analysis." *Urban Affairs Review* 50, no. 4 (2014): 521–552.

Capacity Global. "Diversity." 2007. www.capacity.org.uk/policyandadvocacy/diversity.html (accessed June 2013).

Cheerios. "Heart Healthy." Television Advertisement. General Mills, 2013.

Chun, Yongwan, Yushim Kim and Heather E. Campbell. "Environmental Inequities in a Sunbelt City: A Bayesian Spatial Analysis." *Journal of Urban Affairs* 34, no. 4 (2012): 419–439.

Chung, Su-Yeul and Lawrence A. Brown. "Racial/Ethnic Residential Sorting in Spatial Context: Testing the Explanatory Frameworks." *Urban Geography* 28, no. 4 (2007): 312–339.

City of Baltimore. *The Baltimore Sustainability Plan.* icma.org/en/icma/knowledge_network/documents/kn/Document/301385/The_Baltimore_Sustainabilty_Plan,2009.

Clark, William A.V. "Residential Segregation in American Cities: A Review and Interpretation." *Population Research and Policy Review* 5 (1986): 95–117.

Clark, William A.V. "Residential Preferences and Neighborhood Racial Segregation: A Test of the Schelling Segregation Model." *Demography* 28, no. 1 (1991): 1–19.

Clark, William A.V. "Residential Preferences and Residential Choices in a Multiethnic Context." *Demography* 29, no. 3 (1992): 451–466.

Clinton, William J. "Executive Order No. 12898." *Federal Register* 59, no. 32, February 11, 1994.

CPUC (California Public Utilities Commission). *SCE Tehachapi Renewable Transmission Project.* 2009. ftp.cpuc.ca.gov/gopher-data/environ/tehachapi renewables/TRTP.htm.

Crooks, Andrew T. and Christian J.E. Castle. "The Integration of Agent-Based Modelling and Geographical Information for Geospatial Simulation." In *Agent-based Models of Geographical Systems*, edited by Alison J. Heppenstall, Andrew T. Crooks, Linda M. See and Michael Batty. Dordrecht, the Netherlands: Springer, 2012, 219–251.

Cutter, Susan L. "Race, Class and Environmental Justice." *Progress in Human Geography* 19, no. 1 (1995): 111–122.

Dale, Larry, James Murdoch, Mark Thayer and Paul Waddell. "Do Property Values Rebound from Environmental Stigmas?" *Land Economics* 75 (1999): 311–326.

Daley, Dorothy and David Layton. "Policy Implementation and the Environmental Protection Agency: What Factors Influence Remediation at Superfund Sites?" *Policy Studies Journal* 32, no. 3 (2004): 375–392.

De Smith, Michael J., Michael F. Goodchild and Paul A. Longley. *Geospatial Analysis: A Comprehensive Guide to Principles, Techniques and Software Tools.* Fourth edn. Winchelsea: The Winchelsea Press, 2007.

De Sousa, Christopher. "The Greening of Brownfields in American Cities." *Journal of Environmental Planning and Management* 47, no. 4 (2004): 579–600.

De Sousa, Christopher. *Brownfields Redevelopment and the Quest for Sustainability.* Oxford: Elsevier, 2008.

Deadman, Peter J. and Edella Schlager. "Models of Individual Decision Making in Agent-based Simulation of Common-pool Resource Management Institutions." In *Integrating Geographic Information Systems and Agent-Based Modeling Techniques for Simulating Social and Ecological Processes*, edited by H. Randy Gimblett. New York: Oxford University Press Inc., 2002, 137–169.

Dear, Michael. "Understanding and Overcoming the NIMBY Syndrome." *Journal of the American Planning Association* 58, no. 3 (1992): 288–300.

Department of Economic and Social Affairs of the United Nations. *World Urbanization Prospects, 2014 Revision, Highlights.* New York: United Nations. 2014.

Desai, Anand, ed. *Simulation for Policy Inquiry.* New York: Springer, 2012.

DePass, Michelle. "Brownfields as a Tool for the Rejuvenation of Land and Community." *Local Environment* 11, no. 5 (2006): 601–606.

Dieleman, Frans M. "Modelling Residential Mobility: A Review of Recent Trends in Research." *Journal of Housing and the Built Environment* 16, no. 3–4 (2001): 249–265.

Downey, Liam. "Environmental Injustice: Is Race or Income a Better Predictor?" *Social Science Quarterly* 79, no. 4 (1998): 766–778.

Downs, Anthony. *Stuck in Traffic: Coping with Peak-hour Traffic Congestion.* Brookings Institution Press and the Lincoln Institute of Land Policy, 1992.

Dull, Matthew and Kris Wernstedt. "Land Recycling, Community Revitalization, and Distributive Politics: An Analysis of EPA Brownfields Program Support." *Policy Studies Journal* 38, no. 1 (2010): 119–141.

Eckerd, Adam. "Cleaning Up without Clearing Out? An Assessment of Environmental Gentrification." *Urban Affairs Review* 47, no. 1 (2011): 31–59.

Eckerd, Adam. "Policy Alternatives in Adaptive Communities: Simulating the Environmental Justice Consequences of Hazardous Site Remediation Strategies." *Review of Policy Research* 30, no. 3 (2013): 281–301.

Eckerd, Adam and Andrew G. Keeler. "Going Green Together? Brownfield Remediation and Environmental Justice." *Policy Sciences* 45 (2012): 293–314.

Eckerd, Adam, Heather E. Campbell and Yushim Kim. "Helping those Like Us or Harming those Unlike Us: Agent-based Modeling to Illuminate Social Processes Leading to Environmental Injustice." *Environment & Planning B* 39, no. 5 (2012): 945–964.

Emerson, Michael O., George Yancey and Karen J. Chai. "Does Race Matter in Residential Segregation? Exploring the Preferences of White Americans." *American Sociological Review* 66, no. 6 (2001): 922–935.

Environmental Protection Agency. "Superfund." Last modified September 13, 2013. www.epa.gov/superfund.

Environmental Protection Agency. "Toxics Release Inventory (TRI) Program." Last modified August 27, 2013. www.epa.gov/tri.

Epple, Dennis, Radu Filimon and Thomas Romer. "Equilibrium Among Local Jurisdictions: Toward an Integrated Treatment of Voting and Residential Choice." *Journal of Public Economics* 24, no. 3 (1984): 281–308.

Epstein, Joshua M. "Modeling Civil Violence: An Agent-Based Computational Approach." *Proceedings of the National Academy of Sciences of the United States of America* 99, no. 3 (2002): 7243–7250.

Epstein, Joshua M. *Generative Social Science: Studies in Agent-Based Computational Modeling.* Princeton, NJ: Princeton University Press, 2006.

Epstein, Joshua M. "Why Model?" *Journal of Artificial Societies and Social Simulation* 11, no. 14 (2008). jasss.soc.surrey.ac.uk/11/4/12/12.pdf.

Epstein, Joshua M. and Robert L. Axtell. *Growing Artificial Societies: Social Science from the Bottom Up.* Washington, DC: The Brookings Institute, 1996.

ESRC (Economic and Social Research Council). *Environmental Justice: Rights and Means to a Healthy Environment for All.* ESRC Special Briefing 7, November 2001. www.foe.co.uk/resource/reports/environmental_justice.pdf (accessed June 2013).

European Commission. "Justice: EU and Roma." Last updated November 13, 2014. ec.europa.eu/justice/discrimination/roma/index_en.htm.

Farley, Reynolds, Howard Schuman, Suzanne Bianchi, Diane Colasanto and Shirley Hatchett. "'Chocolate City, Vanilla Suburbs': Will the Trend Toward Racially Separate Communities Continue?" *Social Science Research* 7, no. 4 (1978): 319–344.

Ferreira, Fernando. "You Can Take it with You: Proposition 13 Tax Benefits, Residential Mobility, and Willingness to Pay for Housing Amenities." *Journal of Public Economics* 94, (2010): 661–673.

Fiorino, Daniel J. "Sustainability as a Conceptual Focus for Public Administration." *Public Administration Review* 70, no. s1 (2010): s78–s88.

Fischel, William A. *The Economics of Zoning Laws: A Property Rights Approach to American Land Use Controls.* Baltimore, MD: Johns Hopkins University Press, 1987.

Fischel, William A. "Property Taxation and the Tiebout Model: Evidence for the Benefit View from Zoning and Voting." *Journal of Economic Literature* 30, no. 1 (1992): 171–177.

Franklin, Stan and Art Graesser. "Is it an Agent or Just a Program? A Taxonomy for Autonomous Agents." In *Intelligent Agents III: Agent Theories, Architecture and Language.* Berlin: Springer, 1996.

Freudenberg, William. "Perceived Risk, Real Risk: Social Science and the Art of Probabilistic Risk Assessment." *Science* 242, no. 4875 (1988): 44–49.

Frey, William H. *Population Growth in Metro America Since 1980: Putting the Volatile 2000s in Perspective.* Washington, DC: Brookings, 2012. www.brookings.edu/~/media/research/files/papers/2012/3/20%20population%20frey/0320_population_frey.pdf.

Garrod, G. and K. Willis. "Valuing Goods' Characteristics: An Application of the Hedonic Price Method to Environmental Attributes." *Journal of Environmental Management* 34, no. 1 (1992): 59–76.

Gen, Sheldon, Holley Shafer and Monique Nakagawa. "Perceptions of Environmental Justice: the Case of a US Urban Wastewater System." *Sustainable Development* 20, no. 4 (2012): 239–250.

Ghorbani, Amineh, Pieter Bots, Virginia Dignum and Gerard Dijkema. "MAIA: a Framework for Developing Agent-Based Social Simulations." *Journal of Artificial Societies and Social Simulation* 16, no. 9 (2013). jasss.soc.surrey.ac.uk/16/2/9.html.

Gilbert, Nigel. *Agent-Based Models.* Los Angeles, CA: Sage Publications, 2008.

Gilbert, Nigel and Klaus Troitzsch. *Simulation for the Social Scientist.* Maidenhead: Open University Press, 2005.

Gimblett, H. Randy. "Integrating Geographic Information Systems and Agent-based Modeling Techniques for Simulating Social and Ecological Processes." In *Integrating Geographic Information Systems and Agent-Based Modeling Techniques for Simulating Social and Ecological Processes,* edited by H. Randy Gimblett. New York: Oxford University Press Inc., 2002, 1–20.

Greenwood, Michael J., Gary L. Hunt, Dan S. Rickman and George I. Treyz. "Migration, Regional Equilibrium, and the Estimation of Compensating Differentials." *American Economic Review* 81, no. 5 (1991): 1382–1390.

Grimm, Volker, Eloy Revilla, Uta Berger, Florian Jeltsch, Wolf M. Mooji, Steven F. Railsback, Hans-Hermann Thulke, Jacob Weiner, Thorsten Wiegand and Donald L. DeAngelis. "Pattern-Oriented Modeling of Agent-based Complex Systems: Lessons from Ecology." *Science* 310, no. 5750 (2005): 987–991.

Gross, Catherine. "Community Perspectives of Wind Energy in Australia: The Application of a Justice and Community Fairness Framework to Increase Social Acceptance." *Energy Policy* 35, no. 5 (2007): 2727–2736.

Guetzkow, Harold, ed. *Simulation in Social Science: Readings*. Englewood Cliffs, NJ: Prentice-Hall, 1962.

Gujarati, Damodar and Dawn Porter. *Basic Econometrics*. Fifth edn. Maidenhead: McGraw-Hill/Irwin, 2008.

Hamilton, James T. "Testing for Environmental Racism: Prejudice, Profits, Political Power?" *Journal of Policy Analysis and Management* 14, no. 1 (1995): 107–132.

Hamilton, James T. "Environmental Equity and the Siting of Hazardous Waste Facilities in OECD Countries: Evidence and Policies." Presented at the National Policies Division, OECD Environmental Directorate. March 4–5 , 2003.

Hanlon, Bernadette and Thomas J. Vicino. "The Fate of Inner Suburbs: Evidence from Metropolitan Baltimore." *Urban Geography* 28, no. 3 (2007): 249–275.

Hanson, Gordon H. "Scale Economies and the Geographic Concentration of Industry." *Journal of Economic Geography* 1, no. 3 (2001): 255–276.

Heath, Brian, Raymond Hill and Frank Ciarallo. "A Survey of Agent-Based Modeling Practices (January 1998 to July 2008)." *Journal of Artificial Societies and Social Simulation* 12, no. 4 (2009). jasss.soc.surrey.ac.uk/12/4/9.html.

Hird, John A. "Environmental Policy and Equity: The Case of Superfund." *Journal of Policy Analysis and Management* 12, no. 2 (1993): 323–343.

Holland, J.H. *Emergence from Chaos to Order*. Cambridge, MA: Addison-Wesley. 1998.

Ihlanfeldt, Keith R. "Exclusionary Land-Use Regulations within Suburban Communities: A Review of the Evidence and Policy Prescriptions." *Urban Studies* 41, no. 2 (2004): 261–283.

Irwin, Elena. "The Effects of Open Space on Residential Property Values." *Land Economics* 78, no. 4 (2002): 465–480.

Jacobs, Jane. *The Death and Life of Great American Cities*. New York: Random House, 1961.

James, William. *The Principles of Psychology*. USA, 1890.

Jarrett, Michael, Richard T. Burnett, Pavlos Kanaroglou, John Eyles, Norm Finkelstein, Chris Giovis and Jeffrey R. Brook. "A GIS- environmental Justice Analysis of Particulate Air Pollution in Hamilton, Canada." *Environment and Planning A* 33, no. 6 (2001): 955–973.

Johnston, Kevin. *Agent Analyst: Agent-Based Modeling in ArcGIS*. Redlands, CA: Esri Press, 2013.

Kearney, Greg and Gebre-Egziabher Kiros. "A Spatial Evaluation of Socio Demographics Surrounding National Priorities List Sites in Florida Using a Distance-Based Approach." *International Journal of Health Geographics* 8 (2009).

Keeter, Scott and Paul Taylor. "The Millennials." Pew Research Center. December 10, 2009. www.pewresearch.org/2009/12/10/the-millennials/.

Kersten, Gregory E. "Decision Making and Decision Support." In *Decision Support Systems for Sustainable Development: A Resource Book of Methods and Applications*, edited by Gregory E. Kersten, Zbigniew Mikolajuk and Anthony Gar-On Yeh. Dordrecht, the Netherlands: Springer, 2000, 29–51.

Kim, Yushim, Heather E. Campbell and Adam Eckerd. "Residential Choice Constraints and Environmental Justice." *Social Science Quarterly* 95, no. 1 (2014).

King, Gary. "How Not to Lie with Statistics: Avoiding Common Mistakes in Quantitative Political Science." *American Journal of Political Science* 30 (1986): 666–687.

Kohlhase, Janet E. "The Impact of Toxic Waste Sites on Housing Values." *Journal of Urban Economics* 30, no. 1 (1991): 1–26.

Konisky, David. "Inequities in Enforcement? Environmental Justice and Government Performance." *Journal of Policy Analysis and Management* 28, no. 1 (2009): 102–121.

Konisky, David. "The Limited Effects of Federal Environmental Justice Policy on State Enforcement." *The Policy Studies Journal* 37, no. 3 (2009): 475–496.

Konisky, David and Christopher Reenock. "Compliance Bias and Environmental (In) justice." *The Journal of Politics* 75, no. 2 (2013): 506–519.

Kraft, Michael and Bruce Clary. "Citizen Participation and the NIMBY Syndrome: Public Response to Radioactive Waste Disposal." *Political Research Quarterly* 44, no. 2 (1991): 299–328.

Kriesel, Warren, Terence J. Centner and Andrew G. Keeler. "Neighborhood Exposure to Toxic Releases: Are there Racial Inequities?" *Growth and Change* 27, no. 4 (1996): 479–499.

Krugman, Paul. "On the Relationship between Trade Theory and Location Theory." *Review of International Economics* 1, no. 2 (1993): 110–122.

Krysan, Maria and Reynolds Farley. "The Residential Preferences of Blacks: Do they Explain Persistent Segregation?" *Social Forces* 80, no. 3 (2002): 937–980.

Lazerow, Arthur S. "Discriminatory Zoning: Legal Battleground of the Seventies." *The American University Law Review* 21 (1971): 157–183. www.wcl.american.edu/journal/lawrev/21/lazerow.pdf?rd=1 (accessed August 6, 2011).

Le Page, Christophe, Nicolas Becu, Pierre Bommel and François Bousquet. "Participatory Agent-based Simulation for Renewable Resource Management: The Role of the Cormas Simulation Platform to Nurture a Community of Practice." *Journal of Artificial Societies and Social Simulation* 15, no. 1 (2012): 10.

Lee, Brian H.Y. and Paul Waddell. "Residential Mobility and Location Choice: A Nested Logit Model with Sampling of Alternatives." *Transportation* 37, no. 4 (2010): 587–601.

Legget, Christopher G. and Nancy E. Bockstael. "Evidence of the Effects of Water Quality on Residential Land Prices." *Journal of Environmental Economics and Management* 39, no. 2 (2000): 121–144.

Lewin, Tamar. "Report Takes Aim at 'Model Minority' Stereotype of Asian-American Students." *The New York Times*, June 10, 2008. www.nytimes.com/2008/06/10/education/10asians.html?_r=0 (August 7, 2014).

Ley, David. "Alternative Explanations for Inner-city Gentrification: A Canadian Assessment." *Annals of the Association of American Geographers* 76, no. 4 (1986): 521–535.

Liu, Feng. *Environmental Justice Analysis: Theories, Methods, and Practice*. Boca Raton, FL: CRC Press, 2001.

Luck, Michael. "50 Facts about Agent-Based Computing." Published by the University of Southampton on behalf of AgentLinkIII, 2005. www2.econ.iastate.edu/tesfatsi/AgentLink.50CommercialApplic.MLuck.pdf.

Luke, Sean. "Multiagent Simulation and the MASON Library." Manual, George Mason University, 2011.

Maantay, Juliana. "Zoning Law, Health, and Environmental Justice: What's the Connection?" *Journal of Law, Medicine & Ethics* 30 (2002): 572–593.

Macy, Michael W. and Robert Willer. "From Factors to Actors: Computational Sociology and Agent-Based Modeling." *Annual Review of Sociology* 28 (2002): 143–166.

McAvoy, Gregory. "Partisan Probing and Democratic Decisionmaking: Rethinking the NIMBY Syndrome." *Policy Studies Journal* 26, no. 2 (1998): 274–292.

McCluskey, Jill and Gordon Rausser. "Stigmatized Asset Value: Is it Temporary or Long-term?" *Review of Economics and Statistics* 85, no. 2 (2003): 276–285.

McMillen, Daniel and Paul Thorsnes. "The Aroma of Tacoma: Time-Varying Average Derivatives and the Effect of a Superfund Site on House Prices." *Journal of Business & Economic Statistics*, no. 21 (2003): 237–246.

Meadow, Donella H. *Thinking in Systems*. White River Junction, VT: Chelsea Green Publishing, 2008.

Messer, Kent, William Schulze, Katherine Hackett, Trudy Cameron and Gary McClelland. "Can Stigma Explain Large Property Value Losses? The Psychology and Economics of Superfund." *Environment and Resource Economics* 33, no. 3 (2006): 299–324.

Mill, John Stuart. *A System of Logic*. 1872.

Miller, John H. and Scott E. Page. *Complex Adaptive Systems: An Introduction to Computational Models of Social Life*. Princeton, NJ: Princeton University Press, 2007.

Mills, Edwin S. "An Aggregative Model of Resource Allocation in a Metropolitan Area." *The American Economic Review* 57, no. 2 (1967): 197–210.

Mohai, Paul and Bunyan Bryant. "Environmental Injustice: Weighing Race and Class as Factors in the Distribution of Environmental Hazards." *University of Colorado Law Review* 63, no. 1 (1992): 921–932.

Mohai, Paul and Bunyan Bryant. "Is there a 'Race' Effect on Concern for Environmental Quality?" *Public Opinion Quarterly* 62, no. 4 (1998): 475–505.

Mohai, Paul, David Pellow and J. Timmons Roberts. "Environmental Justice." *Annual Review of Environment and Resources* 34 (2009): 405–430.

Mohai, Paul and Robin Saha. "Reassessing Racial and Socioeconomic Disparities in Environmental Justice Research." *Demography* 43, no. 2 (2006): 383–399.

Morello-Frosch, Rachel, Manuel Pastor Jr, Carlos Porras and James Sadd. "Environmental Justice and Regional Inequality in Southern California: Implications for Future Research." *Environmental Health Perspectives* 110, no. Suppl 2 (2002): 149.

Morello-Frosch, Rachel, Manuel Pastor and James Sadd. "The Distribution of Air Toxics Exposures and Health Risks among Diverse Communities." *Urban Affairs Review* 36, no. 4 (2001): 551–578.

Morello-Frosch, Rachel, Manuel Pastor, James L. Sadd, Carlos Porras and Michele Prichard. "Citizens, Science, and Data Judo: Leveraging Community-based Participatory Research to Build a Regional Collaborative for Environmental Justice in Southern California." In *Methods for Conducting Community-Based Participatory*

*Research in Public Health*, edited by Barbara Israel, Eugenia Eng, Amy Shultz and Edith Parker. Hoboken, NJ: Jossey-Bass Press, 2005, 371–392.

NetLogo. *NetLogo Models Library, Sample Models, Earth Science, Fire*. ccl.north western.edu/netlogo/models/Fire.

Nielsen. "Millennials Prefer Cities to Suburbs, Subways to Driveways." March 4, 2014. www.nielsen.com/content/corporate/us/en/insights/news/2014/millennials-p refer-cities-to-suburbs-subways-to-driveways.html (accessed August 18, 2014).

Nikolai, Cynthia and Gregory Madey. "Tools of the Trade: A Survey of Various Agent-based Modeling Platforms." *Journal of Artificial Societies and Social Simulation* 12, no. 2 (2009).

Nishishiba, Masami, Hal Nelson and Craig Shinn. "Explicating the Factors that Foster Civic Engagement Among Students." *Journal of Public Affairs Education* 11, no. 4 (2005): 269–286.

Noonan, Douglas S. "Defining Environmental Justice: Policy Design Lessons from the Practice of EJ Research." Paper presented at the fall conference of the Association for Public Policy and Management, Washington, DC, 2005.

Noonan, Douglas S. "Evidence of Environmental Justice: A Critical Perspective on the Practice of EJ Research and Lessons for Policy Design." *Social Science Quarterly* 89, no. 5 (2008): 1153–1174.

Okun, Arthur. *Equality and Efficiency: The Big Tradeoff*. Washington, DC: Brookings Institution Press, 1975.

O'Neill, Marie S., Michael Jerrett, Ichiro Kawachi, Jonathan I. Levy, Aaron J. Cohen, Nelson Gouveia, Paul Wilkinson, Tony Fletcher, Luis Cifuentes and Joel Schwartz. "Health, Wealth, and Air Pollution: Advancing Theory and Methods." *Environmental Health Perspectives* 111, no. 16 (2003): 1861.

O'Neill, Tip and Gary Hymel. *All Politics is Local*. London: Crown, 1994.

Openshaw, Stan and Peter J. Taylor. "A Million or so Correlation Coefficients: Three Experiments on the Modifiable Areal Unit Problem." In *Statistical Applications in Spatial Sciences*, edited by Neil Wrigley. London: Pion, 1979, 127–144.

Oreskes, Naomi, Kristin Shrader-Frechette and Kenneth Belitz. "Verification, Validation, and Confirmation of Numerical Models in the Earth Sciences." *Science* 263, no. 5147 (1994): 641–646.

Ostrom, Elinor. "Institutional Rational Choice: An Assessment of the Institutional Analysis and Development Framework." In *Theories of the Policy Process*, edited by Paul A. Sabatier. Boulder, CO: Westview Press, 2007.

Ottinger, Gwen. *Refining Expertise: How Responsible Engineers Subvert Environmental Justice Challenges*. New York: NYU Press, 2013.

Paehlke, Robert C. "Sustainability." In *Environmental Governance Reconsidered: Challenges, Choices, and Opportunities*, edited by Robert F. Durant, Daniel J. Fiorino and Rosemary O'Leary. Cambridge, MA: The MIT Press, 2004.

Parker, Dawn C. and Tatiana Filatova. "A Conceptual Design for a Bilateral Agent-based Land Market with Heterogeneous Economic Agents." *Computers, Environment and Urban Systems* 32, no. 6 (2008): 454–463.

Parker, Dawn C. and Vicky J. Meretsky. "Measuring Pattern Outcomes in an Agent-based Model of Edge-effect Externalities Using Spatial Metrics." *Agriculture Ecosystem & Environment* 101 (2004): 233–250.

Parunak, H. Van Dyke, Robert Savit and Rick L. Riolo. "Agent-Based Modeling vs. Equation-Based Modeling: A Case Study and Users' Guide." In *Multi-Agent*

*Systems and Agent-Based Simulation*, edited by Jaime Simao Sichman,  Rosario Conte and Nigel Gilbert. Berlin: Springer, 1998, 10–25.

Pastor, Manuel, James Sadd and John Hipp. "Which Came First? Toxic Facilities, Minority Move-in, and Environmental Justice." *Journal of Urban Affairs*  23, no. 1 (2001): 1–21.

Pastor, Manuel, James Sadd and Rachel Morello-Frosch. "Still Toxic After All these Years: Air Quality and Environmental Justice in the San Francisco Bay Area." Center for Justice, Tolerance and Community, University of California, Santa Cruz, 2007. cjtc.ucsc.edu/docs/bay_final.pdf (accessed June 2013).

Pastor, Manuel, Rachel Morello-Frosch and James L. Sadd. "The Air is Always Cleaner on the Other Side: Race, Space, and Ambient Air Toxics Exposures in California." *Journal of Urban Affairs* 27, no. 2 (2005): 127–148.

Pearsall, Hamil. "From Brown to Green? Assessing Social Vulnerability to Environmental Gentrification in New York City." *Environment and Planning C: Government and Policy* 28, no. 5 (2010): 872–886.

Pendall, Rolf. "Local Land Use Regulation and the Chain of Exclusion." *Journal of the American Planning Association*  66, no. 2 (2000): 125–142.

Pogodzinski, J.M. and Tim R. Sass. "Measuring the Effects of Municipal Zoning Regulations: A Survey." *Urban Studies*  28, no. 4 (1991): 597–621.

Pohekar, S.D. and M. Ramachandran. "Application of Multi-criteria Decision Making to Sustainable Energy Planning—A Review." *Renewable and Sustainable Energy Reviews*  8, no. 4 (2004): 365–381.

Portney, Kent E. *Taking Sustainable Cities Seriously: Economic Development, the Environment and Quality of Life in American Cities*. Cambridge, MA: The MIT Press, 2003.

Pratt, John W. "Risk Aversion in the Small and the Large." *Econometrica* 32, no. 1–2 (1964): 122–136.

Primorac, Maja. *International Political Economy of E-Scrap Trade and the Basel Convention*. Unpublished dissertation, Claremont Graduate University, 2014.

Pulido, Laura. "Rethinking Environmental Racism: White Privilege and Urban Development in Southern California." *Annals of the Association of American Geographers* 90, no. 1 (2000): 12–40.

Qian, Zou (Joe). "Shaping Urban Form Without Zoning: Investigating Three Neighborhoods in Houston." *Planning Practice and Research*  261, no. 1 (2011): 21–42.

Railsback, Steven F. and Volker Grimm. *Agent-Based and Individual-Based Modeling*. Princeton, NJ: Princeton University Press, 2011.

Rand, William, Moira Zellner, Scott E. Page, Rick Riolo, Daniel G. Brown and L.E. Fernandez. "The Complex Interaction of Agents and Environments: An Example in Urban Sprawl." Conference on Social Agents: Ecology, Exchange and Evolution. Chicago, 2002.

Raper, Jonathan and David Livingstone. "Development of a Geomorphological Spatial Model Using Object-oriented Design." *International Journal of Geographical Information Systems* 9, no. 4 (1995): 359–383.

Reynolds, Craig. "Flocks, Herds and Schools: A Distributed Behavioral Model." SIGGRAPH '87: Proceedings of the 14th Annual Conference on Computer Graphics and Interactive Techniques, Association for Computing Machinery, 1987: 25–34.

Richardson, Harry W., Peter Gordon, M.J. Jun and M.H. Kimm. "PRIDE and Prejudice: The Economic Impacts of Growth Controls in Pasadena." *Environment and Planning* 25, no. 7 (1993): 987–1002.

Ridker, Ronald G. and John A. Henning. "The Determinants of Residential Property Values with Special Reference to Air Pollution." *The Review of Economics and Statistics* 49, no. 2 (1967): 246–257.

Ringquist, Evan J. "Environmental Injustice." In *Environmental Governance Reconsidered: Challenges, Choices, and Opportunities*, edited by Robert F. Durant, Daniel J. Fiorino and Rosemary O'Leary. Cambridge, MA: The MIT Press, 2004.

Ringquist, Evan J. "Assessing Evidence of Environmental Inequities: A Meta-Analysis." *Journal of Policy Analysis and Management* 24, no. 2 (2005): 223–247.

Roback, Jennifer. "Wages, Rents, and the Quality of Life." *Journal of Political Economy* 90, no. 6 (1982): 1257–1278.

Robinson, John and Jon Tinker, "Reconciling Ecological, Economic and Social Imperatives: A New Conceptual Framework." In *Surviving Globalism: The Social and Environmental Challenges*, edited by Ted Schrecker. London: Macmillan, 1997.

Rothwell, Jonathan and Douglas S. Massey. "The Effect of Density Zoning on Racial Segregation in U.S. Urban Areas." *Urban Affairs Review* 44, no. 6 (2009): 779–806.

Röper, Andrea, Beate Völker and Henk Flap. "Social Networks and Getting a Home: Do Contacts Matter?" *Social Networks* 31, no. 1 (2009): 40–51.

Saha, Robin and Paul Mohai. "Historical Context and Hazardous Waste Facility Siting: Understanding Temporal Patterns in Michigan." *Social Problems* 52 (2005): 618–648.

Sawyer, R. Keith. *Social Emergence: Societies As Complex Systems*. New York: Cambridge University Press, 2005.

Schelling, Thomas C. *Micromotives and Macrobehavior*. New York: W.W. Norton & Company, 1978.

Schilling, Joseph and Leslie S. Linton. "The Public Health Roots of Zoning: In Search of Active Living's Legal Genealogy." *American Journal of Preventive Medicine* 28, no. 2S2 (2005): 96–104.

Seig, Holger, V. Kerry Smith, H. Spencer Banzhaf and Randall P. Walsh. "Estimating the General Equilibrium Benefits of Large Changes in Spatially Delineated Public Goods." *International Economic Review* 45, no. 4 (2004): 1047–1077.

Simmons, James W. "Changing Residence in the City: A Review of Intraurban Mobility." *Geographical Review* 58, no. 4 (1968): 622–651.

Smith, Neil. "Toward a Theory of Gentrification: A Back to the City Movement by Capital, not People." *Journal of the American Planning Association* 45, no. 4 (1979): 538–548.

Smith, V. Kerry and Ju-Chin Huang. "Can Markets Value Air Quality? A Meta-analysis of Hedonic Property Value Models." *Journal of Political Economy* 103, no. 1 (1995): 209–227.

Sobotta, Robin R. *Communities, Contours and Concerns: Environmental Justice and Aviation Noise*. PhD dissertation, Arizona State University, 2002.

Sobotta, Robin R., Heather E. Campbell and Beverly J. Owens. "Aviation Noise and Environmental Justice: The Barrio Barrier." *Journal of Regional Science* 47, no. 1 (2007): 125–154.

Starbuck, William H. "Why I Stopped Trying To Understand the Real World." *Organization Studies* 57, no. 7 (2004): 1233–1254.

Stoll, Michael A., Harry J. Holzer and Keith R. Ihlanfeldt. "Within Cities and Suburbs: Racial Residential Concentration and the Spatial Distribution of Employment Opportunities Across Sub-metropolitan Areas." *Journal of Policy Analysis and Management* 19, no. 2 (2000): 207–231.

Strassmann, W. Paul. "Mobility and Affordability in US Housing." *Urban Studies* 37, no. 1 (2000): 113–126.

Theil, Henri. *Principles of Econometrics*. New York: Wiley, 1971.

Thiele, Jan C., Winfried Kurth and Volker Grimm. "Agent-Based Modelling: Tools for Linking NetLogo and R." *Journal of Artificial Societies and Social Simulation* 15, no. 3 (2012): 8.

Thünen, Johann Heinrich von and Peter Hall. *Der Isolierte Staat*, translated by Peter Hall. First edn. Oxford: Pergamon Press, 1966.

Tiebout, Charles. "A Pure Theory of Local Expenditure." *Journal of Political Economy* 64, no. 5 (1956): 416–424. www.jstor.org/stable/1826343.

Tobler, Waldo. "A Computer Movie Simulating Urban Growth in the Detroit Region." *Economic Geography* 46 (1970): 234–240.

Torrens, Paul M. and Atsushi Nara. "Modeling Gentrification Dynamics: A Hybrid Approach." *Computers, Environment and Urban Systems* 31 (2007): 337–361.

US Census Bureau. "US Firms—Ownership by Gender, Ethnicity, Race, and Veteran Status: 2007." 2007. www.census.gov/compendia/statab/2012/tables/12s0769.pdf.

US Census Bureau. *Mover Rate Reaches Record Low, Census Bureau Reports*. Newsroom. November 15 2011. www.census.gov/newsroom/releases/archives/mobility_of_the_population/cb11-193.html (accessed February 16, 2012).

US Census Bureau. "Income." Table 697 Money Income of Families, 1990–2009. www.census.gov/compendia/statab/2012/tables/1220697.pdf.

US Census Bureau. *Households and Families*. Issued April 2012. www.census.gov/prod/cen2010/briefs/c2010br-14.pdf (accessed June 2013).

US Census Bureau. *The White Population: 2010*. Table 1: White Population, 2000 and 2010. 2010. www.census.gov/prod/cen2010/briefs/c2010br-05.pdf (accessed July 1, 2010).

US Environmental Protection Agency. "Environmental Justice, Basic Information." Last updated May 24, 2012. www.epa.gov/environmentaljustice/basics/ejbackground.html.

United Church of Christ, Commission for Racial Justice. *Toxic Wastes and Race: A National Report on the Racial and Socioeconomic Characteristics of Communities with Hazardous Wastes Sites*. New York: United Church of Christ, 1987.

Veldkamp, A. Tom and Peter H. Verburg. "Editorial: Modeling Land Use Change and Environmental Impact." *Journal of Environmental Management* 72, no. 1–2 (2004): 1–3.

Voith, Richard. "Transportation, Sorting and House Values." *Real Estate Economics* 19, no. 2 (1991): 117–137.

Waldherr, Annie and Nanda Wijermans. "Communicating Social Simulation Models to Sceptical Minds." *Journal of Artificial Societies and Social Simulation* 16, no. 4 (2003). jasss.soc.surrey.ac.uk/16/4/13.html.

Ward, Mike. "State Board Denies Using Siting Report: Study Identifies Least Likely Incinerator Foes." *Los Angeles Times*, 1987. articles.latimes.com/1987-07-16/news/cb-4317_1_waste-incineration-plant.

Wilensky, Uri. "NetLogo." Evanston, IL: CCL, Northwestern University, 1999. ccl.northwestern.edu/netlogo/.

Wilensky, Uri. "NetLogo User Manual, version 5.0.5." Evanston, IL: Centre for Connected Learning and Computer-based Modeling, Northwestern University, 2013.Wilensky, Uri and William Rand. "Making Models Match: Replicating an

Agent-Based Model." *Journal of Artificial Societies and Social Simulation* 10, no. 4 (2007). jasss.soc.surrey.ac.uk/10/4/2.html.

Wilson, Sacoby, Malo Hutson and Mahasin S. Mujahid. "How Planning and Zoning Contribute to Inequitable Development, Neighborhood Health, and Environmental Injustice." *Environmental Justice* 1, no. 4 (2008): 211–216.

Wolverton, Ann. "Effects of Socio-Economic and Input-Related Factors on Polluting Plants' Location Decisions." *B.E. Journal of Economic Analysis and Policy* 9, no. 1 (2009): 1–32.

Wong, Grace K.M. "A Conceptual Model of the Household's Housing Decision-making Process: The Economic Perspective." *Review of Urban & Regional Development Studies* 14, no. 3 (2003): 217–234.

Woodworth, James R., W. Robert Gump and James R. Forrester. *Camelot: A Role Playing Simulation of Political Decision Making.* Fifth edn. Belmont, CA: Thomson, 2006.

Wu, Fulong. "Simulating Temporal Fluctuations of Real Estate Development in a Cellular Automata City." *Transactions in GIS* 7, no. 2 (2003): 193–210.

Yücel, Gönenç and Els van Daalen. "An Objective-Based Perspective on Assessment of Model-Supported Policy Processes." *Journal of Artificial Societies and Social Simulation* 120, no. 4 (2009). jasss.soc.surrey.ac.uk/12/4/3.html.

Zeemering, Eric S. *Collaborative Strategies for Sustainable Cities: Economy, Environment and Community in Baltimore.* New York: Routledge, 2014.

Zellner, Moira L., Rick L. Riolo, William Rand, Daniel G. Brown, Scott E. Page and Luis E. Fernandez. "The Problem with Zoning: Nonlinear Effects of Interaction between Location Preferences and Externalities on Land Use and Utility." *Environment and Planning B* 37, no. 3 (2010): 408–428.

Zimmerman, Rae. "Issues of Classification in Environmental Equity: How We Manage is How We Measure." *Fordham Urban Law Journal* 21 (1994): 633–669.

# Index

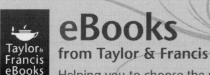